BROTHS TO BANNOCKS

Cooking in Scotland
1690 to the Present Day

CATHERINE BROWN

Illustrations by Martin Knowelden

The publisher thanks
The Famous Grouse Finest Scotch Whisky
for making possible the inclusion of Martin Knowelden's illustrations

JOHN MURRAY

For my mother and father,
Catherine and Barclay Braithwaite

© Catherine Brown 1990

First published in 1990
by John Murray (Publishers) Ltd
50 Albemarle Street, London W1X 4BD

British Library Cataloguing in Publication Data
Brown, Catherine
Broths to bannocks.
1. Scotland. Cookery, history
I. Title
641.509411

ISBN 0-7195-4780-6

Typeset by Colset Private Limited
Printed in Great Britain
by Butler & Tanner, Frome and London

Contents

Is There For Honest Poverty

Is there for honest poverty
That hings is head, an' a' that?   [hangs]
The coward slave, we pass him by –
We dare be poor for a' that!
For a' that, an' a' that,
Our toils obscure, an' a that.
The rank is but the guinea's stamp,
The man's the gowd for a' that.   [gold]

What though on hamely fare we dine.
Wear hoddin grey, an' a' that?   [coarse woollen]
Gie fools their silks, and knaves their wine –
A man's a man for a' that.
For a' that, an' a' that,
Their tinsel show, an' a' that,
The honest man, tho' e'er sae poor,
Is king o'men for a' that.

Ye see yon birkie ca'd 'a lord,'   [fellow]
Wha struts, an' stares, an' a' that?
Tho' hundreds worship at his word,
He's but a cuif for a' that.   [dolt]
For a' that, an' a' that,
His ribband, star, an' a' that,
The man o' independent mind,
He looks an' laughs at a' that.

A prince can mak a belted knight,
A marquis, duke, an' a' that!
But an honest man's aboon his might –   [above]
Guid faith, he mauna fa' that!   [must not]
For a' that, an' a' that,
Their dignities, an' a' that,
The pith o' sense an' pride o' worth
Are higher rank than a' that.

Then let us pray that come it may
(As come it will for a' that)
That Sense and Worth o'er a' the earth
Shall bear the gree an' a' that! [have the first place]
For a' that, an' a' that,
It's coming yet for a' that,
That man to man the world o'er
Shall brithers be for a' that.

Robert Burns

Thanks

My sincere thanks to everyone who has, knowingly and unknowingly, helped me to write this book.

Thanks to all the cooks, professional and domestic, who have taught me their skills, handed on their disciplines, and inspired with their good sense of gastronomic quality.

Thanks to the producers of fine Scottish produce who have not compromised on quality in a modern food processing and producing industry which has not always served the consumer well.

And thanks to those who have given me such good advice and encouragement during the period of writing and editing this book. In particular, my very sincere thanks to my friend Iseabail Macleod, Co-editor of *The Scottish National Dictionary*, for her enthusiasm, when mine flagged, and for her invaluable editing expertise.

Preamble

Soufflé au citron or Crêpes Suzette? Almost everyone goes for the crêpes and waiters wheel in trolleys, light lamps, heat copper pans and deftly remove the juice from halved oranges with a pair of back-to-back forks. The brandy lights. The pans flame.

It is December 1968 and students and lecturers from the Technical College in Elgin fill the dining room of the Stotfield Hotel in Lossiemouth for their annual Christmas meal excursion. It is grand hotel cuisine, the kind which those of us who lecture spend the rest of the year trying to teach.

Before the final spectacle there was a choice of Crème Dubarry or Consommé julienne, then Sole bonne femme, and to follow Gigot d'agneau rôti or Sauté de boeuf à la Bourguignonne. Vegetables were Pommes duchesse and Petits pois à l'Anglaise. All these dishes are well known to the North East catering students for the menu has more or less been chosen from the kind of dishes which could appear in their final exams for the City of Guilds of London.

In catering colleges all over Scotland, England, Ireland and Wales the same French dishes are being taught, the same French system of professional cookery practised in the kitchen.

A strange phenomenon: British cooks and chefs with plenty of early childhood experiences of national, local and traditional food, but thirled to a foreign cuisine which had been many centuries making its way into the cooking habits of the British but has now become the norm.

For teaching City and Guilds our text books were Ceserani and Kinton's *Practical Cookery* and *The Chef's Compendium* by Fuller and Renolds; the dishes in these were 90 per cent French. Classic Scottish broths like cock-a-leekie and Scotch broth appear, but we never taught them. Our heads turned to the crèmes and consommés . . . the flaming crêpes! How absurd it all seemed. How inappropriate. This was Scotland, for heaven's sake, not France.

I remember one of the other absurdities which struck me at the time was General de Gaulle's attitude to English words since he had decided to illegalize them on government documents, street signs *and menus* in his determination to preserve the purity of the French language. There were to be no Franglais words such as fish and chips, Scotch broth, Irish stew or roast beef.

It seemed to me that if the French couldn't see their way to adopting a few of our words which defy translation, why should we be so keen on taking aboard their whole vocabulary to write about food in Britain? So they have the edge over us in running a professional kitchen, but there were also good cooks in Britain cooking good British food. Was there something wrong with the English language that it couldn't be summoned up to describe, imaginatively, food on a plate? Was it that caterers thought customers would have less of an appetite for Roast best end of lamb than Carré d'agneau rôti? Or did they just think they could charge more for the latter?

Though we may feel nationalistically indignant about the sort of wholesale importation of classical French cuisine which occurred in the nineteenth century and reverberated into the twentieth, this was a different influence from the earlier special relationship between the French and the Scots which started in the thirteenth century.

Then it was a to-ing and fro-ing between royal families. Later, at the time of the Jacobite risings, the same thing happened between the many exiled Scots who lived in France for years and must have picked up something of French cooking ways, while the exiled French aristocracy who lived in Edinburgh must also have had an influence.

It is easy enough to isolate the words, particularly in the kitchen – gigot, ashet, etc. – which betray French influence from the earlier Franco-Scottish alliance. There are also a number of Franco-Scottish dishes: Lorraine soup, veal Flory, etc. But it is more difficult to identify the precise French influences on Scottish cooking methods. Except perhaps to notice the very close similarity between the French *pot-au-feu* and the early Scots Strong Broth. In both, an aromatic stock is made first to be used as the basis of future development. In both, the selection of inexpensive cuts of meat, once cooked, may be used as the potential for future meals, and in both, root vegetables and aromatic herbs are cooked slowly to extract maximum flavour. It was the inspiration: the starting point for both French and Scottish cooking.

But this natural interchange of culinary habits was a different thing to the wholesale importation of a cuisine which was the problem in the sixties. It was not long after the Stotfield affair that I abandoned a career teaching the art of *cuisine classique* to young Scottish cooks. Armed with Meg Dods's *The Cook and Housewife's Manual*, F Marian McNeill's *The Scots Kitchen*, Heptinstall's *Gourmet Recipes from a Highland*

Hotel and a little book of *Traditional Recipes from Scotland* written by an Aberdonian, Janet Murray, I set off for the wilds of Wester Ross in the spring of 1969 to see what could be done in a country house hotel on a shooting and fishing estate on the shores of Loch Torridon. To be honest, Escoffier's *Modern Cookery*, Salunier's *Repertoire*, Montagné's *Larousse Gastronomique*, Renolds and Fuller's *Compendium* and Ceserani and Kinton's *Practical Cookery* came too. But I was determined to write menus in English and cook as many dishes as I could which were traditionally Scottish in nature.

When I arrived, the fruit and vegetable van drew into the courtyard once a week with a sad array of invariably dead-beat fruits and vegetables that had been travelling in the van (unrefrigerated, of course) for several days since leaving the Glasgow market. It explained the need for extensive deep-freeze space in hotel larders: safer to reach for a packet of deep-frozen peas than risk the tired and possibly bacteria-ridden vegetables from the van. Salads were a nightmare.

Fresh fish came once a week from Dingwall about sixty miles away when someone went to the market for meat. The rest of the time fish on the menu seemed to be breaded haddock fillets and flabby rainbow trout – frozen, of course. Tasteless factory bread came from Inverness and had to be inspected carefully round the edges, even after only twelve hours of arrival, for mould! It was not a good start.

Undeterred, I felt that though there were considerable practical difficulties, there were also one or two rather special qualities about the more available raw materials in this part of the world. And if these ingredients could be put to best use then there was some possibility of achieving something worthwhile.

I didn't know a lot about cooking game when I arrived, but among the people who lived in the area was Mary Holmes who had cooked on Highland estates practically all her life and knew everything I needed to know. And there were kind stalkers who brought in the beasts and who also knew a thing or two about game cooking. Traditional game dishes, even venison tripe, which the Gaels called poca buidhe (the yellow bag), livened up the menu and satisfied customers. We described it with its colourful Gaelic name, giving a translation and telling them what it was.

Properly handled, there was no finer game to be found in Europe than from these wild majestic West Coast mountains. Feeding on rough grasses and heather, shot in its prime and carefully hung, it was this in particular which impressed Continental guests who would happily have eaten it every night of the week. The Aberdeen Angus beef and Blackface lamb which we bought by the carcass from the market in Dingwall was always superb quality.

Another unique raw material was the fish. It was a greater problem since there was no regular system of delivery from the nearest port of Gairloch, thirty single-track miles away. The fresh fish was ice-packed and hurtled south to Billingsgate. None of the other local hotels seemed interested in this valuable commodity on their doorstep. But boats were fishing in the loch. It seemed the only answer was to intercept the fishermen, personally, and persuade them to drop off some for the hotel.

Then there were the Gaelic-speaking West Highlanders who became friends and who still cooked the old dishes: Mary Macdonald's croppen heads, Alice Mackenzie's tatties and herring, Rhoda Mackenzie's sheep's head broth, Peggy Maclean's clootie dumplings, and the raw pickled herrings, cured in vinegar and brown sugar which old Murdo Mathieson kept in a plastic bucket in his caravan in Shieldaig, to be eaten at ceilidhs along with malt whisky tasting of nectar from an unlabelled bottle.

All this lent enthusiasm to the cause and a new-found confidence in native dishes and local produce at a professional level. One of the best things was allowing the excellent quality of the game, fish and meat to rejoice in its freshness, uncluttered by rich French sauceing. We stuck to simple methods and down-to-earth dishes, authentic soups, stews, pies and puddings. This was a comfortable West Highland country house, once the laird's ancestral home, frequented as a hotel now mostly by outdoor types who were there for shooting and fishing or for the stunning mountain scenery. It was no place for French – or any other for that matter – high-falutin cuisine.

It is now nearly twenty years on (1986) and we sit this time in the dining room of one of Edinburgh's most prestigious hotels where a menu boasts its 'Legends of the Scottish table'. We are again at the sweets and puddings and the waiter has just wheeled the laden trolley over to us and is decribing the array: 'And this is Cranogan. It's a meringue basket with some fresh fruits and a Drambuie flavoured cream on top.'

It's on occasions like this that I wish the poor old harvest-home Cranachan – so brutally corrupted – had never seen the inside of a restaurant kitchen. Better to let it slip into oblivion than have it turn up in such a setting: a million miles from the simple family celebration when everyone gathered to enjoy a bowl of fresh whipped cream mixed with nutty toasted oatmeal, ripe juicy black brambles, heathery honey and a slurp of the local whisky to lubricate.

Better not to have encouraged the patriotic fervour without first establishing the culinary discipline. Of course there have always been – as there will always be – those who muck about with classic dishes and foods either out of a lack of knowledge, or sheer laziness, or just from a need to swim with the tide whatever the direction. Scottish, French, or anything else they can lay their hands on – all is in danger.

As food writer, Derek Cooper, once remarked about the 'Lochalsh kipper' which he was presented with for breakfast in the Kyle of Lochalsh Hotel: 'As everyone living in Lochalsh knows the only thing they smoke in this town are cigarettes!'

But the fraudulent Cranachan was appearing in an establishment which ought to have known better, just as the Lochalsh Hotel ought to have known better than to claim a kipper cure that didn't belong.

Are we to be plagued by a gang of ignorant and pretentious workers in the kitchen set to destroy the real potential of Scottish cooking by their ludicrous antics?

What had started as the need to flee the French mumbo-jumbo on the menu and to make more effort on the Scottish front could very easily be destroyed by this kind of indiscriminate gimmickry causing even greater menu confusion than before. Even if the old French rules were unnecessarily rigid, at least you knew what to expect of crêpes Suzette when they appeared on a menu. But the movement, not just in Scotland but in Britain as a whole, to a more distinctly national style has now attracted so much attention that inevitably there have been both good and bad interpretations. The rising blood pressure of patriotism on the food front brings with it, inevitably, the perils of sentimentalism and misguided enthusiasm. Just as Sir Walter Scott had encouraged the whole of Scotland and the visiting Hanoverian king to get into a kilt and boast the tartan, the real origins of this exclusively Highland tradition were overlooked, dismissed as unimportant to the cause.

However honourable the intentions may be, there is always the threat of exploitation. Opportunities for tourist commercialism leading to disastrous 'Cranogans' are being made by those who care nothing for authenticity.

It was in the late sixties, while I worked out for myself the practicalities of promoting Scottish food in the professional kitchen, that a number of factors came together and started this momentum back to an interest in national cuisine. British producers, naturally, wanted cooks to buy British. And the powerful propaganda machine behind the Tourist Boards and the British Tourist Authority wanted visitors to Britain to be able to find more British food among the ethnic variety. These were the people most interested in the development of a British awareness in the professional kitchen.

Having already written a classic textbook on French cuisine, *The Chef's Compendium*, in 1963, along with Master Chef Ted Renolds, John Fuller, Professor of Hotel and Catering Management at the University of Strathclyde's Scottish Hotel School, had the idea of setting up a research project which would explore the possibilities of establishing a British Culinary Code. It was an ambitious plan: to search out the relationship between the natural resources of the land and the dishes which had evolved, as well as the political and social influences which had affected the diet. The idea was to bring together the history and origins of British food and to establish a system of professional cookery based on authentic British dishes: a project, sponsored by the British Farm Produce Council and the British Tourist Authority, which I worked on as Research Assistant in the early 1970s.

By the time it was published in 1976 as *British Cookery* the Director of the Scottish Tourist Board, Lester Borley, had already come up with the idea of providing a list of hotels and restaurants for the visitor which would direct them to places serving Scottish food. The wheels of commercial tourism were moving in the same direction as Fuller's project, and the 'Taste of Scotland', to be followed later by the 'Taste of England' and the 'Taste of Wales', took off.

These schemes heightened the awareness of national cookery and directed the attention of the travelling public to establishments of special British character. They also persuaded chefs and cooks that there was absolutely no need to have an inferiority complex about British food. Some of our dishes could undoubtedly hold their own in competition with French or any other national cuisine for that matter. But during the years that I worked for the 'Taste of Scotland' as food consultant and chief inspector, its strengths and weaknesses became more and more evident.

I left the scheme at the time of the 'Cranogan' incident in 1986. That was one problem. How could you police it properly from the limited resources of what amounted to one project in the tourist board's marketing budget? Catering education as a whole needed to get in behind the idea if it was really to succeed. Adapt the French methods: move with the times. Start thinking in English instead of French in the professional kitchen, and make sure that all students at least knew what a proper Cranachan was all about by the time they left college.

But even if they knew what it *ought* to be, there was still the question of what they would actually end up presenting on the plate. A mush of tinned raspberries in the base of a glass, with a dollop of cream on top, was what I was presented with quite recently as a 'Cranachan' in a well-frequented Reo Stakis hotel in Glasgow. Never mind the fraud, what about the gastronomic quality?

Though the Epicurean philosophy of appreciating the full pleasure of good food through balance and self-control is not native to the Scots, or indeed the British, this is not to say that there are no gastronomes in Scotland. Those who mind what they eat, as much as they mind about anything else, find food both fuel and fun. Their senses of taste and smell are sharpened by constant practice which extracts the full enjoyment of well-cooked food accompanied by appropriate wines. They have developed an ear for gastronomic quality, frequently offended by gastronomic discord which might not be noticed by others. Because they practise the art, they are never loth to spend time (and money) at the table.

It is all very well whipping up interest in authentic national food, writing books, and running 'Taste' campaigns. But unless a good palate is also fostered, then those talented cooking Scots, both professional and domestic, who cook using all their senses to practise the kitchen art with balance, restraint and common sense, will be left to sing their song to the desert air. It is a far more difficult thing to educate the palate of the nation to reject mushy tinned rasps and cream than to persuade it to fall in with Cranachan *et al.*

Looking at Scotland's own cooking assets and the question of how to establish a distinctive style that would prevent national characteristics falling into undeserved oblivion – which has always been a threat since political union with England three hundred years ago – there are a few things to consider clearly and selectively. For example, whatever we think ought to be preserved, patriotic fervour must not be allowed to dominate culinary excellence and nor should it be allowed to sweep aside the authenticity of the Scots kitchen. Keeping within the Scottish idiom, while at the same time refining and developing to produce the best food, is the trick. Modern tastes and dietary needs must be considered too and traditions adapted to appeal to a much more health-conscious nation.

My own feelings about the special Scottish assets in the kitchen are to do with simplicity. It was a well-established custom in the past that celebrated the fine natural flavour of the meat, game or fish on its own. A glance into the cooking pots of Scots in the past, which has been my aim throughout the historical part of this book, shows that simplicity which was the essence of Lord Cockburn's eighteenth-century suppers: the hens, the oysters, the cold roast beef, and not another thing to detract from their excellence. Sir John Foulis, the MacDougalls, Burns, Scott, the young Blackwoodsmen – they all understood about simply letting the food speak for itself.

When the late Duncan Macrae was taken to the Savoy Hotel for dinner one night after his play's performance he was presented with the *carte*, several pages long and all very high-falutin French gourmet cuisine. He took one look at it and turned to the waiter: 'Just bring me a pheasant – and a cup of tea.'

Don't let over-complicated styles camouflage real character: let the beef taste of beef, the hens taste of hens, the pheasant taste of pheasant. There is surely a need for a large measure of this kind of restraint, for a few more straight-talking Duncan Macraes if the natural gastronomic quality which is inherent in Scottish raw materials is not to be lost to too much tricksiness on the plate.

If there has been a focus for Scottish food through the ages, it is in the big cooking pot: so important in the Scottish kitchen for it establishes an idiom on which to latch a whole range of native dishes. If a distinctive style of Scottish food is to survive the pot must play a central role.

And out of it should come food which has been cooked with care, not boiled to death. To English minds the very idea of boiling suggests boiled suet puddings and tasteless watery food. This nation of roasters, who sometimes find difficulty in understanding the different habits of the Scots, ought not, because they dislike the notion themselves, to ridicule the Scots' desire to 'boil everything'. If they are good Scots cooks they don't anyway, but understand instead the need for a languid simmer. To those who criticize such habits I can only suggest that they look to established gastronomic geniuses in the kitchen: the French masters, who will tell you that a stock pot is everything; without it nothing can be achieved.

And if you question them more closely you will find that while their great dishes start out with careful cooking-pot extraction of flavours, the greatest influence in their cooking lives has not been some kitchen guru, however inspiring, but their own mother's family cooking.

I have a special respect for those chefs who have kept true to their roots of family cooking, keeping alive homely dishes which they themselves enjoy eating as much as cooking – refined and developed, of course, but still retaining the character of the original. Such chefs operate a kind of brake on the 'new' improvisers, bringing us back to the intrinsic goodness to be found in the commonplace.

I have only come across it a few times in hotel restaurants, but the idea of presenting the main course of a meal in the kind of deep broth-trencher or large soup plate which Scots have always used as a receptable for the contents of the cooking pot strikes me as one – commonplace – Scottish habit which deserves attention. The meat and vegetables piled up in the middle of the plate, surrounded by natural cooking juices, are eaten first with a knife and fork, then finished off with a soup spoon – a fairly universal peasant custom, after all, which you may meet with almost anywhere in the world where old traditions survive.

Most recently I encountered it at a celebration lunch when a young Frenchman, Daniel Galmiche, was awarded the *Glasgow Herald*'s Master Chef Award for 1988. Astutely searched out by Raymond Gardner, the *Herald*'s 'Trencherman', Chef Galmiche cooked what was arguably one of the top gourmet experiences of the year in Scotland. There were many well-known Scottish gastronomes present who thought so, and in homely *pot-au-feu* tradition, the main course of the meal came in a deep old-fashioned soup plate.

However delighted we may be to welcome the cooking French to our shores, the future of the Scots kitchen lies, nevertheless, in the hands of the cooking Scots who produce from deep within their pots the slow, measured combinations, the uncluttered presentations, the feeling for good raw materials, the proper respect for ancient customs. Their natural instincts lead them to produce the dishes which harmonize with the country and bring out the best accents of its character. There ought to be some sort of preservation order on such food: on the Bawd bree (hare broth) from the pot on Mary Holmes' cooker in her tiny stable cottage in Wester Ross, a wide deep plateful of the rich dark velvety liquid, collops of tender hare meat surrounding a large potato, its floury whiteness exploding through the skin – a meal in a soup plate dominated by the flavour of a well-hung mountain hare. Eaten with knife, fork and spoon, as the disintegrating potato mixes with the broth, all the subtle blends of textures and flavours balance to satisfy the senses of the most critical gourmet.

We need only celebrate such cooks to justify the excellence of Scottish food; to rescue it from the gang of impostors who will hide behind old romantic-sounding Scottish names when all they have done is flavour some cream with Drambuie.

Catherine Brown
July 1990.

COOKING IN SCOTLAND 1690 TO THE PRESENT DAY

1
The Old Simplicity
1690

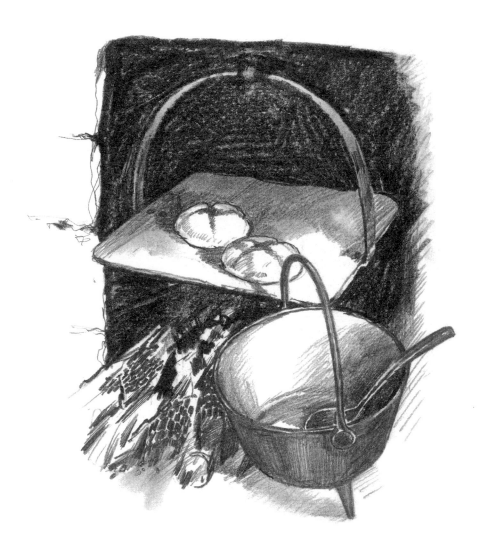

Marie hitches the handle of the muckle black pot onto a hook over the open coal fire in the basket grate. The smoke catches in her throat and waters her eyes whilst coiling upwards and – hopefully – out of the hole in the roof. She fills the pot almost full with three gallons of cold water carried from the well in a wooden luggie. It heats up slowly.

A wide baronial archway separates the fire and pot from the main kitchen where she goes now to cut the meat from a leg of fresh beef. It is early autumn and she has been up since five o'clock getting the fire lit, the water in, the vegetables washed, the breakfast organized. By the time the family sit down to their morning brose at eight her broth will already be half cooked.

Now the large pieces of beef and the chopped up bones go into the pot, then three Strasburg onions stuck with a dozen cloves, and a bundle of sweet herbs which the servant-lassie has brought in from the garden. The lid is put on as a protection from soot drips. Marie lifts it to skim as the scum rises and damps down the fire so the broth will not boil.

Cooking 'softly' is how she describes it. The secrets of a good 'strong broth' are an instinctive part of her cooking life – the nub, in fact, of most of the dishes she prepares. Success, she will tell you, is mostly to do with long, slow, careful cooking. For she takes for granted the fact that she has the best raw materials in succulent beef, flavoursome hens, good barley and oatmeal, and freshly picked vegetables and herbs from the garden.

The stone-flagged kitchen where she spends most of her working life is in the modest country house of Ravelston, built by George Foulis in 1624, and set in gentle rolling farmlands on the northeast shoulder of Corstorphine Hill. The city of Edinburgh, about two miles away, is still surrounded by a medieval wall with a twenty-four hour guard on the city gates.

Functional, rather than highly decorative in appearance, there are distinctive details such as the crow-stepped gables. The front doorway is intricately carved in stone with a family motto. Rooms are sparsely furnished: no curtains or carpets, some family portraits on the walls, and the handsome, country-carved, oak trestle tables and high-backed chairs filling the rooms with their solid character.

The sashless windows are deep-set and small, the walls are natural stone with linen hangings or wood panelling, and the ceiling rafters are decoratively painted in the main living room only. Dark rooms, though, where draughts blow, log fires blaze, and men thicken the air with pipes of tobacco.

Living with his family in this house is George Foulis's grandson, John, the third Baronet of Ravelston. In August he married his second wife Ann Dundas. The mother of his fourteen children, Margaret Primrose, died in April. Sir John is fifty-two.

He is privileged to enjoy the best things in life, simple enough pleasures but exclusive to his rank. From the details of his expenditures and other notes which he wrote up daily in his household book over a period of thirty-eight years a number of clues emerge about himself, his lifestyle, and the history of the period. There are many gaps, of course, but enough of the jigsaw to see something of the whole.

He is not wealthy in money terms. From evidence in other account books of the period, his shows that he spends less than other high-ranking families of the day on expensive furnishings, foreign tapestries and sophisticated furniture. But he is a bon viveur, a connoisseur of French claret and brandy, with a cellar well stocked with wines, sack, Canary wine, rum, brandy, beer and herb ale. He spends on his cellar double what he spends on his farm and garden.

A considerable amount is also spent on eating out, or just drinking in Edinburgh taverns. He also gambles at cards with his friends, and loses money betting on his game of golf at Leith. For country pleasures his expenses involve falcons for hawking, deerhounds for hare coursing, and tackle for trout fishing on the River Cramond. He frequently buys chestnuts and gingerbread at the fairs for his children, gives them money to buy curds-and-whey and buys sweetmeats for his wife.

The garden, we learn from his seed buying, is well stocked with parsnips, leeks, turnips, potatoes, asparagus, carrots, salad vegetables, parsley and syboes (spring onions). And there are apple, pear, plum and apricot trees in the orchard. The larder is a rich storehouse of hams, fifteen-pound Irish cheeses, barrels of salt herring, pickled oysters, dried fish, solan geese (gannets), anchovies, loaf sugar, butter, salad oil, vinegar and salt. There are dried figs, prunes and raisins, nuts, aniseed, chestnuts, lemons, oranges and pomegranates, and spices such as cinnamon, mustard seed, cumin, cardamoms and fenugreek. Tea, coffee and chocolate are not bought in great quantity and only rarely. Expensive wheat bread is bought occasionally from the baker in Edinburgh.

For Marie there is the farm produce as well as that from the rented lands where rent was paid in kain (kind). Her cooking is based on simple mild broths subtly seasoned with herbs and vegetables from the garden and grains from the field – a pastoral cooking. Infusions of the peasant cooking pot are more common than roasts from the feudal spit.

But breakfast is over now and Marie returns to the kitchen to prod around in her seething broth. The onions are in a mush, the pieces of beef just tender, and the liquid reduced by half. She strains the broth through a large wooden sieve, then lifts off the beef and puts it onto a cold shelf in the larder. Onions and herbs have done their task of flavouring and go out. Bones and excess dripping are kept aside for beggars at the back

door. Meat is something they will taste rarely, if at all. These twice-boiled bones are better than nothing to make a frugal pap: the poorer they are the thinner it will be. It is seldom, if ever, that they taste the kind of meaty broth which Marie cooks up in the laird's kitchen.

She calls this strained liquid, which is so powerfully flavoured, 'strong broth'. Now it goes back into the muckle pot on the chain. The morning is getting on when she adds half a pound of barley to the broth, five heads of chopped celery and a couple of handfuls of marigold petals. They cook softly for an hour and the petals release their orange colour to the broth. Now she adds three large kain (rent) hens.

By twelve-thirty the broth is smelling good. The barley has lithed (thickened) the amber liquid, the hens are just tender, and she removes them to another ashet (oval serving plate). She adds a few handfuls of fresh young sorrel leaves and all is poured into an immense charger, the steaming liquid scenting the kitchen with herb and meat aromas.

It is carried now, at around one o'clock, by one of the man-servants through to the laird's dining table and placed before him – still steaming – to be served out to family and servants. Marie has already taken through the ashet of cold beef from the first boiling plus a kebbuck (whole cheese) from their own farm, a stone jar of freshly churned butter, baskets of soft bannocks, and a bowl of ripe plums from the house orchard. Oysters newly dredged from the Forth are piled high on a wooden board.

Pewter broth-trenchers are round the table. The indoor servants sit at one end, the family at the other, with Sir John presiding in his high-backed, carved oak chair: head of the table at this simple but satisfying daily meal. Everyone is served a share of the ambrosial liquid along with a morsel of hen and a slice of beef. The servants drink home-brewed ale, the family and children drink claret from a pewter stoup (flagon) taken from a hogshead (barrel) in the well-stocked cellar.

This is the main hot meal of the day. Around four o'clock they stop for 'four-hours', a quick snack, when servants sit in the kitchen with a tankard of ale and some bannocks; Sir John and friends in the living room with brandy and shortbread; his wife with wine and a slice of yeasted wheaten bread which is something of a luxury in this unleavened bannock-eating household.

As the day draws to a close Marie escapes the scrubbed kitchen's noise and bustle, its smoke and its smells, and goes down the neat path to the kitchen garden. Past plots of fragrant lavender and onion rows, she ducks under heavy-hung apple branches in the orchard, and lifts her apron through the long grass.

The old gardener is sitting against the sunny south wall in the warm orchard and they talk of the growth and ripeness of the fruits and vegetables. Some cabbage-lettuces to pick now, the beetroot soon. The fruit is ripening fast on trees and bushes. The apples and pears they will store; some they will send to market in Edinburgh along with surplus vegetables. There are still prickly black tangy barberries to be picked and made into jam. Picking, preserving and putting by for winter – there is no other time of the year, they both agree, that so much has to be done in so short a time.

Supper at seven is a relaxing meal. In winter and cold summer days the pot of broth goes back onto the fire and another charger of hot soup and sappy (succulent) meat satisfies the household before they go to bed. Sometimes they just have a pot of mealy pottage (porridge), but tonight it is a cold meal. The cabbage-lettuces, some syboes, mint and pennyroyal which she picked as she came back through the herb garden. A good flavoured dressing is mixed with oil and vinegar. There are the leftovers from yesterday's roasting of small game birds, moorfowl and partridges plus a chunky earthenware pot of sharp redcurrant jelly for eating with the game. Still some oysters left, the bannock baskets are filled up, the cheese and butter back on the table.

Daylight is fading as she clears up. The tallow candles are already lit in the living room. A dozen candles sit in their holders on the table in the wood-panelled hall, waiting to be collected by the family as they make their way stairwise to cosy beds and sleep. Tomorrow, Sir John and his family go to Leith. A visit to his wine merchant to taste and choose some new wine, stock up on brandy, play a game of golf with his sons. The women will visit dressmakers and friends and then everyone will ride up into Edinburgh at the end of the day for a tavern supper.

It makes a break from the daily treadmill of feeding this large hungry household and Marie makes up her mind to get a fire going the next morning in the old brick oven. It is now seventy years old and recently bricks have been inconveniently falling out of the brick-lined roof during a baking. Something will have to be done. She would also like something done about the fireplace. A proper built-in chimney is what is needed so that coal smoke is reliably removed from her newly scrubbed kitchen floors and tables. Too often, when the wind gusts in the wrong direction, black clouds descend, be-sooting food, people, everything. (It is another three years before the new chimney is built.)

She is not bitter about these problems. They are minor inconveniences when she thinks of the plight of the starving poor begging daily at the back door. There is plenty to be thankful for without making a fuss about a smoky chimney and a crumbling oven. She has good raw materials to cook with, no shortage of supplies, and an appreciative family with hearty appetites who enjoy the pies and pastries, the pickles and preserves, the oatcakes and bannocks from her girdle and the daily changing delights of her superb pots of broth. The laird too is a generous and considerate man, the household is well run, and she will just wait patiently till things are fixed.

Sir John's generosity is not confined to his own family but extends to the distressed poor who come to his back door. No one is turned away: destitute seamen, poor scholars, old servants, poor widows, the poor Irish, gaberlunzies (registered beggars), dispossessed 'Episcies' who have been put out of their livelihood with the deposition of James VII last year and the re-establishment of the Presbyterians under William and Mary who have banned the Episcopal Church. He hands out money to them all, noting the amount, and he sends money to poor prisoners and for the relief of slaves. He also gives to the poor on a Sunday morning as he comes out of the Tron Kirk in Edinburgh. And he defies the sober dictates of the Presbyterians who have forbidden the giving of money for singing and dancing at fairs and celebrations by constantly rewarding the unpaid players and musicians who are dependent for their livelihood on such good will.

In his lifestyle there is precious little, it would appear, of the sober kail-and-brose cult of the dour-faced Presbyterian clergy and their followers. There is so much inbred generosity and *joie de vivre* in this zesty, eventually four times married, Scots laird. If there are others around like

him it is hard to believe how the Protestant Reformation was so successful in its attempts to stifle the sensual pleasures of the Scots. Those whose
wealth give them the power to cock a snook at some of the ridiculous
dictates of the Presbyterian church – like forbidding players to be
paid – appear to pay little attention to what the church thinks about their
behaviour. They continue to enjoy good food and wine, to patronize the
arts, and to make trips abroad to collect fine furniture and tin-glazed
earthenware to decorate their elegant houses.

There are many signs that the Scottish love of beauty and style was not
destroyed by the puritan ethic: in the architecture, and in the fine designs
of quaichs and mazers (drinking vessels) and communion cups which
show high levels of artistic achievement by Scottish silversmiths and
wood carvers.

The crackdown by the church was principally concerned with immor-
ality and the strict enforcement of the Sabbath. There were to be no
taverns, no dancing, no profane music, no walking, no business done, no
washing clothes, no brewing ale, no baking bread. All were punishable
offences on this sacred day and if the law officers didn't catch you then
the church searchers who went out looking for 'sinners' would.

It was more than a hundred years since John Knox had set the country
on a new spiritual course. The previous ecclesiastical corruption of
the Catholic church – the gluttonous monks and grasping bishops,
and the exploitation of land at the expense of the poor – had turned
Knox to Calvinism. What he wanted was social as well as religious
change. He demanded moral discipline, education of the young, and care
of the deserving poor, old and sick. There is no doubt that the exertions
of the Knox-founded church led to changes in Scottish society. Preaching
the virtues of high morals, hard work and a frugal lifestyle hit a chord in
many a serious-minded Scot. Educated at the parish school in such
principles, and on many occasions to high levels of academic achievement, Scots made best use of this advantage which was to be the foundation for much intellectual and business success in later centuries.

But the disadvantage, from the point of view of the preservation and
practice of the sensual pleasures of eating and drinking, was in the way
the church interpreted frugality. Knox preached against the excesses of
eating and drinking but he never actually set out to banish enjoyment.
The frowning church which followed his reforming zeal suspended
ministers because they were found cooking a roast of mutton on the
Sacred Sabbath! It was a church which had become fanatical to the point
of derision. No doubt many Scots lost out on the appreciation of fine
food and wines as a result: too many raised on a diet of porridge-and-the-
Shorter-Catechism than was good for culinary advancement. But a lack
of reverence for such church philosophy also saw to it that many others

9

continued to make the most of life. In the chapbooks of the second half of the eighteenth century there is ample evidence of disrespect for the church by the peasantry. The woeful piety of the gloomy ministers is a great source of ribald mirth. And later Burns leant his brilliant wit to satirize this hypocrisy in the Holy Willies of the church.

The pleasures of life were there to be enjoyed. Musical entertainment was such an integral part of the Scottish way of life. How did the church imagine that by stopping the pay they could possibly stop the play? Though there is evidence of John Foulis' extremely hospitable nature not once does he indicate any socializing with the clergy.

Until his death in 1707, aged sixty-nine, Foulis continues to write up in the leather books much the same pattern of living as before. But in the final seventeen years of his life the country suffers the misery of universal famine after a series of disastrous harvests in the 1690s. At a conservative estimate one fifth of the population dies of starvation. In addition to this catastrophe the Darien scheme to found a new Scottish colony in the West Indies which has attracted considerable sums of the country's limited wealth, fails. At the turn of the century Scotland is in dire poverty, a famished nation with a stagnant trade, crude manufactures and a profitless industry. In 1707 it is more or less forced to relinquish the Scottish parliament.

Now Parliament men and their families take the road to London which the Crown men took a century before. Sir John Foulis is one of the last of the stay-at-home lairds: unaffected and unimpressed by foreign ways. His life revolves round the old simplicity: his game of golf at Leith, his fishing on the River Cramond, his tavern suppers in Edinburgh, his fine brandy and mature claret, the artless pleasure of oysters and ale for breakfast, the favourite trencher of beef broth and hens. 'Contented wi' little, and cantie [cheerful] wi' mair.'

2
A Highland Table
1715

Time moves forward to summer 1715, but the manner of living steps backwards from the settled household of the Lowland Baronet of Ravelston. Scots in the remote and roadless Highlands are less influenced, materially, by the open shop window on the European world which now attracts Lowlanders to more and more Continental goods and cultures. Highland life is in contrast: physically cut off from Lowland influences and deeply Celtic in its culture. Two separate peoples speaking different languages exist within one small land. And now the divide deepens. Jacobite Highlanders fighting, as is their custom, for the clan cause – a deposed Stuart king – while more law-abiding Lowlanders make a compromise of token loyalty for the foreign king.

At the ancestral home of the Clan MacDougall lives the twenty-second chief, John, known as Iain Ciar (dark John), with his wife Mary. The castle is a solid square six-foot-thick walled tower on the edge of a sea cliff overlooking the northern entrance to Oban Bay – the site of a fortress since at least the seventh century. A steep stone staircase leads from the ground-floor vaulted cellar to the main hall, a wide-arched window views out across the Firth of Lorn to the mountains of Mull. More steep stairs lead up to the sleeping quarters and battlements: the look-out place, not for romantic gazing on splendid vistas, but to check whether advancing boats contain friend or foe.

When needs must, guns discharge on the unwelcome. The great door is barricaded when the family comes under siege. For Iain Ciar, like other Highland chieftains of the day, settles wrongs by force rather than by negotiation. He is a proud chieftain, with a reputation for personal bravery among his clansmen. His training has been a rigorous one in the wild mountains of the west: hunting for deer, skirmishing with rival clans and raiding for cattle. Both he and his men are strong and fit. He is a good leader, respected by clansmen, loved like a father, and in times of trouble, a helper. He and his men take up arms to defend land and honour in the ancient way, above all other considerations.

On this last day of August 1715 Iain Ciar is twenty-five. In the three years since his marriage to Mary, a MacDonald of Sleat, three sons have been born at the castle. On 9 August Mary, just nineteen, gives birth to their first daughter, Cathrine (Kettie).

In the manner of the country the chieftain's home is home to a great many others besides: family relations who live here permanently, many visiting friends, as well as the dependent clanspeople who work as servants for their keep. It is a patriarchal society, the castle being the centre of activity.

Here, a special welcome is prepared for occasional visitors, whether family or stranger, for they bring with them news and gossip as well as their judgements and opinions on the world outside. Highlanders look upon their home and whatever they have to offer in the way of food, drink and comfort as a symbolic offering of friendship. Whoever comes under their roof must receive the best they have, even if they turn out to be foe instead of friend. Hospitality will not be denied. A firmly held religious belief in giving generously is expressed in the old Gaelic rune: 'Often, often, often, goes the Christ in stranger's guise'.

There may appear a paradox here with their warring nature, but the hospitality-from-the-home principle was a matter of trust and honour, and something which they would not break whatever they might find out about their guest in the course of his visit. This was one of the reasons why they did not speir (inquire) too much about a stranger's background. On one occasion a chieftain discovers that he is harbouring his son's murderer, but even then hospitality is honoured and the guest comes to no harm.

Free and open private hospitality of this kind where anyone could knock on a door and be sure of a welcome was a delightful attraction for the traveller. ('In heaven itself I'll ask no more than just a Highland welcome,' says Burns after his tour in 1787.) Knowing that there would always be something to eat and drink and a place to sleep with a Highland family meant that there was no need for public inns. Such inns, if there were any, were mostly for stabling horses rather than catering for travellers. Travellers in the eighteenth century speak highly of the way they are entertained, privately. Those that do find their way into an inn find it an uncomfortable and clarty (dirty) experience.

Many speak, in astonishment, of the plenty and the quality of the food on the tables of private households, and of the variety of the wines and spirits. Travellers are accustomed to thinking of the Highlands, as one chronicler puts it, as 'the birthplace of famine'. They find a different reality.

Plenty food at Dunollie: the great front door opens into a well-stocked storehouse at ground level, a single narrow slit of light penetrates the gloomy arched space stacked full with barrels of salt fish, cogs of salt butter, rounds of cheese sitting on planks in movable frames hanging on the walls, harvested vegetables lying in heaps. There are kists (cases) of meal and hogsheads of wine. Dried fish, herbs and seaweed hang from hooks in the roof. Space still, when besieged, for cattle, sheep, goats and horses, hurriedly herded in. But up the stone stairs to the hall is where the household's daily living, eating, and cooking takes place.

Two rough stone hearths are set in opposite walls, one for cooking, the other for sitting at. Not a large room, the ceiling is low-beamed, the walls a natural grey sandstone. The castle is well furnished and the details carefully kept in the family inventory of household possessions which are, according to custom, valued at the time of the chief's death.

Not only are travellers in the Highlands at this time surprised at the plenty on the table, they are also impressed with the style of the house furnishings of the clan chiefs and they comment on sophistications which they did not expect to find. According to the inventories there were a number at Dunollie: a glass decanter and a dozen drinking glasses plus two flagons; a dozen silver spoons and half a dozen other smaller ones; a china punch bowl; eight Delph plates and five dishes; a small Delph posset dish and two Delph bowls. This was in addition to such basics as a couple of large trestle carved wooden tables and three smaller ones; two dozen chairs; two old 'armed' chairs; an old dresser where the table linen was kept: nine tablecloths and thirty napkins; and twenty-two yards of a kind of table linen from Tournai with a geometric design which they called Dornick and which they used for special occasions when they put the tables together. Everyday eating dishes and cutlery on the dresser included fifteen broth pewter plates and forty-two wooden ones, six knives and forks, many horn spoons and wooden bowls, a dealing spoon, a salt dish and a mustard dish.

At the cooking-hearth nearest the staircase were two big 'potts'; a cauldron; a big three-legged pot; two small 'potts'; two small copper skillets; two brass pans; a frying pan; an old girdle; a brander (grill); three pairs of tongs; a ladle; a strainer and a grater. In the fireplace was a roasting rack and three long spits which rested on hooks above the stone arch when not in use. There were shelved stone recesses in the walls to store everyday essentials like salt and meal.

Upstairs were nine four-poster beds and one box bed. Only three of the beds had feather mattresses, pillows and bolster; the others were of straw or heather. There were eight sets of bed linen and twenty-two pairs of blankets, two pewter chamber pots and two earthen ones.

Not lavishly furnished, but there are the essentials of comfort, enough table linen and crockery to set up a civilized table with refined delftware and silver adding to the style. The kitchen was equipped for feeding large numbers of people, four large pots catering for their basic needs. The smaller copper skillets were used for such refinements as sauces, while the brass pans dealt with preserving fruits. Roasting was done on a spit, and baking was confined to the girdle or to one of the three-legged pots which were buried in burning peats for all-round heat.

As summer draws to a close, light dawns around five and the day's work begins: peat-cutting on the hill, water-carrying from the burn, milking animals where they stand grazing, and the children searching out new-laid eggs among the nooks and crannies of outbuildings and courtyard. Now the pot of mealy porridge heaves and bubbles. The clanswoman who cooks for the chief's household carries it to the table and they stand round supping from the pot then dipping spoonfuls into a bowl of thick fresh cream. It is a good contrast, this hot porridge and cold cream that they eat from deep-bowled hand-carved horn spoons. Delving deeper till satisfied, then they sit down to crack some freshly boiled eggs and eat them with a hard bannock and a slice of soft goats' milk cheese. Milk, buttermilk or ale they drink from tankards or horn tumblers while men swig potent whisky from the stone bottle which appears at every meal.

Today's breakfast is a simple affair for there are no special guests. But when there are, the breakfast table staggers with cold roast meats, fried fish and pickled meats as well as fruity preserves. And to drink there is a special concoction of Auld Man's Milk: egg and milk beaten together in a Delph bowl, sweetened with sugar and zested with whisky – or sometimes brandy or rum, if they have it.

These spirits are among the luxuries bartered from foreign luggers when they happen to sail into remote Highland sea lochs, exchanged tax free – no crime is so common or respectable as 'fair trading'. They may also pick up some Dutch tea and coffee, Oriental spices, dried figs, raisins, liquorice and sweet candies – all fair exchange for their barrels of salt herring and local cheeses.

In summer another source of new foods for the table comes from the custom of taking animals (sheep, cattle, goats, and horses) to the shielings (rich hill grazings) so that crops get a chance to grow and ripen in their unfenced fields. Butter and cheese are made by the women who escape, with animals and children, to pastures new for a few months. And while they are kept busy with their cows and goats their children run wild among the rocks and burns gathering lichens, mosses and roots. Boiling them up in the cauldron they learn the ancient art of dyeing wool. Then mothers card, spin, and knit warm stockings for the winter. Strong, weather-beaten, peat-burnished faces they have, these women who make this temporary home for themselves in beehive-shaped shelters of rough stone and turf. There may not be much in the way of comfort, but there is enough to eat: meal for porridge and bannocks, butter and cheese, buttermilk to drink, wild mountain berries with rich cream and soft cheese. As dusk falls, they huddle for warmth round the glowing peat embers, and amuse children with strange stories of old Celtic folk-tales and sing to themselves the sad songs of the Gael.

Today, one of the women from the shielings arrives at Dunollie with some fresh sheeps' milk cheese and butter by way of rent for the chief. The cheese is safely stored on the wooden shelves in the cool cellar and the butter, packed into a barrel, will be sent off to the Lowland market for much needed cash.

Already the day's broth simmers on the peat fire in the castle hall. A good time of year this for the broth pot: wild herbs, garlic, sorrel and watercress to be had growing wild for the picking and young tender shoots of seaweeds when the tide ebbs. She stirs and plots over her steaming pot.

The seeds sent from Glasgow in March have grown into cabbages, carrots, parsnips, turnips, beetroot, parsley and radishes in the castle garden. There is no shortage of meat either: today's pot is full-flavoured with some well-hung venison. The scrag ends, bones and skinned head have already been simmering in the pot since early morning; now she strains off the hot liquid and thickens it with beremeal (a hardy Northern form of barley). Thin collops (slices) of venison from the haunch are fried in butter in the copper skillet till well browned, and then tipped into the thickened broth. Just before it is served some chopped sorrel and syboes (spring onions) are cooked lightly in some butter; the herb and onion tang sharpens up the final flavour of the dark brown gamy soup-stew. The cheeks which she picks from the head, regarded as a delicacy, go back into the pot along with some fresh green chopped sorrel and a few slices of sharp lemon.

Dinner is the main meal of the day and this gamy broth-pot, flavours carefully balanced, takes central place on the thick oak table. Boiled salmon left over from the previous day is put out, beremeal bannocks, butter and the sheeps' milk cheese fresh from the shielings. There is a large bowl of fresh cream and a bowl of blaeberries which the children enjoy mixing together in their little wooden porringers.

When there are guests, roast game – partridge, grouse, hare, duck, mallard, woodcock and snipe according to the season – fills the table. On special occasions there will be rich cream and egg fricassees of chicken, fried collops of beef and mutton, creamy possets and syllabubs with rich summer milk – the season's plenty in the good things to eat.

After dinner, while the fire is still hot, there is a baking to be done on the girdle. Huge round girdle-sized soft bannocks of barley are wrapped in a cloth while still steaming, harder cakes made with meal and water are shaped thin and toasted dry and crisp in front of the fire till their edges curl. Because of their hardiness barley and oats are the commonest meals and the ones she uses most; both, she grinds between the round stones of her quern.

But now the clanswoman cook has had enough of hot fire and black pots and it is time to breathe in some fresh sea air for an hour or so. A creel (basket) on her back, she leaves the castle and makes her way down to the shore. Scrambling barefoot among the rocks she stops, every now and again, to lift slippery seaweed, looking for lurking partans (crabs) and catching them quickly by their backs before they scuttle for cover. She picks off clusters of shiny dark blue mussels, she digs with a sharp stone for the horse mussels that burrow at the lowest ebb of the tide, scooping up handfuls of little whelks, pulling at bunches of caragheen, sea tangle and dulse. When she reaches the golden sands of Ganavan Bay she tucks up her skirts and cools her feet in the lapping waves. The sand moves and she stamps her foot quickly on a flurrying flukie. The creel is almost full.

No need for any more cooking today for the remains of the broth can be heated up again for the men back from the hill. The salmon, bannocks, cheese and butter can go back on the table and just before the meal begins the shellfish can be boiled up quickly. She strains off the shellfish bree (cooking liquid) into another pot and piles up the hot steaming mass of sea-plenty in a large charger. When sand and sea debris have settled in the pot, she decants off the bree and pours it among the shellfish and finally tosses in a few stalks of red dulse which the children like to chew. What is left of the salty bree goes into a jug and is drunk with the meal.

Those beside the sea are luckier than those inland. None are wealthy in money terms, living out their lives without much need or desire for it. The produce of their animals, the wool which they spin and weave into clothes and the crops which they grow provide everything they need. In the richer pastoral Lowlands the laird of Ravelston might spend £200 on some occasional items of furniture. But when Iain Ciar dies the total value of his house possessions amounts to only £50. He can sell cattle, butter and cheese to buy salt, candles, an iron girdle and a black pot if he needs one, but as one chronicler puts it: 'They have everything here but money'. When wind and rain destroy crops the chief takes responsibility, as best he can, for feeding both starving people and animals through long hard winters. It is an economic system which depends on the plenty of land and sea and the benevolence of the clan chiefs.

As the household retires to bed it is not the worry of a failed harvest which troubles Iain Ciar but the certainty that the exiled James Stuart will soon make a bid for the throne. How will his young wife cope? How will she manage to defend the castle? With a baby just born and three other young children it is the worst possible time for this to happen. Only God can protect them for clan honour comes before family needs.

Today, he has received a letter dated 27 August from the Duke of Argyll, the king's Lord Lieutenant of the county, warning of the dangers of the 'intended rebellious attempts to destroy our Religion and liberties'. The Duke, intent on rallying support behind King George, writes the same letter to all the 'gentlemen of the shire of Argyll' indicating that, in the event of trouble, he will expect their armed support.

On 23 September Iain Ciar receives a letter from Campbell of Dunstaffnage, who has already pledged support to Argyll and has been made a Deputy Lieutenant, to 'be in readiness to march with me to Inveraray against monday next . . . I hereby order and desire that you and your men do meet me at Kilmore'. Campbell is still uncertain which side Iain Ciar supports.

'Send me some arms for my men,' writes back the bold MacDougall, already under instruction from Stewart of Appin who is rallying the Jacobite side. But Campbell will not give out arms till he sees the men at Inveraray and pleads with his young friend and neighbour to 'behave yourself so as to oblige the Duke of Argyll who certainly will have a particular regard to such as desire well of him, as he cannot but take notice of those who do otherways'.

The few remaining days before his departure are spent organizing provisions and arms. A blacksmith has been working secretly in a cave putting swords and other arms in order. But his other concerns are for his young wife and children and he spends time teaching her the practicalities of barricading the castle to survive a siege.

For these brief three years prior to the uprising, young Mary MacDougall and Iain Ciar have managed the day-to-day provisioning of this household, casting a net ingeniously in the search for food to provide a table of rich Highland plenty. When the chief and his men march off from the Dunollie lands to join the Jacobite army in Perth at the end of September 1715, with them goes an old way of life which never returns.

For Mary MacDougall there are a hard twelve – landless – years ahead. She survives the first winter in the castle despite several attacks, but eventually retreats to a bothy on the island of Kerrera. Her husband returns, furtively, which accounts for the births of three more children. But the rest of the time he, like many other clansmen, spends long years in exile before being finally caught and put in Newgate prison along with Stewart of Appin and Rob Roy MacGreggor. They receive the king's pardon the night before transportation to Barbados.

Iain Ciar is given back Dunollie Castle, but not his lands. He lives for another ten years with his wife and children at the castle and they survive as best they can – mostly from their own efforts. But the table no longer heaves with past plenty. While they lived a self-sufficient lifestyle, from the growth of the land, the wild game from the hills, fish from the sea, and the produce of their cows, sheep, goats and hens, they survived well, and their people were cared for in times of famine. Though this has worked in the past, times are changing and agricultural improvements beginning in other parts of the country. What the Highlands need is capital investment to develop, and professional advice on how to work out more efficient forms of agriculture to feed the growing population. What they have is a ruling class lacking the necessary financial resources, many deprived of their lands (sometimes totally destitute and living out their final days in the Edinburgh Poorhouse). It is a recipe for disaster which reflects on the Highland table in the years to come.

3
Edinburgh Tavern Eating
1786

It is 1786. Mary and Iain Ciar's grandson Patrick, later the twenty-fourth chieftain, is forty-four and practising at the bar in Edinburgh. Not too successfully, it seems, for despite help with food from home – barrels of oatmeal, kegs of whisky and sixteen-pound cheeses – he writes to his father continually for more money. In a series of acrimonious letters over a number of years the final ultimatum comes: this expensive lifestyle in Edinburgh will have to come to an end for the estate resources can no longer support it. The old man gives his final words on the subject: 'Consider that my funds are one way or another exhausted'.

But pessimistic letters from the errant son continue, full of gloomy prophecies of the debtor's jail and ruin and starvation for his wife and two young children. Despite this, he seems to make ends meet for the next eleven years until, in 1798, he finally goes back to Argyll to take over the running of the estate from his eighty-five-year-old father. But, for the moment, he lives with his wife, Louise, and their children, in part of Lady Stair's House, tucked in behind tenement lands on the Lawnmarket.

Edinburgh is changing: there have been many changes in his own time, and many more since the kindly Baronet of Ravelston sat in taverns around the turn of the century, drinking and betting and slipping fresh Forth oysters down his drouthy throat.

The Scots Parliament is gone. Edinburgh still officially accommodates residencies for five times more noblemen and gentry than does Glasgow, but they all now live for the best part of the year in London. Edinburgh no longer hosts the most colourful occasions of the noblest in the land; the Canongate and High Street are no longer brightened by brocaded aristocrats, jostling with judges, caddies, and dandering street beggars, on their way to and from the Palace of Holyrood and their tenement lands. The earnest political debate in Parliament House has ceased. The military has suppressed the violent uproar of the crowd protesting against a Union which they do not want.

Now it is the avidly sociable legal intelligentsia who are in privileged positions. Judges rate as noble lords in the social hierarchy. Already the 'Golden Age' of Scottish intellectual enlightenment has made its mark: philosopher Hume is dead ten years, economist Smith is an unsociable old man, philosopher Fergusson is sixty-two, biographer 'Jupiter' Carlyle and dramatist Home are both sixty-four. The poet Burns is twenty-seven, the future novelist Scott is just a young boy of fifteen. There are bookshops and publishers now which were not around in the laird of Ravelston's time. Though he does buy paper for writing, and books for his children, never, in all his thirty-eight years of accounting, does he record buying a book for himself.

The completion of the North Bridge in 1772 has started the shake-out from the old cramped and disorderly medieval walled town into the new spacious classical houses in symmetrical squares and circuses. By 1786 speculative builders have already built some of the New Town. Many thought them mad, for who would want to live so far away from the High Street and the Canongate, so cut off from the camaraderie, the sociability of hurrying humanity? Hemmed in though they are in the Old Town, beneath overhanging tenements, this is the centre of city life, where every social class knows one another as they pass the time of day on the common stair.

Many of us living in the impersonal twentieth century might harbour a longing for these old and apparently delightful sociable times. But not so delightful were the inconveniences of the life: the daily carrying of household water up five narrow flights of stairs or the stench of rotting refuse in the streets. Were we, by some magic, to step back into the eighteenth-century Canongate we would find the experience extremely upsetting.

Holding noses was the thing to do, or priming with snuff to shun the smells. But the constant threat of soiled clothes and shoes, not to mention the diseases which spread like wildfire, must, at times, have been beyond bearing. In this city of 70,000 odd souls, sewers run openly. Dogs, cats and pigs scavenge for food among the refuse. Wooden luggies (pails) outside doors on stairheads are filled daily with every kind of household waste; stinking debris, chucked out the window at night, lies in the streets till scavengers turn up in the early morning to take it away. English travellers visiting the city write home with some revolting details of the streets of Edinburgh and complain that they can't sleep at night for the smell which Boswell describes in his diary as Edinburgh's 'evening effluvia' and others nickname the 'flowers of Edinburgh'.

However disgusting the streets, there are some attractive homes in the old tenements where all classes are sandwiched together in the one house or 'land'. Ground floors are let to the lower classes; the middle floors, with the best rooms, are reserved for professionals and aristocrats. Not large rooms, but they are dignified, with painted beamed ceilings, decorated stone walls, finely carved wide stone fireplaces, curtained four-posters, and comfortable high-backed oak chairs. Sleeping arrangements are cramped: servants sleep in beds under dressers, in pull-out drawers, and in hinged beds that fold up to the wall during the day. Higher up the tenement, the smaller plainer rooms belong to shopkeepers and merchants, and above them are the tiny cramped attics and garrets where artisans and labourers live with their large families. The destitute burrow themselves into a basement underworld, shunning the light of day in windowless dens as dark and gloomy as their own fate.

At the other end of the social strata is the legal profession, a class which has, in some respects, taken over the role of court and parliament. The Scottish system of law, along with the church and education, is one of the few remaining vestiges of national independence. The future twenty-fourth chieftain of the Clan MacDougall lives and works alongside these convivial – occasionally kenspeckle (conspicuous) – characters of the profession. They include some of the most intelligent and enthusiastic intellects of the day, sophisticated, highly trained, often at Continental universities and politically well connected. Some have published works of philosophy and written elegant essays.

Their daily lives are spent in a constant to and fro between court and tavern around Parliament Square and St Giles. No judge is too lofty in rank or position to take a pew in the most unpretentious taverns (even drink himself under the table if he feels inclined and lose no face for it). In windy wynds, down dark stairs and up dingy closes – as on the common stair – all classes mingle in social tavern, howff (pub), and laich (basement).

Cramped living conditions make these places more popular than homes which are often much less comfortable. All the family frequent them during some part of the day, many will eat in them every night of the week. Here is the quintessence of simple hospitality: chairs and tables in a plain room with an open coal fire for heat in an iron grate, a kettle for hot water on an iron chain over the fire, a cluster of tallow candles for light in a wooden chandelier hanging from the centre of the ceiling, shelves on the walls for spent bottles, hooks for drinking vessels such as pewter tappit hens, chopins and mutchkins. There is no idle ornament or decoration. To every tavern there are a number of similar rooms, some windowless, some partitioned with screens of thick brown paper to give visual privacy at least; the kitchen and living quarters of the owners are out of sight though not out of bounds.

A boy comes in for hot water to pour into his bowl of brose. People choose which dining room to eat in: in one room cheap tripe suppers, boiling hot pennyworths of black and white puddings, hot pies or kail (broth) suppers; and in another the more expensive roast turns on a spit and is carved to order. An old beggar at the doorway chews on a dried up spelding (salted, dried and smoked fish).

With the shortage of 'office space' in the Old Town these two thousand odd hospitality-houses of mostly respectable reputation are not just places for daily eating and communal nocturnal jocosity. They also hum through the day with the city's business affairs, as merchants strike deals, patients consult doctors, and men of the law argue their cases.

A typical day for Patrick MacDougall starts in Robert Clerk's in Parliament Close where he spends the early part of the morning over breakfast and meeting up with his clients. By 7 a.m. taverns are open, the streets filling up with traders pushing their hurlies (barrows) and laying out goods on wooden boards supported by barrels, others covering the street beside them with their wares. Most of the city will mingle in the street buying their daily food from these street-sellers. Servants are already queueing to collect water from the barrels. Along with the smells, there is noise and clatter: 'Oranges! Braw Oranges!' they shout for the streets are bright this cold December with mounds of the juicy fruits. 'Hot peas and beans!', 'Potatoes all hot!', 'Pies piping and reeking!', 'Caller ou! [fresh oysters], Caller partans! [fresh crabs]', 'Caller cockles and whilks!'

For warmth, Patrick sups his 'drap o' parritch' (porridge), followed by eggs and bacon, mealie puddings, cheese, oatcake farls (quarters) and wheaten bread with orange marmalade from a large earthenware pot, and he drinks ale and brandy.

Eleven-thirty finds him still here as the 'Gill' Bells ring out from St Giles and clerks and writers leave their desks. And taverns fill up as they down their morning gill – whisky or ale – and nibble at a saucerful of freshly boiled mussels, then back to work. Patrick sits on gossiping with friends which he finds a great deal more enjoyable than arguing his cases in the High Court. Soon the 'Kail' bell rings for dinner and he stirs himself across the High Street and into the quiet little alley off the Writers' Court. Catching hold of the greasy rope hand-rail which guides him up the dark stair, he enters the welcoming atmosphere of Clerihugh's, where serious and not so serious business is discussed in yet more convivial talk with his colleagues over the sixpence (2½ p) 'ordinary': a good dinner of broth and beef, roast mutton and boiled tatties, and a bottle of claret.

From here he retires, along with some more cronies, to John's Coffee House in the 'Piazza', a colonnaded walk, somewhat inaccurately termed, at the northeast of Parliament Close. Popularly known as the 'Peaches', it sells tea, coffee, and a dish of thick fatty chocolate. Tea is still an expensive luxury at 6 shillings (30 p) a pound, while a pint of whisky is around one shilling (5 p), and claret about 10 pence (4 p) a bottle.

First opened in 1688, the Peaches has been a hot-bed of political discussion and argument for nearly a century. Wooden racks hang on the wall with well-thumbed newspapers and magazines. The London papers are there too with every day bringing new issues for heated debate.

It is nearly six o'clock now but Patrick decides not to go home: not just yet. The ladies will still be at their tea and cards, and that could go on till nine o'clock before there will be any supper at home. The ritual tea-drinking is not something he cares for much, with all its paraphernalia: the pretty china teaset, the silver teapot, sugar and milk, the tea in a locked casket, the japanned tray which the tea things are set out on, the light crisp little common biscuits made with eggs and sugar, the heavier buttery shortbread, the rich and spicy plumb cake. As far as he is concerned the ladies can keep this genteel little party to themselves. Much better to get legs properly under a table for something more lively to drink, more substantial to eat, more informal in atmosphere. He thinks – along with most of his sex – that the delicate non-alcoholic drink is no substitute for the pleasures of a full-tasting claret which the legal profession, in particular, drinks in enormous quantities. 'I always feel at my best after six [pint] bottles of claret,' maintains one of the leading judges of the day.

But it is dark now as street-sellers dismantle their makeshift stalls, load up barrows and head for home; fishwives humph up the leather strap around their mutched heads (covered with a starched cotton bonnet) and go swinging down the hill to Newhaven, creels creaking. Shopkeepers wind up for the day and make for the nearest tavern and supper.

Tonight, Patrick stays away from the card tables on account of his lack of cash and instead dives, along with some other legal wits not quite drunk yet not quite sober, into the dark defiles of Stewart's, one of the many popular Oyster Cellars down the Fish Market Close which have

opened in the last twenty years since he first came to Edinburgh. There will be a good night's entertainment; singing and dancing as night deepens the sociability; good company too: the literati with their publishers and printers, and parties of well-bred women who have abandonned the dainties of the teatable for an oyster-ploy. For the manners of the day permit women to be 'appropriately and elegantly drunk' without any loss of face in this gutsy atmosphere of the Old Town, where the ability to appreciate good drink is as vital as the company and the food.

But first the oysters. In attempting to satisfy the Old Town's insatiable appetite Stewart gets through a good few thousand in a week. Fresh from Newhaven, the large opened 'natives' are piled on a round wooden board in the centre of the table, with vinegar and pepper in cruets, plates of buttered bread, drams of gin, and pots of porter. Claret is not usually drunk with oysters, but when the company has had its fill, and to finish off the night, there appears the final warming draught of punch made with sugar, lemons, ale, brandy or rum to fortify against winter's chill. As Stewart deposits the enormous bowl (sometimes as large as five gallons) of hot steaming punch in the centre of the table everyone reaches out for a small glass which is filled up with the punch ladle. As the level ebbs the fun livens.

Fishwives sing their strange sea-songs, fiddlers play melancholy Highland airs, genteel ladies sing Lowland love songs. They birl some energetic reels:

> Wi' quaffing and laughing
> They ranted an' they sang,
> Wi' jumping an' thumping
> The vera girdle rang.

Then the ten o'clock drum for closing sounds in the streets and they make for home, picking their way carefully in the dim light from occasional burning torches, wary of rogues and whores and other nightly nuisances descending from above. Patrick climbs up the High Street into the Lawnmarket and through the close to home and bed. But some of the ladies, spirits still high, go off in the opposite direction. They come to a deep shadow falling across the street and fancy to themselves it is a burn. With much jesting and shrieking they take off shoes, lift up skirts and 'wade' across the shadow!

Not all frolic and jollity ends at the ten o'clock drum. Not all drinking houses stop customers imbibing either. In the interests of business many carry on – furtively – till late into the night, and, frequently, till customers are abandoned under tables to sleep it off till morning. At John Dowie's in Libberton's Wynd, half way down to the Cowgate, the rowdy chorus of gossip and jest carries on. Tonight there is a visitor who has taken a fancy to this place and whose witty conversation has kept things going here well past The Drum.

Robert Burns, on his first visit to Edinburgh, has come from Ayrshire seeking approbation from the great and illustrious in the land. Already he has made a good impression on the intelligentsia and they clamour to invite him to their private social functions at the Assembly Rooms and St Cecilia's Hall. But the truth is that, while enjoying the adulation, he finds their affairs unbearably stiff and formal. Though he needs their help, their accolade means little to him – a bubble quickly burst – and he would much rather spend his time socializing in the less sophisticated taverns where the atmosphere is more relaxed, where the homogeneous mix of social classes allows Lord Provost to sit with humble caddie, where people meet on equal terms regardless of who or what they are. It is in such taverns that his genius has picked up so much material for the bawdy lyrics – totally unfit for publication – which capture the riotous spirit of the age.

The tavern fare is more to his taste too, and particularly at Dowie's. Not a claret and French fricassee man, he describes brandy as 'burning trash'. His drink is ale and the 'rascally' Highland Gill, not yet fully nationalized as whisky. Illicit distilling of whisky is rife in Edinburgh: hundreds of displaced Highlanders are making it in improvized stills hidden in the cellars of the city. Dowie's food is noted for its fine quality, as is that of many other Edinburgh taverns. Some are run by characterful tavern landladies, known as luckies, who cook up good things in the kitchen and have poems written about their wonderful hospitality and excellent fare.

Tonight Burns is ensconced with his cronies, Willie Nicol and Allan Masterton, in one of Dowie's recesses known, on account of its shape, as The Coffin. Along with the excellent 'Edinburgh Ale' brewed by Archibald Younger they have already eaten some of Dowie's famed, and jokingly named, 'Nor'loch trout' – not trout at all, but fresh haddock coated in breadcrumbs and fried in butter (the Nor'loch is a stagnant pond, now Princes Street Gardens). Johnie Dowie takes great pleasure in hospitality and every sort of kindliness and discretion. He is one of the finest landlords Burns has come across; in caring for his customers nothing is too much trouble.

Tonight the smiling John brings in a fine gamy dish of jugged hare, and a rich apple pie flavoured with lemon and cinnamon, raisins, almonds, and some finely chopped lemon and orange peel. They have this around nine o'clock, and then later Dowie tempts them to a tangy Welsh rarebit: his wife melts some ripe hard cheese on a plate in the hot hearth and then mixes it with ale and secret spicing while Dowie toasts the bread in front of the glowing coals.

It is not the hamely (homely) Ayrshire fare that Burns is accustomed to. His family are poor farmers and food is limited to the daily contents of the kail (broth) pot along with bowls of brose (meal and hot water) for filling up and hard oatcakes and ripe cheeses for taking to the fields. But the fare at Dowie's, though much richer, is still hamely enough with good broths and stews, the ubiquitous oatcakes and hard cheeses. It is certainly more familiar than the rich and fancy French dishes which Burns meets on the tables of the wealthy.

He has eaten a number of suppers since he arrived in Edinburgh on 29 November, not all at Dowie's or at the fashionable dinner tables. He has been to the Oyster Cellars, and he has eaten juicy sparerib steaks cooked by cheery luckies – butchers' wives, who get the best steaks from their husbands – in the noisy taverns of the Flesh Market Close. Their fires glow hot from morning to night, gridirons clatter, beef steaks sizzle, and customers wait in anticipation till the wooden trenchers are rushed through steaming with the crisp, browned, juicy meat. These are the less familiar city foods for the Ayrshire farmer.

Not long after he arrives in Edinburgh an Ayrshire friend, the merchant Andrew Bruce, invites him for a family supper. Bruce's wife has made haggis puddings that day specially for the supper. Using the pluck (innards) of the sheep which she bought from the Flesh Market first thing that morning, she has spent the best part of the day boiling, chopping, and then stuffing stomach bags, until the muckle pot is eventually filled full of plump haggis puddings tumbling in the bubbling boil. And they eat them that night, appreciating their quality and feeling the statisfaction of eating something good made out of odds and ends – bits and pieces which separately have no real value. Appearance is not the first consideration: what matters is the taste – a principle which applies generally to tavern food in the eighteenth century.

Tasty food may come out of pots, or turn on spits, or grill over hot coals, but it is served up and eaten, by twentieth-century standards, in a rough-and-ready way. Attractive presentation has no meaning as long-boned chops of mutton are grasped from the broth pot and chewed on unceremoniously. Slices of meat carved off roasts on spits are eaten with fingers, potatoes are eaten in the hand, communal eating from a central pot still goes on, and two people will share a basin of broth. We would have found both streets and table manners a problem, though we might well have enjoyed the taste of the food.

To celebrate the haggis and the special supper with his Ayrshire friends, Burns writes a tribute to the 'Great chieftain o' the pudding-race!'. 'The Address' appears in the December issue of the *Caledonian Mercury* and in the January issue of the *Scots Magazine*.

And now this everyday pudding is elevated by the bard to national importance. He could have chosen other dishes. Haggis, though common enough, was by no means any more of a special Scottish dish at this time than roast beef an English one. English cookery books still give recipes for haggas (*sic*) puddings in the late eighteenth century and the Scots certainly liked a bit of roast beef when they could get it. So why did Burns choose to nationalize the haggis? We can only assume that Burns, the iconoclast, looked around for the best example of Scots ingenuity and thrift, the most plebeian dish that would best symbolize honest peasant food. He needed a worthy challenge to the cityfied food fripperies and their attendant pretentions which he so detested. He found it in the haggis.

Edinburgh, apart from the influence of the taverns on his bawdy lyrics, did not excite much other poetry on this first visit in the winter of 1786, while he was working on his second edition of poems with William Creech. The real bard of the Old Town had died tragically, in only his twenty-third year, some ten years previously. Burns was distressed and appalled to find in the Canongate Churchyard where Fergusson is buried that the Edinburgh literati had neglected to put up a proper headstone on the grave of 'poor Robert Fergusson'. He goes to see about a proper headstone which he pays for himself, remarking in a letter to the stonemason that since it is one penniless poet putting up a gravestone for another, he is very lucky to be paid at all! Whatever the so-called literati might think, he regards Fergusson as 'by far my elder brother in the muses'. It is Fergusson who makes, in his long descriptive poem 'Auld Reekie', the accurate observations and the humorous asides which capture so brilliantly the spirit of the Old Town. And it is Fergusson who celebrates the delight of tavern comfort and 'caller oysters':

> Auld Reekie's sons blyth faces wear;
> September's merry month is near,
> That brings in Neptune's caller cheer,
>   New oysters fresh;
> The halesomest and nicest gear
>   Of fish or flesh.
>
> Whan big as burns the gutters rin,
> Gin ye hae catcht a droukit skin,
> To Luckie Middlemist's loup in,
>   And sit fu' snug
> O'er oysters and a dram o' gin
>   Or haddock lug.

4

Old and New
1822

It is 4 February 1818. A group of civic dignitaries and their wives gather along with Sir Walter Scott and his daughter in a room in Edinburgh Castle to witness the unlocking of a box.

Abandoned for nearly two hundred years, the useless and forgotten contents are the crown, sceptre and orb of the last Scottish monarch. The British government – persuaded by Scott – have set up the commission to find these old Scottish regalia. Not everyone present feels, as Scott does, the solemnity of the occasion. As the box opens a Commissioner lifts out the crown and playfully makes to put it on the head of one of the ladies.

In a tone which his daughter describes as something between anger and despair, Scott shouts out: 'By God. No!' And the commissioner, respecting feelings 'with which,' says Scott's daughter, 'he had not been taught to sympathize', the man puts the crown down in embarrassment and Scott leaves. Walking home the short distance between the castle and his house at 39 Castle Street, he takes his daughter's arm. 'He never spoke all the way home,' she says, 'but every now and then I felt his arm tremble.'

His next patriotic ambition was to bring the reigning monarch, George IV, to Scotland which he achieved four years later in 1822. No monarch had been in the country since the young Charles II was crowned king in 1651, but on 15 August, one hundred and seventy-one years later, the royal ship sailed into Leith harbour. Scott was taken out to meet the ship and welcomed on board by the King, who claimed when he heard who was coming, that 'Sir Walter Scott is the one man in Scotland that I want to meet'.

The procession from Leith through the city, masterminded by Scott, was a tremendously exciting spectacle for the thousands who watched. None had seen anything more than the odd military parade or the annual trouping of the Law Lords up the High Street, tripping over their swords and clutching at their wind-threatened wigs. But this was something quite different: a flame of pageantry which had burned in Scott's imagination for many years. Now it had become a reality.

For a brief spell the capital revelled. Scott, in his enthusiasm for patriotic revival – possibly as a symbolic gesture to the long lost Jacobite cause – persuaded the Hanoverian George to don the full Stuart Highland dress for a levee at Holyrood on 17 August.

A portrait was painted of the tartan-clad king on the occasion, tactfully omitting his legs for he had insisted on wearing a pair of pink tights with short tartan socks! He presented the picture to the Duke of Buccleuch by way of thanks for the use of Dalkeith Palace during his stay, and the picture hangs today in the study in the Buccleuch house of Bowhill just outside Selkirk.

Scott's son-in-law and biographer, John Gibson Lockhart, thought the whole tartan thing overdone, but Scott regarded it as a valid way of proclaiming national identity in an extremely colourful way. No matter that Highland and Lowland cultures were historically poles apart, no matter that the majority of Lowlanders had no more natural right to be associated with a Highland clan tartan than a Hanoverian king. Scott's fight was against the flood of modernism accompanied by new wealth and more sophisticated lifestyles. Burns was against this too. But his approach was more direct: an outright condemnation of pretence, and an appeal to value 'Sense and Worth', to stay with 'hamely fare' and think of plebeian haggis puddings. He would have made short shrift of be-kilted Hanoverian kings in pink tights!

But Scott continued to worry that there should be a merging of Scotland with the rest of Britain, an un-Scotching; and that she would become dull and boring as a result, her distinctive character lost. All around him in Edinburgh he could see a city dividing, into Old and New; the rich classes continuing to move out of the Old Town's cramped tenement lands and into their smart new spacious houses in the New. Large parts of the Old were devastated by the great fire in Parliament Square in 1824. Though Scott had many followers there were also the hard-headed, sceptical Scottish Whigs. Reforming, and much less nationalistic, they opposed the arch-Tory Scott with his passion for feudalistic romance and times past.

The leading political opinion-former in the city until 1817 was the Whig *Edinburgh Literary Review*, published by Archibald Constable from his offices in the High Street. It was a highly respected manual of wisdom and good taste. Scott supported the rival publication of the Tory *Quarterly Review*, ushered into the Edinburgh literary world by the London publisher of Scottish origin, John Murray.

But just moved into a large airy suite of rooms at 17 Princes Street was William Blackwood, a shrewd and intelligent man of middle age who had resolved to contend the monopoly of the Whig review with a more challenging Tory magazine than the John Murray publication. As he sat at his desk in the Oval Saloon behind the retail business at the front of the shop, he had noticed, amongst the throng of literary society browsing and gossiping, two young briefless barristers who joined the lively company almost every day on their way home from Parliament House to the New Town.

One was a tall man of impressive leonine form with flowing yellow hair and ruddy complexion; the other was younger, slimmer, dark, with fine features and an air of self-contained elegance. John Wilson and John Gibson Lockhart were just the sort of highly intelligent youthful spirits, touched with a streak of reckless dare-devilry, that he was looking for.

Blackwood knew that he must produce something more nimble, more frequent, and more familiar, to oppose the challenge of the weighty *Quarterly Review*. After a number of false starts the first number of *Blackwood's Edinburgh Magazine* (*The Maga*) appeared in October 1817.

It was a huge success, causing a stir and excitement in Edinburgh exceeding Blackwood's wildest dreams. The first issue carried a brilliant piece of satire, the notorious *Chaldee Manuscript*, a pithy, symbolical account of the strife between Toryism and Whiggism. Its attacking style ridiculed the Whig establishment who were absolutely furious. Wilson and Lockhart had been joined in writing it by James Hogg (Scott's friend 'The Ettrick Shepherd') and the three of them were to provide much of the material which ensured *The Maga's* success until Hogg's death in 1835.

And the most popular item – the one which had people queueing in the streets as it came out each month – was the vivid, racy, imaginative talk between the three half-fictitious characters who met of an evening at Ambrose's Tavern in Gabriel Road in the New Town: Christopher North (Wilson), the Shepherd (James Hogg) and Timothy Tickler (Robert Sym, Wilson's uncle).

It had started one night very late, after a particularly amusing and well-lubricated evening in the company of Blackwood and others, when Lockhart declared that it was a great pity that a shorthand writer had not been there to take down their conversation. In the edition of March 1822 there appeared the first *Noctes Ambrosianae*, written by Lockhart but later taken over completely by Wilson who found in it the perfect medium for his racy, humorous, satirical style.

The rollicking manner of the intellectual gladiator, North, against Hogg's rural freshness expressed in the vernacular Doric provided two highly original characters, leavened by Tickler's more conventional, more mature line.

The leading High Court (Whig) judge of the day, Lord Henry Cockburn (brother of Robert Cockburn the wine merchant in Leith who supplied the Prime Minister), generously described North's dialogues as 'bright with genius', and his interpretation of Hogg's Scotch dialect as 'the best Scotch written in modern times'. The young Blackwoodsmen, along with Blackwood, were frequent guests at Scott's literary dinners; Lockhart had married Scott's daughter in 1820.

On the whole, Scott supported their efforts, though at times he objected to the harshness of their literary criticism. But particularly important to Scott was North's ability to write so brilliantly in the vernacular. Too many, for his liking, had let the national language sink from something of which to be proud into a provincial dialect of which to be ashamed. Scott welcomed *The Maga* as an important venture in the fight to keep Scotland Scottish.

Scott still followed the old pattern of eating. Up early, before six, to write or to spend some time with the men discussing estate business, before returning between eight and nine for the large breakfast which Lockhart describes:

His table was always provided, in addition to the usual plentiful articles of a Scottish breakfast [by which we must assume porridge, cream, oatcakes, bannocks, butter, marmalade, jams and jellies] with some solid article, on which he did most lusty execution – a round of beef – a pastry – or, most welcome of all, a cold sheep's head, the charms of which primitive dainty he has so gallantly defended against the disparaging sneers of Dr Johnson. A huge brown loaf flanked his elbow, and it was placed upon a broad wooden trencher, that he might cut and come again with the bolder knife . . . He never tasted anything more before dinner, and dinner he ate . . . sparingly.

Like most men he left luncheon to the fashionable ladies of the day. They thought it an attractive diversion which also allowed them to push the dinner hour later into the evening. And as it gradually moved from the late afternoon, it took over from the elegant little suppers previously enjoyed around nine or ten o'clock.

There were many who disliked the new fashion. Lord Cockburn was an old-fashioned impromptu supper-party man. At some point during the day he scribbles the following note to half a dozen friends: '14 Charlotte Square, Saturday. My Dear ———,' then he sketches out the layout of the supper table: an ashet of Cold Beef at one end, Two Hens at the other, Oysters in the middle with four rather badly drawn tankards, all containing punch, at strategic points on the table. Mrs Cockburn sits at one end, 'Me' at the other, and the guests are named in their places. Then there is a line drawn and underneath the final detail: 'Tonight before 10.'

This was the kind of artless supper which the cronies who met at Ambrose's also enjoyed around ten o'clock when the sliding doors of the Paper Parlour opened and 'douce, civil, judicious' Ambrose appeared with the ashets of fish, flesh and fowl.

The *Noctes* epicures – the Shepherd, North and Tickler – had no time for the 'corner' dishes with French names which appeared as table-fillers and which Elizabeth Grant of Rothiemurcus describes in her *Memoirs of a Highland Lady* (1797–1827) as the 'various abominations . . . which were merely libels upon housekeeping'. The Shepherd felt likewise though he was more taken up with the effect on his appetite: 'I like to bring the haill power o' my stamach to bear on vittles that's worthy o't, and no to fritter't awa on side dishes, sic as pates and trash o' that sort.'

The well-filled ashets of roasts and boiled food were enough of an attraction in themselves. Placed, at the one go, on the table – to avoid the interruption of 'instalments' to the flow of conversation – the glistening brown spit-roasted, the steaming-boiled meats, the humble ashets laden with food. All looked good enough to eat and no need to shadow them with fancy towering tureens and forest-like epergnes, which many a society hostess now used to decorate her table. Another thing which the *Noctes* epicures disliked about new food fashions was the movement away from the old traditional thick broths.

Shepherd That's hotch-potch – and that's cocky-leeky – the twa best soups in natur. Broon soup's moss-water – and white soup's like scaudded milk wi' worms in't. But see, sirs, hoo the ladle stauns o' itsel in the potch – and I wish Mr Tickler could see himsel the noo in a glass, curlin up his nose, wi' his een glistenin, and his mouth watering, at the sight and smell o' the leeky.

They liked mustard with their steaks, apple sauce and mashed potatoes with their roast goose, their turkey devilled, their potatoes mealy, their cheese well ripened and toasted, their Christmas mince pies soaked with brandy and set alight, their oysters by the hundred . . .

Shepherd Hoo mony hunder eisters are there on the brod, Mr Awmrose? – Oh! Ho! Three brods! – One for each o' us! – A month

without an R has nae richt being in the year. Noo gentlemen, let naebody speak to me for the neist half-hour, Mr Awmrose, we'll ring when we want the rizzers – and the toasted cheese – and the deevill'd turkey – Hae the kettle on the boil, and put back the lang haun o' the clock, for I fear this is Saturday nicht, and nane o' us are folk to break in on the Sabbath. Help Mr North to butter and bread, – and there, sir, – there's the vinnekar cruet. Pepper awa, gents.

They enjoyed a variety of drinks throughout the evening. Jugs of toddy with 'het water and broon sugar' are called for frequently. Bowls of punch come after the meal, and they have the odd sip of the Auld Port (very common and very cheap) when they feel like it. There are bottles of Ale and Porter, 'lang shamblers [tumblers] o' ale' and pots of draught. Berwick Ale they thought had a 'ripe, racy, and reamy richness' while Giles Ale is 'pure spirit of unadulterated strength'. The caulker (dram) is always Glenlivet; the coffee, when it appears, only half-fills the cup, to be topped-up with more Glenlivet.

Claret has by now lost its position, mainly because of unfavourable laws aimed against France which make it more expensive. Those who still drink it look for named growths of good vintages for special drinking rather than for six-bottles-a-day sustenance. Claret appears only once in the Paper Parlour when an English friend is entertained with a grand dinner. Duty on whisky has been reduced from seven shillings (35p) a gallon to two shillings and tenpence (14p) which helps the dram take over from claret as the new national drink.

Frugality also comes into their ambrosial nights and there is much debate about their approach to good food. Will they be considered gluttons? Tickler loses his appetite when they start discussing the state of the poor one night as winter approaches. There is hunger in Scotland, to be sure, some of the poor living on no more than a plate of porridge in the day, and too many going home to an empty cupboard and a cold hearth. But they believe that the poor are not actually starving to death although they are much worse off than the poor in England.

If casual observers, travelling between Scotland and England, are to be believed there are greater signs of poverty among the Scots, an endemic problem for centuries, which the *Noctes* set, in their debate, decide is better dealt with by the Scottish Poor Laws. The Scots are more charitable. They reckon, the 'haves' are much better at handing out to the 'have-nots' in Scotland than they are in England.

For themselves they give thanks that they are fortunate to be able to eat in a manly Scottish way with a keen appetite and sufficient discrimination: not to growl too loudly over a bad dinner nor exhault too highly a good one. They are neither fastidious gourmets nor sinful gluttons, but healthy enthusiasts for the traditional no-nonsense dishes; enthusiasts for seasonal dishes, enthusiasts for good quality raw materials, enthusiasts, above all, for the perfection of Ambrose's cooking:

Shepherd Beef and greens! Beef and greens! O, Mr North, beef and greens!
North Yes, James, I sympathise with your enthusiasm. Now and now only [winter] do carrots and turnips deserve the name. The season this for rumps and rounds. Now the whole nation sets in for serious eating – serious and substantial eating, James, half leisure, half labour – the table loaded with a lease of life, and each dish a year. In the presence of that Haggis, I feel myself immortal.

During the ten years that Wilson turned out his monthly serial there is no doubt that the crisis between old and new deepened, threatening the simple way of traditional Scottish eating as new foreign cuisines and more sophisticated eating habits made their influence felt. The setting had something to do with it too.

By 1835 the taverns of the Old Town were practically deserted by the professional and upper social classes who now meet in plush Princes Street hotels and the likes of Ambrose's. The Shepherd, while he is waiting for North one day in the Saloon, sits on the damask-cushioned settee and wonders at the strangeness of the feeling when all he has ever been used to is a hard chair and a rickety one at that. The grand mirrors with their gilt mouldings, the cut crystal chandeliers with their galaxy of wax candles, and the Turkey carpet are a far cry from old John Dowie's Tavern in Liberton Wynd (demolished in 1824).

But despite the plushy grandeur of the decor, at least Ambrose continues to cook the same old tavern favourites from a more spacious and better equipped kitchen in this new hotel in Picardy Place. The fact is that the *Noctes* set have only moved here from the old place because of Ambrose and his cooking. They constantly mourn the snugness of the old howff and pay sentimental visits to the room where they originally met in Gabriel Road just for old time's sake.

Scott's passion for the preservation of old traditional ways and the talent which the Blackwoodsmen had for immortalizing their ambrosial nights gave an important boost to national awareness of the distinctly Scottish kitchen. Around the time that all this was going on a minor novelist of the day embarked on writing up a system of Scottish cookery which paid particular attention to the national palate and national dishes. *The Cook and Housewife's Manual* by 'Meg Dods' was first published in 1826. It turned out to be a bestseller for the remainder of the century, going into at least sixteen editions and bringing the author – Christian

Isobel Johnstone – much more success as a cookery writer than she had ever had as a novelist.

Though Scott did not have a very high opinion of her novels he seemed pleased at her original idea of using one of his characters, Mistress Margaret Dods (Meg Dods), from his novel *St Ronan's Well*. Meg Dods was based on the fiery but brilliant cook, Marian Ritchie, at his local howff, The Cross Keys in Peebles. Mrs Johnstone chooses to write anonymously, using Scott's Meg Dods as the central character of the cookery book.

It is unclear whether Mrs Johnstone and Scott ever met, whether she asked his permission to use his character, and whether in fact he had anything to do with writing the introduction to the book. She is described as an 'extremely retiring' person. But in a note to the new edition of *St Ronan's Well*, published after the first edition of the cookery book, Scott says:

Meg Dods has produced herself of late from obscurity as Authoress of a work on Cookery, of which, in justice to a lady who makes so distinguished a figure as this excellent dame, we insert the titlepage. – Though it is rather unconnected with our immediate subject, we cannot help adding, that Mrs Dods has preserved the recipes of certain old dishes, which we should be loath should fall into oblivion in our day.

It may be that Scott over-romanticized, but there is no doubt of his passion for the preservation of a Scots identity. It is in a large part thanks to him that the Blackwoodsmen have left such a vivid picture of Scottish eating habits of the time, and that Mrs Johnstone felt motivated to preserve through Meg Dods the old Scottish dishes. Much of it is still relevant: no need for it to fall into oblivion in our day.

5
Highland Disaster and a Fishwife's Creel
1840–90

In the decades following the surge of Scott-generated nationalistic emotion the Highland situation deteriorates. His Highland stories *Rob Roy* and *The Lord of the Isles* tell of stirring times long past, of warrior-Highlanders like Iain Ciar and of an old clan system now in decay. They are about the romance of tartan-clad Highlanders, about scenic grandeur, and about the idea of a benevolent chief caring for his clansmen. They create the appealing image which brings Landseer to paint Highland scenery and Mendelssohn to visit Fingal's Cave. But the popular idea of the Highlands is far removed from the reality of bankrupt chieftains forced to sell their ancestral lands, of wealthy industrialists who want neither the people nor their produce but only the land. The desire for prestigious sporting playgrounds and gigantic sheep farms is what they have in mind: the land under threat, the people under sentence.

Of course some of the chiefs stay. The MacDougalls of Dunollie hang on to their lands though their letters are constantly filled (yet again) with anxieties about money and how to economize. 'Keeping the land in good heart' is what Patrick's son, John, the twenty-fifth chief, sees as the most important priority. Their lifestyle is frugal, the chieftain's wife making money for essential items by selling the butter and cheese from her cow. They keep up appearances as best they can, but do not fall into the trap of keeping up with the extravagant social lifestyle of their more affluent English counterparts.

There is a feeling in the MacDougall family that 'comfort means ruin', a philosophy which, though it may have saved them from bankruptcy, causes problems when a wealthy and high-ranking distant relative comes to stay. They are not 'at a loss for meat and drink' but a cook and manservant must be hired from Edinburgh. Wax candles, a bottle of Madeira, some claret and one dozen white ivory-handled dinner knives must be bought specially for the visit. Accommodation is the greatest worry. They fear that he will think them vulgar for they have not spent, as many others have, on building a more elegant house or even furnishing the existing one with fine furniture.

Those who have, and who live above their means, are forced to make their estates more profitable. There is nothing romantic about the reluctant exodus of the Gael as the clan chief takes away his fertile strips of land and mountain shielings for the sake of more profitable grazing for sheep. Rural exodus, to be sure, is taking place throughout the whole country as a natural result of the population expansion and the need for urban workers in industry. But unlike Scottish peasants in other parts, many of whom want to leave a life of dirt and toil for what they imagine to be a better one, the Gaelic-speaking Highland clansman does not willingly leave his land. Clan loyalties and a strong identity with his land are bonds which have to be broken – tragically in many cases – by force.

Though the greatest compulsive exodus took place in the 1840s it continued steadily throughout the next three decades as it became more and more impossible for the Gael to make a living from his decreasing strip of croft land.

Travellers in the Highlands took back stories of what a miserable, filthy, lazy lot the Gaels were. Courteous, generous and hospitable, mind, but living in such hovels and in such awful peat reek! Looking and smelling like smoked hams! They would really all be a lot better off if the young men got themselves into the army and the women took themselves into domestic service in the city. They ought to be grateful to the landowners who were prepared to pay a passage to put them on an emigrant ship.

Such misinterpretation of the situation by visitors to the Highlands had been a problem since General Wade's roads first penetrated the mountainous land and brought the curious to investigate the wild places in the eighteenth century.

The travellers' tales gave a distorted picture of the truth since it was difficult for them to get the true picture of reality when all honoured guests, as they were, sat down to the most bountiful table that could be mustered. However hard-up, Highlanders treated their visitors royally with the traditional Highland Welcome.

According to many reports, and especially the widely-read Johnson journal of the journey in 1773, it appeared as if the clan chiefs were living in the lap of plenty. The truth was all too often – as for the MacDougalls of Dunollie – the exact opposite. What the travellers saw were the final remnants of a way of life which had been in decline since the first Jacobite rising.

The English travellers spoke no Gaelic so they only reported what they saw, not what the people thought or felt. Strange customs were never properly explained. (It is still a problem today and the philosophy and habits of Highlanders are often a puzzle to casual observers.) Also, it must be remembered that these early travellers judged what they saw by their own standards of a settled English countryside with picturesque market towns and a much more sophisticated lifestyle. They were ill-equipped by prejudice and the inability to communicate. They provided little analytical comment of any depth on the real situation in the Highlands; their reports record some of the basic facts but their impressions, on the whole, are fairly superficial.

This lack of understanding led to some appalling attitudes towards Highlanders when it came to selling the lands. Derisory London estate agents wrote frank articles in *The Times* warning prospective buyers from purchasing some estates on account of the 'irrepressible crofters'.

They advised against buying anything in the Western Isles, and perhaps on a few of the sea lochs, where the properties were more or less 'swamped in squatters'.

It was not until the 1880s that there was some effective local ferment against such injustices to the Gàidhealtachd (Gaeldom). It resulted in the Napier Commission of 1883 (set up by the government) which took details of the squatters' plight and presented the evidence of their grievances. But the outcome was not satisfactory. Whilst the crofters' case was seen to be a just one – they were given security of tenure for land and house, a guaranteed fixed rent, and the right to heriditary tenure – what they really needed was capital investment and some proper system of agricultural improvement as had happened in the Lowlands. The Highland crofter, not rich in money resources, was left with a too small, uneconomic croft and the reluctant exodus continued.

Their unwillingness to leave a difficult and unrewarding kind of existence seemed strange to those who came into contact with the situation. It was difficult to understand the Highlander's emotional ties, nor could others grasp the idea of putting homeland before wealth. But the Gael had never really known the value of cash in his hand and had little idea of the comforts which might lie beyond his remote Highland glen. He was also peculiarly suited, physically and temperamentally, to the harsh unrelenting climate. What were regarded as hardships by others were, to him, an acceptable and natural way of life.

What if winds blew and snow drifted; without wishing to romanticize the picture, there was warmth from the glowing embers of the peats heaped up in the middle of the room. There was the gentle smoke reeking pleasantly of heady peat bog scents as it wafted its way upwards. There was the comforting sight of the black iron pot, hanging on the end of a rope fixed to a rafter, quietly steaming away with a grand meal of light mealy potatoes in the bottom, and on top a thick layer of fat herrings which had been salted in the autumn.

When the pot was drained, the family fell on the huge pile of herrings and potatoes, relishing them as they picked with their fingers. A potato in one hand, they would take a bite and then a nip from the fish flesh; it was a delightful contrast this mealy potato and tangy-rich herring.

They were happily fed, they were cosy enough, they loved the land, the community, their animals, the solitude and peace of a beautiful country. They had known hardship and survived; before the troubles they had known an even better life.

The Highland quality of self-reliance which allowed these people to make best use of the outstandingly varied produce from the land and sea was now under serious threat. The best resources of the land and sea had been at the disposal of the MacDougall clansman of 1715. He was skilled

at operating the system to provide a rich and varied table.

But poor Highland crofters of the 1880s are now reduced to a potato-based diet, some milk and oatmeal if they are lucky – always the herring. Shielings are gone and with them cheeses and cream dishes. The game and salmon belong to sportsmen now. There is not enough land for goats, sheep or hens; those who have the means hang on to a cow for milk; the remaining narrow strips of land are taken up with growing enough potatoes to give the greatest yield. There is no room for the other vegetables which had been grown in the past; no seeds for cabbages, carrots, parsnips, turnips, beetroot, parsley and radishes come from Glasgow now as they had done to Dunollie in 1715. But there are still the wild things, the herbs, berries and fruits, the edible seaweeds and the shellfish from the shore.

Just as potatoes are now replacing the milk cow and the oat field, the travelling van and the grocer's shop later force this ingenious race away from their ancient ethic of self-reliance.

Some of the displaced crofters-fisherfolk from the sea coasts resist the emigration boats and travel to the Eastern seaboard where there are plenty of thriving little fishing villages and good white fishing. On the Easter Ross seaboard the fishing villages of Shandwick, Hilltown and Balintore provide refuge for victims of the Highland Clearances. The populations of some towns double as a result. And there is a rich harvest from the North Sea as the community helps the incomers build new houses for their families.

In the house-style of the village, walls are built of large round stones gathered wherever they can be found, carried back in creels, and bound with red clay from the various clay-holes. Timber for rafters is from the local woods; there are no ceilings. The thatch is woven to make a watertight roof and they have some comfort and protection against the elements. The coastline is stormy, so ropes are thrown over the thatch and weighted down with boulders as the only safeguard against the distress of having the roof blown away during a gale.

Floors are made of grey clay which comes from other nearby clay-holes. They clean easily with a sprinkling of sand and a good brushing. The praze (chimney) is set against an inner wall with a wooden canopy stretching from ceiling height and overhanging the whole fireplace like a huge hood so the smoke finds its way out through a small wooden chimney pot. The open fire of wood or coal sits in an iron basket grate supported on each side by two stone and clay hobs for pots and pans. The chain and crook for the cooking pot hang from a wooden beam across the flue. This is a much more orderly arrangement than that in their old windowless Highland black-houses with central clutter round the fire in the middle of the room.

Windows are nevertheless tiny. Doors have no locks. The walls are innocent of plaster but lime-washed a brilliant white. There is the aumry (cupboard) where provisions and utensils are kept, the skelf (a wooden frame containing shelves) where the crockery is arranged, a kist (chest) containing family clothes, a box bed with its sliding doors. The kitchen table sits by the small window for light, a muckle chair with arms for the man, high stools for women, and creepies (low stools) for children. There is a girnel of oatmeal, and a barrel of salt fish, and crusie lamps with their supply of fish oil and dried pith from rushes to light the winter nights. The family Bible, a copy of Robert Burns's *Poems* and Bunyan's *Pilgrim's Progress* lie on a table.

From black-house to white-house these displaced West Highland families begin a new life, a much more organized fishing lifestyle than the haphazard fishing affair on the West Coast which was only a small part of their working life. Here it occupies their every waking hour.

From the 1840s to the 1880s the fishing is good and East Coast fisher-folk prosper. In the summer months the men go to the herring. The unmarried women follow the fish from Shetland to East Anglia, gutting, packing and salting the silver darlings which are then exported in millions of barrels to the salt-herring eaters in Russia and Scandinavia. For the rest of the year it is the weekly round: gathering bait, baiting lines, fishing, drying, smoking and selling.

Gathering bait is women's and children's work and they must follow the ebb tide even if it means getting up at 1 a.m. to catch it. They find sand eels near home when the tide is out, but they also have to travel round the coast to Tain, Inver, Arboll and Fort George for mussels. At Nigg Bay they also get mussels, cockles, lug worms, and small flat flukies (flounders) which children love to catch with their feet. Limpets are scraped from the rocks near home and put in a basin of cold water for a week; this allows the hard edge to become softer and therefore easier for the fish to take.

The next job of the day, also timed by the tide, is preparing the line for sea. Everything stops for two hours while man and woman steadily clear and hook the line.

They sit on low stools, the woman to the right-hand side of the man. He clears the line of used bait and it falls in loops onto his right-hand side. She sits with basins of shelled bait at her feet and a plate with more on her leather-aproned lap. The line passes through her fingers and she catches up a piece of bait for each hook, the line falls into a creel on her right-hand side and every now and again she throws layers of chopped grass in to stop the hooks snagging each other.

When the fisherman is ready to go to sea he takes with him a keg of water and enough oatcakes and cheese in a canvas bag with a drawstring – his pocken mor – to keep him going for twenty-four hours. His wife takes off her boots and stockings, hitches her skirts above her knees and goes down to the shore to push off the yawl (boat). Then her husband climbs onto her back, for he is wearing long leather sea-boots unsuitable for wading through salt water, and she picks her way carefully into the water to deposit him in the floating boat. It is the 1890s before a harbour is built at Balintore. Until then, women push off boats and carry men once a day.

Three men work in one yawl. Sailing to the fishing grounds, rowing if there is no wind, they know the best places to go, sometimes just out from the villages, sometimes to Tarbat Ness, sometimes to Helmsdale. The line is cast and left for half an hour or so before being pulled in, hopefully full of fish: cod, haddock, mackerel, whiting, cuddies (young coalfish or coley), soles, flounders, skate and dogfish. One man rows the boat while another pulls in the line as the third removes the fish and recoils the line to prevent tangling. In rough weather great skill is required; in fog they must study the direction of the waves to find their way home, for every seventh wave is a directional one and the land lies at right angles to it.

Safely back, the catch is laid out on the beach and divided evenly into heaps for each fisherman in the boat. Now the fresh fish for selling is packed into the fishwife's creel and she sets off round the country.

A couthy character in her white mutch (bonnet) tied under her chin, the starched and ironed frills framing her brown weather-beaten face. She wears stout knee-high leather boots and black woollen stockings. Her skirt is navy worsted and she wears an apron on top, a blouse and woolly cardigan. On cold days she slings a shawl round her shoulders. Then she ties a string round her skirts about half-way down her hips, ties it tightly and hitches up her long skirt and petticoats. Once pulled up, the thick material at the back makes the pad to take the weight of the fish-laden creel as she walks inland for many miles to sell the day's catch.

The farmwife is glad of some fresh fish to relieve the monotony of their oatmealy diet. The fishwife guts the fish, and may even fillet it. Then there is a cup of tea and chat and a bite to eat if she wants it. She barters her fish for cheese and butter, some meal, fruits and vegetables in season, eggs or crowdie, occasionally a piece of venison: self-sufficient women extending their family food supplies. The creel ends up as heavy as it was when she started out.

For these intrepid fisher-women their toil is not ended as they make their way home through the pine woods to the tide coming in across the sands of Shandwick Bay. In the remainder of the evening there is still work to be done: the rest of the day's catch has to be prepared for smoking tomorrow, the lines have to be baited for the next day's fishing, and children and husbands have to be fed.

The best of the catch has been sold but there are enough small flounders, whiting and a few wings of skate to make a 'fry': not fried, but grilled, in their favourite way which takes no time at all, across the brander on top of a good 'red' fire. The whole family eat them along with fresh-churned farm butter and the boiled floury potatoes which were cooked before she went off to 'the country'.

On other nights there is more time to make up a good fish stock flavoured with onions and potatoes for a fish broth. Once the large haddock and cod have been deheaded for smoking or salting, the heads can be stuffed with a mixture of oatmeal, onions and the fish livers, and then boiled in the pot to make a dish of 'croppen heads'. Sometimes she makes potato soup and vegetable broth from bones and sheeps' heads or pigs' trotters – all cheap dishes, but satisfying without straining the family finances. Butchermeat is not as plentiful as fish but they eat lots of rabbits. The odd cormorant, tasting of wild duck, occasionally finds its way into the broth pot.

The only method of baking is on the girdle. Oatmeal or barley bannocks (round and thick) and oatcakes (triangular and thin) are baked on the girdle and dried off on a trivet or toaster hooked onto the fire bars. 'Loaf bread' is not much eaten. When children come in from school they have a slice of sweet yellow turnip from the broth pot on a crisp oatcake, or they slice some fresh butter, lay it on an oatcake and spread with crowdie for a feast of flavours and textures in crisp oatcake, soft creamy butter and crumbly sharp cheese.

For festivities they make a boiled suet pudding in a cloth, a 'clootie dumpling'. If times are hard it contains just flour, suet and a little spice and soda dissolved in water. When they can afford it, the pudding is richer, with more spices, sugar, syrup, treacle and dried fruit. The mixture is wrapped in a scalded cloth which has been coated in flour and is boiled in the pot over the fire for three hours or so. They eat it hot, with a knife and fork, sprinkled with sugar. The leftovers are eaten cold or fried up with bacon and egg.

Because there is plenty fish they do not eat much else from the seashore now, just cockles and whelks and cuvie (a rope-like tangle) which they peel with a mussel shell and then crunch. They also eat dulse, dry-roasted on the brander till it is crisp, or put into the broth for flavour. Carageen they still dry and make into a jelly and eat with plenty of thick cream. Though frugal, it is a nutritious diet which serves them well through the strenuous days of their industrious lives.

Sunday, of course, is for the church and no one fishes or does anything much besides reading the Bible and praying. Mondays, the fishwife stays at home to get some housework done and to see to the smoking. Each fishwife owns a bothan (a wooden smoking shed), usually on the strip of land between the front of the house and the sea. The floor is of earth and in the centre is a hollow where the fire is laid. There is no chimney, so as the fire burns the shed fills with smoke. Along with her collection of hard woods, she likes to have plenty of fir cones to make up the fire for they give the best flavour to the fish and some of her customers will have them no other way.

The haddock are gutted, split open, and the heads taken off. They are then laid in a shallow tub of fresh water and scrubbed to remove all traces of blood from around the backbone. Now they are put into another tub along with salt and sometimes a little brown sugar and left for half an hour. The prepared fish are hung to drain on speets (spits), the point stuck through the 'ears'. Then the shed is filled up like the shelves in an oven, the speets hanging on runners at the side. The fire must be watched carefully to keep it smoking properly and the speets moved about as some fish are done sooner than others. Fish are smoked two days a week, Mondays and Thursdays. Tuesdays, Wednesdays, Fridays and sometimes Saturdays are days for 'the country'; everything else has to be fitted in round this weekly routine.

The fishwife's Moray Firth speldings travel to far distant parts beyond hinterland farms. Bothan-smoked fish are eagerly sought after in the best fishmarkets in the country. Though she also smokes salmon and herring for kippers it is the speldings which are the native cure. Later they become more commonly known as Finnan haddocks after a fishing village further south on the Kincardineshire coast.

Displaced Gaelic Highlanders, now East Coast fisherfolk, they gather round a blazing coal fire in their new white-house, their old life gone for good. Though the toil is hard here, this new living is not a bad one, but still there is a longing for mountains, glens and old clan kinship:

> That old lonely, lovely way of living
> In Highland places . . .
> The yearly rhythm of things and social graces,
> Peatfire and music, candlelight and kindness.

6

French Food for a Queen
1900

It was Prince Albert who took a liking to the Scottish Highlands, perhaps as much for the sporting facilities as for the beauty of the scenery. But whatever the reason, the building of Balmoral Castle meant that the royal household made a temporary home in this part of the Highlands in the spring and for the best part of September and October each year, Queen Victoria continuing with the twice yearly visits after Albert's death.

At the age of eighty-one, and in the autumn before her death in January 1901, she journeyed from London to Balmoral for the last time. With her on the royal train was a select group of servants picked from the three hundred necessary to run the Buckingham Palace operation.

At Balmoral the style would be simpler. Not exactly a holiday for the staff, but they would have more free time and a slightly less stressful existence than the London routine. Among the servants on this final trip was the French *chef de cuisine*, Menager, who had replaced Charles Elme Francatelli. Menager had chosen to bring with him a young Swiss apprentice, Gabriel Tschumi, who had been working in the palace kitchens for nearly two years and was showing some talent for cooking along with the necessary dedication to the rigours of the job.

Tschumi, just sixteen, had arrived in London from his native Lausanne with no English, no cooking experience and no earthly idea of what an apprentice kitchen post in the royal household meant. Neither had he any concept of the complicated social structure which operated among the British servant classes of the day: a below-stairs society with as many rigid social castes as the one upstairs that it served.

It took Tschumi some time to get to grips with it all: the boredom of spending most of the day fetching and carrying for the master chefs, the long hours standing peeling vegetables (no stools or chairs were allowed in the kitchen), the relentless heat from the huge coal fires as he patiently basted revolving roasts.

To help him learn 'his place' and the clearly defined responsibilities of each member of the servant household, as well as the intricate details of palace protocol, he had his cousin, Miss Louise Tschumi, who had been one of Queen Victoria's dressers for many years.

As this opulent empire drew to a close the royal system was copied by other rich households of the day. A house steward, the Master of the Household, hired and fired the men, paid bills and wages and kept household accounts; the Housekeeper was the Steward's counterpart on the female side and had charge of storerooms, ordering and handing out supplies to the housemaids. She was in charge of the still-room, she candied and bottled fruit, made preserves and pickles, lavender water, rose water and the pot-pourris used to scent the rooms.

Along with the still-room maids, she also made the scones, cakes and sandwiches for the drawing room afternoon tea. In terms of authority she was something between a headmistress and a mother superior, extremely dignified and strict, but not above practical help if servants were in trouble or ill. She had the rudiments of first aid and could make up healing lotions and potions for minor ailments.

Next in rank was the Butler, who was responsible for the plate chest and its inventory, the wine cellar and the cellar book, and the table arrangements at all meals, as well as serving the meal and the wines. He usually slept in a small room beside the silver plate safe and was – like the housekeeper – not allowed to marry. Along with the Groom of the Chambers, the Valet, the Ladies' Maid and the Chef, these were the Upper Servants who enjoyed certain privileges of comfort and privacy in their daily lives. Beneath this hierarchy of Upper Servants was the vast army of workers – Lower Servants – who carried out their orders.

By the time Tschumi found himself travelling to Balmoral in the autumn of 1900 – at the age of eighteen – he was no longer delegated to menial kitchen chores but learning the art of *cuisine classique*, a style of cooking common in all the wealthy households of the land.

The chefs' day begins at 7 a.m. when they meet in the kitchen to prepare breakfast. This is a very different affair to the Continental roll and coffee which Tschumi has been accustomed to at home in Switzerland – a minor snack in comparison with this breakfast ritual. Rumour has it that Queen Victoria eats a simple boiled egg from a gold egg-cup, which may be a dieting gesture on her part (her waistline is reputed to be 54 inches) but the rest of her family and guests see their way through the daily five-course breakfast which is regarded as essential stoking up for the rigours of the day ahead. With a lifestyle that involves much physical effort, and with no central heating, no labour-saving devices, no motor cars, there is a need to consume a great deal of fuel to provide energy and keep inner fires burning – unless, of course, you happen to be an overweight and inactive monarch.

By 7.30 coal ranges are hissing-hot, spits skewered with chops, cutlets, steaks, sausages, chickens, and small game birds. Roast-cooks are basting and deftly removing spits from fires, and with a long sharp fork sliding the roasts onto huge hot ashets. Elsewhere, egg dishes are stirring-up, fresh fish grilling, bacon frying. Queen Victoria's boiled egg is timed to the second.

The choice of five courses, plus tea, toast and preserves, starts with Eggs. Then there is Bacon, then Fish, a grilled Finnan haddock or kipper, then the Roast Platter, chops, steaks, or sausages, then the Game in season, or chicken.

After breakfast, Menager sets to work finalizing the menus for the day, reviewing the contents of the larder and planning ahead for the next few days. The draft menus, written into his menu book, are taken by a footman to his mistress for approval. Lunch is not as elaborate as dinner since many of the household are out for the day fishing or shooting and a picnic will be taken to them. But for both lunch and dinner the kitchen must produce the statutory eight courses which late nineteenth-century households of any pretention regarded as the essential length of a decent meal.

For Her Majesty's dinner tonight, Tuesday 9 October 1900, Menager has suggested:

Potages: De faisan aux quenelles/Purée de choux-fleurs
Poissons: Cabillaud aux oeufs/Merlans frits
Entrées: Mousse de jambon aux concombres/Pojarky de volaille
Relevés: Boeuf rôti/Choux braisés/Kallrs Nuszmet Ralm
Rôti: Dinde farcie
Entremets: Les haricots verts sautés/Les choux de Bruxelles au beurre/Spurutz Gebacknes
Le Dessert
Sideboard: Hot and cold chicken/Boiled tongue/Cold roast beef/Salad

This is a modest dinner by Buckingham Palace standards where the average meal ran to four soups, four fish dishes, four removes, eight entrées – a break here for some water ice to rest the stomach before the serious part of the meal – three roasts, six removes, and fifteen desserts. And if that did not satisfy there was still the chance of a slice from the sideboard rib roast of beef or leg of roast mutton.

For dinner tonight Tschumi has been given the task of preparing the pheasant consommé with quenelles. Work on the soup began two days ago when he boned out the breast fillets of four pheasants that had been used as an entrée. The carcass remains he threaded onto the spit and roasted till well browned before putting them into the stock pot with a knuckle of veal, a pound of lean ham and enough water to cover.

While this was coming to the boil he sautéd some chopped carrots, a sliced onion, two turnips, a head of celery and a leek in a stewpan with some butter till all the vegetables were a golden brown. When the stock rose to the boil he skimmed off the grey scum carefully, then added the vegetables, three cloves, a piece of mace and a bunch of fresh aromatic herbs. Then he left it on a gentle part of the stove, languidly simmering for three hours, before straining it.

Yesterday he removed the fat, and carefully picked the meat from the bones of the birds. He worked silently. Menager was a strict disciplinarian and did not permit unnecessary talking in the kitchen which might distract from the concentration required for complicated and delicate culinary operations. While Tschumi worked, he wondered if those who were (hopefully) to enjoy this consommé, had any idea of the effort and time involved in its preparation. He loved the work in the kitchen now that he had more interesting things to do, more challenging dishes to prepare, and it was enough to receive praise from Menager for tasks well done. But he still thought it odd that there was not more comment from Upstairs. None of them came near the kitchen, none of them ever sent a comment on whether they thought the food good, bad or indifferent. At home in Switzerland it was considered rather rude not to say that you had enjoyed a meal. Why did the British never say that they liked the food that so much time and effort had been spent preparing? Tschumi put the meat through the mincer till it was very fine and then returned it to the strained soup with some egg whites to make it crystal clear. 'A good consommé,' Menager had instructed him, 'must be as clear as whisky.'

So, today the soup is more or less ready. Now he has to make the *quenelles*: first, some finely minced chicken, then a thick white sauce – a panada – and half a pound of fresh butter. He pounds all this vigorously in the mortar till smooth, adds salt, enough grated nutmeg to cover a sixpence, some pepper and an egg. Then more pounding. Finally he puts it into a bowl and whisks in another egg and two yolks and a tablespoonful of béchamel sauce (flavoured white sauce). To check that the seasoning and texture is just perfect, he cooks a small spoonful in a pan of boiling water for three minutes, takes it out, cuts it, and tastes.

It is a complicated procedure for the eighteen-year-old apprentice and he is nervous of making mistakes. A recent disaster was the filling for an Apple Charlotte. The mixture of apples, sugar and butter had been on the stove when the alarm was raised in the kitchen that a rat was loose. Grabbing a frying pan for a weapon and abandoning his apples he joined the chase – rat killed but apples burnt. Start again was the thing to do in this kitchen if disaster struck. There was always plenty more of everything, even Beluga caviare and French truffles. Tschumi soon learned the kitchen philosophy: in the complications of *cuisine classique*, if something goes wrong it is merely the price of producing a Master of Cuisine, and he should feel no guilt about the waste.

For the *quenelles*, both mixing and cooking are tricky. He needs two teaspoons, a knife, and a jug of hot water to mould the mixture. Each spoonful is smoothed over with the knife, and then the other teaspoon is dipped in hot water and used to scoop the mixture out of the first spoon. He puts each tiny *quenelle* into the base of a buttered sauté pan, and when the pan is filled he holds the lid of a pan in a slanting direction towards the inner part of the edge to protect the very delicate textures, and pours boiling water carefully into the pan. They are poached for a few minutes then drained on a cloth before he puts them into the base of the soup tureen to be filled with his now bright whisky-clear pheasant consommé. Striving for perfection, it has taken Tschumi almost two hours just to produce the garnish for the soup. But Chef Menager has no time for apprentices who are in too much of a hurry to get things done, and Tschumi knows well enough that there is no point in cutting corners.

Now the dinner must be served. Course after course is carefully timed and sent off. Silver-domed ashets of hot food are all meticulously checked by Menager and rushed along corridors by liveried footmen to be served in the royal dining room before the food cools. This extravagant lifestyle has taken centuries to develop, but lasts only briefly into the twentieth century.

By the time of Edward VII's death in 1910, Buckingham Palace no longer supports the three hundred servants of Victoria's reign but the French style of food which the Queen liked has survived. So familiar, so well established, the French chefs so thoroughly professional in their approach to this discipline in the kitchen that British gourmet eating remains exclusively *cuisine classique*, transferred more and more now, as the century advances, from the houses of the aristocracy and nobility to the grand hotels. It is to them that these talented and dedicated French chefs now direct their skills.

Edward had followed the cooking of Escoffier and the comfort of Ritz's hotels round Europe. He was a bon viveur in the French mould, believing wholeheartedly in the French view that *'la bonne cuisine est le fond de la vie'*. Though Queen Victoria had made suggestions about the content of the menus she approved each day, and though she certainly had her likes and dislikes, she did not share her son's enthusiasm for gastronomy.

Edward was a discriminating, well-practised gourmet who had eaten his way round the top eating establishments in Europe. When he took over from his mother he made much more pertinent comments to the kitchen.

He had likes and dislikes too. Sophisticated *cuisine classique* – yes – but what about some of the good British cooking traditions? He introduced the custom of serving roast beef and Yorkshire pudding with plain roast potatoes and horseradish sauce on Sunday nights. It relieved Downstairs from the nightly ten-course marathon and was hailed as a huge success by the royal household Upstairs who were possibly quite relieved to be excused one night of the week from the rich French cuisine.

There was more interest too in what was going on in the kitchen. Queen Alexandra frequently side-stepped royal protocol and arrived in the kitchens with her daughter to investigate what the chefs were up to and how they cooked certain dishes. Her mother-in-law would have been horrified, but Tschumi rather fancied that had she not been queen, she would have liked cooking.

Had Edward's reign been longer, or had he held more sway with his French-loving mother, there could have been a much needed revival of the best traditional British dishes led by the monarchy.

As it was, Edward was followed all too soon by a son, George V, who was obsessed with hot curries which he had learned to love during a spell in India. Indian chefs cooked them in the palace kitchens and they appeared on every menu – royal taste buds deadened by chilli-hot food. (It must have seemed rather a waste spending three days preparing a delicately flavoured pheasant consommé with gossamer light *quenelles*.) George V's wife, Queen Mary, it has to be said, was a gourmet in the Edwardian mould and later, when she was living in Marlborough House as a widow, Tschumi went to cook for her and discovered then her extremely discriminating palate.

But along with Tschumi and the other servants the Indian curry-chefs make their pilgrimage to the Scottish Highlands each year on the royal train. As his grandmother had appreciated Menager's French-cooked *potage de faisan aux quenelles*, now George V relishes India's spicy cuisine. The leading family in the land employs foreigners in the kitchen who cook with prime Scottish raw materials but do not understand or practise the cooking art of the country. Scottish cooking traditions neglected, Sir Walter Scott's fears materialized.

This disastrous situation was not helped, from a British point of view, by the prolific number of French cookery books which were published in English. The influential French chef Louis Estache Ude from Crockfords, one of London's most famous clubs, had produced *The French Cook* in 1813. Other giants in the kitchen – Francatelli, Soyer and Escoffier – followed, and the French invasion of the traditional British kitchen was irreversible.

So what of Mrs Beeton? You may well ask. Though her collection of recipes was massive it was written for the sound, solid and sensible, middle-class Victorians whose real ambition was to employ a French chef, or at least imitate the style as much as possible. There is actually very little in her collection of distinctive national or regional dishes or their origins. How to 'command the household' is dealt with in great detail but not the history of native dishes.

In contrast the Scottish 'Meg Dods', *The Cook and Housewife's Manual*, written anonymously in 1826 by Christian Isobel Johnstone, was much more concerned with the subtleties of national eating and cooking. An entertaining introduction illustrates the distinctive Scottish eating traditions of the day as practised by the gourmets of the Cleikum Club whose pertinent comments on the food continue as footnotes throughout the book. She also isolates national cuisines in chapters on Scotland, Ireland, Wales, France, Germany and Spain. She wanted to enhance the value of the book for the practical cook by setting out a culinary system which would be superior: drawn from the combined excellences of Britain and other countries. But even such praiseworthy efforts had little lasting effect on the French march into the British kitchen.

When F Marian (Flossie) McNeill wrote *The Scots Kitchen* a century later in 1929 her concern echoed cries of Scott and Johnstone: to preserve for the sake of their excellence as well as their nativeness, dishes which were in danger of slipping into undeserved oblivion. She scoured the land in her capacity as a folk historian for the dishes of the people, searching out the historical background to Scottish cookery. The result is the most complete collection of classic Scottish dishes yet produced which has had as lasting an effect in the twentieth century as *Meg Dods* had in the nineteenth. A really delightful source of Scottish traditions, its success in the 1970s and 80s is sadly not appreciated by its author who died in 1973. But though it was widely read, and cooks and chefs dipped into it for something distinctly Scottish when the occasion demanded, it too, like all the other British books, failed to provide the kind of technical expertise necessary to direct and influence those cooks who cooked for a living and set the professional style.

The food traditions of a country are rarely to be found in rich houses, or in the professional kitchens of hotels and restaurants. We must look elsewhere.

7
Urban Plenty and Want
1920s and 30s

Hunger marches follow the General Strike of 1926. In Dundee, fathers who are too expensive to be employed in the mills become housekeepers: the 'kettle-bilers'. For the kettle has replaced the cooking pot, and it is boiling water which now hums on black iron hobs where once fragrant brews simmered and stewed. In their cramped tenements, one room is bedroom, parlour, kitchen and scullery combined. An upturned tea chest is their only table, some empty tin cans their only drinking vessels.

The men are not bad cooks – when they have something to cook. A 'poor relief' hand-out is two pounds of jam and a loaf of bread. The fact is that their traditional oatmeal is expensive and a loaf of white bread cheaper. They don't need any fuel to cook the bread either, so, working it out, all in all, the household finances will simply not stretch to old staple, however much they might long for a bowl of porridge and milk. Milk? Well, that is more expensive than the water that comes out the tap.

What little money there is goes on some tea instead, for it has become much cheaper. Sugar is cheap too. In tea and on slices of white bread it is just about the only sweetener in their poverty-stricken, hunger-marching lives.

They buy their tea from 'wee shoppies' on every tenement street corner, many of them supplied by the Dundee Tea and Coffee Merchant, James Allan Braithwaite and Sons, whose shop selling retail and wholesale is tucked in under the Adam-designed Pillars in the town square.

The quarter-pound packets of the cheapest tea at threepence (1½ p) are what they supply to the shoppies, but the rest of Dundee come here for their fine blends of tea and coffee. While the British Empire survives, the country enjoys the pick of the tea and coffee crops, secured in oriental japanned tea bins which line the polished mahogany shelves in Braithwaite's shop – treasured tastes and aromas of distant lands. To find the shop, a blind man in the street need only follow his nose and the wafts of coffee-roasting smells. Inside, the scents of astringent teas and mellow coffees mingle.

James Braithwaite has a finely tuned tasting-palate and buys only the best. He has many customers further afield than Dundee and he tastes and blends, balancing the flavours. He uses the local water which his customers send in bottles, knowing that different water affects the delicate taste of the tea and that he must blend to suit.

It is all part of the service. Like making up small bags of drinking chocolate, a special and popular mixture of cocoa, icing sugar and vanilla essence, and his own blend of butter and margarine which he sells cheaply to those who can't afford butter. There is a display cabinet with a twelve-bin selection of biscuits and above it a smaller one with a selection of quality sweeties. From the three dozen hives of bees that he keeps as a hobby there are jars of heathery-tasting amber honey and waxy combs too.

As he shuts shop on Saturday night it is well after seven o'clock. He walks down to Dock Street, passing through the thronging Greenmarket on his way to the station and the train home. The market is thick with people: a rendezvous for townspeople and farm workers on Saturdays, in for the day from the surrounding countryside. The stalls are open till around eleven o'clock on this, the busiest night of the week.

Shoeless, ragged street urchins are everywhere, begging, stealing, living by their wits. They seldom enjoy the simple pleasure of buying food for themselves. They all know Mr Bratty-Tattie, as they call him, not just because he is a well-known shopkeeper in the city, but also because of the Quaker Sunday School which he runs for them on Sunday afternoons, when they flee the cold streets and sing hymns for an hour, and sometimes imagine there may be more to life than the misery they see all around them.

If they are lucky to get a penny, there is the 'Buster' stall, named after the digestive effects of the saucers of piping hot peas which it sells. They eat them with a teaspoon, sitting on benches at trestle tables inside the tent. The chip stall is a covered tent too, where a salt-and-vinegared poke from Italian Mr de Gernier costs a penny. Hot chestnuts and roast potatoes are another winter treat, ice cream in the summer.

The street kerb is their club. Most of the street food comes from barrow-pushing Italian immigrants who make wonderfully rich and creamy ice cream and pour red raspberry sauce over it which the street-wise children call 'the Tally's blood'. It is cheapest from the barrow but there is a sit-down Italian shop in the Overgate now.

Pressing noses against the window they gaze in wonder at the Fourpenny Specials made up in big fluted glasses the size of flower vases and filled with layers of flavoured ices and preserved fruits, topped with mounds of red juice-dripping ice cream and fancy wafers. A threepenny (1½ p) 'het peh' (hot pie) from Wallace's in the Vaults is also beyond their means and they must be content with just a sniff of the huge plate-sized semicircles of the best steak-filled 'het bridies' for they cost the small fortune of fivepence (2 p).

James Braithwaite, as he passes through the Greenmarket this Saturday, goes for the exotic fruits brought in on jute-carrying and other foreign boats. By this time of the day they are at a bargain price, as stall-holders start to get rid of those they have not sold (it was just this sort of bargain that attracted the Dundee grocery family of Keillers in 1700 to buy up a lot of sour Seville oranges which started them making the first commercial marmalade in this jute and jam-famous city). For the seven

Braithwaite children there is a Saturday night surprise in their father's bag. Will it be pineapples, mangoes, pomegranates or peaches?

These are the luckier children of Dundee: once a week fruit-treats, a penny for a het peh and poke of chips, and plates filled daily with good food. They live in the village of Barnhill on the sandy stretch of coast just five miles from the centre of Dundee. The Braithwaite's house, Sunnybank, is a five-bedroomed villa which looks out to the beach and the Firth of Tay. They have a dozen hens in the back yard, an allotment where they grow vegetables, a greenhouse for tomatoes, a front garden full of apple trees, and beehives which are brought down from the heather moors in winter.

Providing three meals a day for the large hungry household, Christina Braithwaite has been most influenced, since she married James Braithwaite and came to Barnhill from her native Kilmarnock, by the fishing port of Broughty Ferry, just a short ten-minute walk along the Esplanade. Though they ate fish in Kilmarnock, it was never so plentiful, so fresh, or so readily available as here. Twice and sometimes three times a week Kate, the fishwife, arrives at her back door. She comes first to Mrs Braithwaite who, she knows, will relieve her of a good few pounds of fish and not just the haddock, whiting and cod, for Mrs Braithwaite is willing to have a go with some of the more unusual fish.

Kate tips the fish 'fresh and louping in the creel' into the deep sink in the scullery. Some *are* actually still alive for Kate has come straight from the boats. They talk about cooking the fish and Christina, though an intuitive and talented cook, learns new ways and gets good advice from this fish-cooking fishwife.

Sometimes Christina will buy Arbroath 'smokies', the coppery smoked haddock which have been hot-smoked over a smouldering oak fire. Unlike the Finnans which are split open, these fish are smoked with the bone in. Sometimes they are eaten cold once the skin has been removed with boiling water or they are heated up with butter in the oven. The fisherfolk cook them in milk. To make the fish go further, Christina cooks up a kedgeree with rice, hard boiled eggs and lots of butter and cream. Kate's kippers are good too grilled simply with butter.

Other good things to eat come from the hens. Fresh eggs every day and a well-matured hen now and again for a pot of rich-tasting chicken and rice broth. Between the cheap and plentiful fish and the ready supply of newly-laid eggs there is not a great deal of butchermeat eaten. A leg of farm-cured bacon, wrapped in a muslin cloth, hangs in the cupboard under the stairs. Hungry children home from school take a few slices for a fry-up with some eggs or a slice of the sweet haggis pudding which their mother makes with oatmeal and dried fruit. There is always potted hough (shin of beef) or potted rabbit in the larder at the end of the scullery, which they have with tea and piled-up plates of hot buttered toast. In a cupboard upstairs there are rows and rows of home-made jams, jellies and chutneys, a girnal (storage chest) of flour and one of oatmeal, a barrel of apples which the children delve into when hungry and some tins of bully beef and tinned fruit but only for emergencies.

The day starts with porridge and boiled eggs, or fish, tea and toast. Always there are soft white floury baps from the bakers and home-made oatcakes. Children come home from school for dinner (lunch) in the middle of the day. Walking to and from the Grove Academy in Broughty Ferry they pass tempting fruit-laden gardens on the jute lords' mansioned-slopes which they raid relentlessly to the despair of gardeners and the annoyance of the owners, neither of whom are smart or quick enough to catch the nimble culprits. At home there is a plate of broth and some mince and carrots with creamy mashed potatoes.

School finished for the day and back home, there is a plain tea between four and five o'clock: bread and butter with something eggy or black and white puddings with bacon, always with bread and butter and jam, home-made pancakes, scones and oatcakes. The final meal of the day is around eight o'clock when they all sit down together with their father home from the shop. It is always fish for supper, along with a plate of porridge and milk.

Sundays are different with a special roast beef dinner in the middle of the day. A huge tureen of chicken broth is to start. The puffy Yorkshire puddings are next. Then comes the ritual carving of pink slices of succulent beef, crisply edged with glistening fat, and the half dozen vegetable tureens which are filled with garden-fresh greens and roast and boiled potatoes. Finally there is a burnished lemon meringue pie. Most of the cooking is done on the Triplex in the kitchen which has an open coal fire and three ovens, though there is also a gas cooker in the scullery.

At New Year there are more than twenty round the table, a goose at each end or a giant turkey, and a massive clootie dumpling with lurking silver threepennies for every child. Following tradition, it is on Hogmanay that children expect Santa to come down the chimney and they hang up a pillowcase at the end of their bed for presents. At Easter they roll painted boiled eggs down hills till they crack open. Summer is for picnics.

Family ones in the train for day trips to Arbroath, smokie capital of the East Coast, where fish smoke reeks through every alley and every wynd. Then they walk along the cliffs to Auchmithie where descendants of Norse seamen still smoke haddock in the ancient way.

Half-barrels have been dug into sunken pits in the ground, a fire lit in the bottom, and the fish, headed and tied in pairs, hang across speets (spits) laid on the edge of the barrel. Once the fire is just the right heat, the whole thing is covered with layers and layers of black, smoke-impregnated hessian sacking. The fire is regulated by these layers of sacking: if too hot on a dry windy day more layers must be piled on to exclude air and slow it down; too slow on a wet muggy day and they must give the fire more air. Good smokers have an instinctive sense born of long practice, for the smokie must not be burnt to a frazzle, nor too lightly done. Auchmithie is one of the oldest fishing villages along this coast where tiny but-and-ben (two-roomed) fisher houses cluster at the cliff's edge overlooking the sheltered harbour and pebbly beach with exciting caves for adventurous children.

But the summer picnic of the year, the one everyone looks forward to and the whole of Barnhill turns out for, is the picnic for the eighty odd street-urchins from Mr Bratty-Tattie's 'ragged' Sunday School. The children who never see the outside of Dundee from one year's end till the next all make their way to the station. Tin mugs for their tea hang round their necks on a piece of string. The guard locks the doors on the train compartments to remove temptations as they stop along the way. At Barnhill they are released for a day of freedom at the seaside.

The local shopkeepers have been warned and take the necessary precautions. Sandcastles are built. Races are run. Then there is 'The Scramble', the highlight of the picnic when, for some brief moments the sky rains pounds of sweeties as Mr Bratty-Tattie showers the mob from a huge box he has brought from the shop. And the grassy part of the beach is a scrambling mass of sweetie-chasing children. Tea follows in the Bratty-Tattie garden: tin mugs filled with milky tea to be drunk along with their bag of goodies – a round jam-filled butter biscuit which is not a biscuit at all but a kind of huge flat bun, a Coburg cake, a queen cake and a doughnut.

It's a happy day for these children so cruelly deprived, many wearing no shoes, winter or summer, their clothes always in tatters. Today they are on their best behaviour: no need for mischief, no need to steal and beg for food, no need to do anything but enjoy themselves for a few brief hours.

These children belong to the generation of urban poor who are now deprived of past eating traditions: for them kettles and tea instead of pots and porridge. On the poverty line they must sustain themselves on a miserably inadequate diet, picking up what they can from the more interesting variety of foods on the streets. But the quality of their food is so poor, the facilities for cooking so bad and the cooking-women who once stirred pots now spinning and weaving jute in factories.

Dundee was one of the worst examples of this change in the working-class way of life – past country rhythms gone – where urban deprivation for far too many caused ill health and a serious deterioration in Scottish cooking traditions. Not that the whole urban population was living at this poverty level, but many were forced into bad eating habits which have reverberated into present times. A recent survey of diet in Dundee revealed that 30 per cent of men never eat any vegetables!

While the poor could not afford to maintain their traditional foods, the rich jute lords preferred to eat sophisticated French food or any other foreign food novelty which they could lay their hands on – high-falutin extravagancies on their cut-crystal and shining-silver decorated Queen Anne tables and not much virtue in homely fare.

But at the Dundee tea merchant's table the quality and traditions of Scottish food meet with more respect. Discriminating eaters – a father with an adventurous and highly tuned tea-and-coffee-tasting palate and a dedicated and skilled cooking mother – they both pay attention to the details of freshness of ingredients. Their children are educated at the table to enjoy the simple natural tastes of the best quality ingredients: richly flavoured Angus beef, garden vegetables, orchard apples, Carse of Gowrie soft fruits. They understand how to handle the fishy delicacies from the cold North Sea. They preserve the traditions of good things from pot and girdle, and to start and end the day eat a plate of comforting porridge. It is at this table (my grandparents') that an important part of my early conceptions of Scottish food are formed.

Postscript: Though James Braithwaite died in 1939 his two sons James and George carried on the tea and coffee business but not in the stately old Adam Pillars which were pulled down. They moved to a new shop in Castle Street which today still sells teas and freshly roasted and ground coffee, and is managed by George's son, Allan Braithwaite. All the old beautifully crafted traditional shop fittings were moved from the Pillars to the new shop and are still in use. My grandfather's coffee grinder still grinds in the window, his ornate brass scales still weigh out tea on the original shop counter, the handsome japanned tea bins still survive after nearly a century of use – all museum pieces now in a plastic world of designer shop-fittings.

8

Glasgow Good and Bad
1940s and 50s

For dinner at one o'clock there is a plate of thick meaty broth: ham bone with lentils, or the stock from a boiling chicken thickened with leeks and rice, or Scotch Broth made with pearl barley and a piece of nineholes (flank) of beef: always the cheapest cuts of meat, always the threepence-worth (1½ p) of vegetables and parsley, always a warming plateful.

Meat and potatoes are for Sundays: an oxtail stew, tender meat sliding of its own accord from sculptured bones left on the plate; or rich brown oniony mince with misshapen mounds of grey-white suety dumplings, or chewy tripe in milk and soft boiled onions – all cooked in the pot which sits on the black iron range in the cramped kitchen of my Glasgow tenement-living grandmother.

Through two World Wars, and the subsequent repercussions on food supplies, through a Depression which hit hardest at this urban population, it was quite astonishing that these fundamental Scottish cooking traditions should have been so well preserved in this tenement lifestyle which I grew up with in the 1940s and 50s.

Of course much was lost. But the old habits of Scots frugality saw this generation through their difficulties, some better than others, their powers of ingenuity stretched by the relentless scrimping and saving which went on to make ends meet. Their attitude to waste as a criminal offence also helped them to survive. It developed their hard-headed approach, which made them so splendidly thrifty – valuing occasional luxuries, but always realistic of the horrors around the corner which were all too visible on suffering faces in city streets.

To say that the Scots can't cook, but are nevertheless quite good bakers, always seems to me to dismiss too lightly the ancient tradition of cooking in a pot, which survived despite serious obstructions, if the things which came out of my urban grandmother's and my mother's pots were anything to go by.

Their ideas on cooking were quite sound. They had an intuitive talent for making good things out of a little, which requires clever cooking skills rather than just the ability to slap out a scone for the girdle or make a crisp round of shortbread. How much easier, also, to stick a roast in the oven, fry up a steak, grill a lamb chop, than gently coax the flavour from meat and vegetables, blending with patience and discretion the delicate combinations.

This was clever economy cooking, using the least amount of fuel, extracting the maximum amount of flavour. It is a more advanced method of cooking than primitive roasting on the spit. It is a method understood in the higher echelons of gastronomy. In France, more than in any other country perhaps, there is a long history of respect for the pot on the fire, the *pot-au-feu* – the foundation of the cooking.

There were other food influences around, of course, for the young generation who played the streets and back courts of Glasgow tenements at the end of the Second World War, but there is no doubt that for the fortunate the focal point of the eating day was the cooked dinner from the pot. We never saw such things as roasts. Vegetables went into broths or were cooked in the stews, but hardly ever appeared separately, except sometimes a cabbage, or a tin of peas. It is, I fancy, the main reason why so many Scots of this generation have a mental block about eating vegetables on their own.

Street food, if it wasn't a 'piece in a poke' (white bread and jam in a paper bag thrown out of the window to hungry children in the back court), was from 'chippies' (fish and chip shops) or 'Tallys' (Italian ice cream cafés) or there was always the baker selling hot pies, sausage rolls and gravy.

At the ancient street-market complex where people eked out a living selling from barrows there was more street food for hungry children along with second-hand clothes and books, rusty mincers, crystal wireless sets and all the clamjamphry of odds and ends that makes up the 'Barras'.

Developed as one way of fighting poverty and unemployment in the nineteenth century, it later became an established part of the city life, which it remains today: a pantomime of fast-talking barrow men and women. Selling is the thing. Holding the attention with whatever antics are most novel and the typical Glasgow sceptic in the crowd quips back: 'See him . . . could sell the Pope a double bed, so he could.'

We indulged in toffee apples, poky hats (ice cream cones), hot peas and vinegar, pea bree (cooking liquor), hot pies and gravy, bags of whelks, plates of steaming fishy mussels with cups of mussel bree. As we lived so much of the time in constant city smoke, sulphurated air and wintertime pea-soupers, just to put our heads round the door of the Oyster Bar in the Gallowgate as the huge pans of black mussels and whelks were tipped onto wooden slats on the floor to drain, was to take us back to nostalgic salty scents of the sea.

For those who struck some sort of balance between this street/shop-cooked and home-cooked food, the diet did not lack variety. Vegetables eaten raw were certainly rare. But the city streets, especially on Saturdays, were full of fruit and vegetable barrows. Much of the produce came from the Clyde valley, a fertile source of vegetables, plums, apples and pears, tomatoes, strawberries and raspberries. Fruit was our treat in those days of post-war rationing when we never knew sweets and never missed them.

Of course there were those, inevitably, who ate more fish suppers from the chippies in the week than was good for them – like every night because their mothers were out working all day. Their diet suffered, though nutritionists have established that fish and chips make a well enough balanced meal.

While broths and stews were for dinner, shop-cooked foods were for the teatable at night. You went out to smart tearooms where a black and white uniformed waitress would ask if you wanted a 'plein or a heigh tea'. But tea was just tea at home. There was nothing 'high' about it.

White bread and marge with a huge pot of brewing tea on the hob. Fish, pies, black and white puddings were always with chips. Bacon was with eggs, or tattie (potato) scones, herrings were in oatmeal, squerr sausages (square sliced Lorn sausage) were with fried potatoes, cheese was scrambled with eggs, kippers and boiled eggs were with toast. The standbys were either sardines, or for a special treat, tinned salmon.

Salads were virtually unheard of, the only nod in that direction being a solitary Clyde valley tomato which appeared along with a plate of cold meat. The meat was invariably gammon (ham), a smoky cure which came from a grocer who sliced the cold meats with a long sharp knife.

White bread with jam was a staple – a habit developed early in the century as a deprived urban population looked for cheap sustenance which did not require cooking. The bread we ate was always a well-fired Square loaf, Plain, rather than Pan, its blackened crust, crisp and crunchy, the 'heel' tough and chewy. This Plain loaf was made by the old-fashioned batch method of baking without tins where all the loaves are cooked together, then separated where they join. A Pan loaf made in a bread tin was regarded as rather pretentious and in the slang of the streets used to describe anyone who acted too posh.

Traditional craftsmen bakers made the bread, rising the dough with a long yeasty fermentation. It was not until the 1950s that the factory (Plant) bread – which now makes up two thirds of the bread eaten in Britain – established itself. It was in the fifties that the largest milling companies, Spillers and Rank, saw the opportunity of setting up large-scale bakery plants, of buying up vulnerable small bakery businesses hit by heavy capital taxes, and using these retail outlets to sell their factory bread. It was the death knell of the craftsman baker in Britain. It was the beginning of the end for good-tasting bread.

The end came in the sixties when scientists and food technologists at the Flour Milling and Baking Research Association at Chorleywood in Hertfordshire created the Chorleywood Bread-Making Process (CBP), the process now used to produce most British bread.

Using sixteen times as much yeast as normal, higher temperatures, and a fast dough mixer, the process cuts down the first fermentation of the dough from a few hours to a few minutes and can produce a finished loaf in less than ninety minutes when it would take six hours by traditional methods: an advantage in commercial terms but the reason for our tasteless bread.

Put in a small quantity of yeast, leave it to ferment naturally, and it will multiply with moisture and warmth and ripen the dough adding acidity and flavour. The longer it has to work, the better the flavour, texture and crust of the bread. Some bakers I know leave their bread maturing for several days before baking. It is this natural maturing, as with wine, which produces the taste and character which no amount of additives can create artificially. (And neither can it be created in today's hot bread shops or supermarket in-store bakeries. Both may conjure up alluring smells to attract custom, but merely sell, on a smaller scale, the same instant CBP bread. It just costs more.)

The urban bread-and-jam eating habit which had developed in the first half of the century was later perpetuated as bread lost its flavour and it became necessary to lash on the butter, jam – anything – to give it a taste. We used to spread on margarine and a few well-salted and vinegared chips for a chip sandwich. Did we really eat these carbohydrate calamities? We did. We even ate macaroni cheese, dare I say it, with chips!

But it wasn't all such unhealthy-sounding heavy stodge. The light floury scones, just off the girdle, were fabulous. And golden hot pancakes – butter dripping – equally delectable. Thin lacy crumpets the size of saucers were rolled up with butter and strawberry jam, also while they were still hot, the butter melting into the jam and oozing out at the ends.

For Saturday night tea there was also a plate of 'fancies': shop-bought sticky iced French cakes, creamy filled meringues and dusty sugary cream-cookies. The full-blown tea, scones, pancakes, fancy cakes, etc., appeared only once a week when the 'clan' gathered in my grandmother's kitchen. Even with two sittings there was precious little elbow room at this indulgence of good Scottish baking; the scarcity of expensive protein amply compensated by the generosity of the cheap carbohydrate.

When people get nostalgic about old-fashioned teas it is as well to remember that tea at night for the Scottish working classes originally developed as an inexpensive filler for hard-up hard-working people. The poor-relief handout during the Depression had seen to it that, for those with nothing at all, there was no alternative but a starchy and sugary unbalanced disaster.

What damage was done to the cooking traditions of a nation when family cooking was abandoned to tea and white bread. What damage to health when a diet so overloaded with carbohydrates and fats was universally eaten by the working people.

The wealthy and fashionable were also addicted to this style of eating though it was much more elegantly presented. Seen at its most refined in the Glasgow tearooms which developed at the turn of the century and flourished as fashionable meeting places until their decline in the 1950s, the polite 'heigh' tea was the thing. Three-tiered cake stands towering on teatables with a bounty of bread on the bottom, teabread on the one above, and on top, pinnacle of desire – the 'fancies'. It was a special but short-lived ritual, for a brief spell immortalized in the unique tearooms invented by the energetic Kate Cranston.

She established the originality of the setting with rooms designed by the most innovative architect of the period, Charles Rennie Mackintosh. She stimulated public interest in the arts by decorating the walls with pictures by some of the most talented artists of the day.

Both Kate Cranston and her husband, Stuart, were Chartists. He had owned the Crow Hotel in George Square where the Merchant's House now stands. These 'temperance' pioneers were concerned that there should be an alternative to the pub.

Stuart Cranston started the gentleman's Smoking Room, attached to tearooms and hotels, where men could go without having to buy an alcoholic drink. She developed the tearoom, also as a place where couples could go without the obligation of drinking alcohol. In this sense the Glasgow tearoom developed out of a need to combat the serious drinking problems of the city. An alternative to the pub during the day and in the early evening but not as any particular celebration of the tea meal.

By the 1960s restaurants for evening dining out were becoming more popular with the younger generation lured by the novelties of Indian curries, Chinese stir-fries and Italian pasta. Tearooms in the old style disappeared. One or two of the originals survived into the sixties, but they were mostly the domain of stylishly be-hatted ladies of the heyday tearoom generation.

It does seem a pity that the elegance of the Cranston tearooms had to go, also the celebration of proper tea drinking out of china tea pots (speaking as a tea merchant's granddaughter). Besides, it was the one meal which commended the skills of Scottish bakers.

Of the few tearooms left in Glasgow today there are some who have imaginatively adapted their menus to emphasize salads rather than greasy fries. Some have taken the girdle and baking specialities off the tiered cake stand and put them into display cabinets. Some have inventively made them an integral part of a snack meal, such as the Tattie Scone and Toasted Cheese which the Glasgow bakers, Bradfords, sell in their elegant Coffee Shop in Sauchiehall Street, as near as you will get to the old style (and not a stone's throw from Kate Cranston's original Willow Tea Room, now renovated). A brigade of black and white waitresses provides the service and if nostalgia gets the better of you there is even a tiered cake stand.

Making use of these old Scottish baking specialities by incorporating them into snack meals, while at the same time taking a more balanced nutritional approach, seems to me a good way of moving forward. But those who claim that Scots cooking skills are confined to baking must look deeper. Centuries-old habits of pots on the fire are not so easily destroyed.

So let's take up the opportunity, still existing, to keep the good things alive – bury the bad – and prove that even from the most unlikely places there is something worth handing on.

9
Historic Orkney
1988

The shore-lashing gale has destroyed a large part of the dyke. Repair is urgent. This dry-stone blockade which normally encircles the entire coastline of North Ronaldsay is to keep sheep on the beach. It is the only protection the island's grass and crops have from the seaweed-eating sheep which inhabit this northernmost isle in a group of seventy which make up The Orkneys.

Here, the community responsibility is such that when disasters strike, able-bodied men from other islands leave their work and spend what time and effort is required to get the dyke mended as quickly as possible: several days' hard work, in this case, manipulating the stones back into place.

And as they leave, the grateful islanders throw a couple of bulky sacks into the boat – this small island population showing their appreciation with a couple of carcasses of their very special sheep. Unlike any other sheep on any other island, or in any other part of Scotland for that matter. Nowhere else do sheep eat *only* seaweed – thanks to the dyke. Nowhere else produces sheep of such flavour as this close-knit island community where Orkney people rally to the needs of others.

Forged out of a more brutal age of Picts, Vikings and early Scots they live differently now, these distinctive Orcadians, in this scatter of islands between Scotland and Shetland: a land of curious sheep, strange stones, mercurial northern light, and sea – everywhere.

To get to it you must first cross the turbulent waters of the Pentland Firth, the stretch of water where Atlantic meets North Sea and which has strong men reaching for the sea-sickness pills on a rough day.

But there is little more than a gentle heave as the *St Ola* crosses between Scrabster and Stromness this fine sunny day in the late September of 1988. In such calm weather it is much the best way of arriving in Orkney. The ferry boat, taking a westerly curve, passes close in to the thrilling red sandstone cliffs of Hoy, the beach of Rackwick, the Old Man, St John's Head, The Kame. And then there are yet more gigantic cliffs on the 'Mainland' island further west. The flat and fertile island of Grimesby is to the east and finally the boat steams into the sheltered waters of Hamnavoe – the haven bay – and the waiting pier of Stromness.

Passing ships, sailing in and out of this last watering hole before Iceland, Greenland, Canada and the Arctic, have shaped the character of the town: whalers, explorers, sea-going expeditions, wartime sailors, peacetime fishermen – all men of the sea, reliving the sea-life of their Viking ancestors. Though they have come and gone they have left us Stromness.

A treasure of a town as it unfolds: The Street follows the curves of the shoreline, rising and falling, twisting and turning, so always there are new vistas: too narrow for much traffic but if cars appear they crawl at walking pace. The pedestrian rules, tramping the old flagstone paving, past tightly packed tall stone houses set end-on to the sea with waterfront stone piers and steep slipways. The wind blows strong from the southeast and the gusts hit as they surge up the gaps between every block. There is refuge in one of the closes which lead to more houses and gardens up Brinkie's Brae behind – a maze of narrow wynds with steps and stairs, one of them is called the Khyber Pass!

The shops, set into the ground floors of domestic houses are modern enough inside. In the grocers and bakers the shelves speak of the uniformity of our food supplies.

But yet . . . but yet . . . outside The Fish Shop, on this fine day, hangs a foot-long salt-encrusted dried fish. Inside is Raymie Manson, Smoker and Fish Curer. He has trays of good-looking fresh fish, some creamy orange-roed scallops, deep dusky red partans (crabs), blue-black mussels and little pots of pale pink prawns. But it is the dried salt fish which I am interested in.

Is it just a good curiosity-rouser at the shop door or something that people actually eat regularly? He laughs, good humouredly; the Orcadian enthusiasm for old unchanging customs is like a shot of sanity in a world of crazy food happenings.

'Goodness, me! Everyone eats salt fish here. We love a good salty piece of ling. That's what's outside.'

His voice lilts at the end of sentences in the gently questioning and delightful tone of the native accent.

'I dry and salt some of it myself. But not enough, so I have to get more in from Aberdeen.' How would I cook it? 'Well, you just soak it overnight then boil it up in fresh water. Eat it with plenty of good mealy potatoes mind. Lots of butter too, Orkney butter if you can get it. Then what we do is make up enough for two days and mash all the leftovers together. My, but it makes really grand fish cakes too.'

I buy a pound and make my way up The Street in search of mealy potatoes and Orkney butter. An elderly woman standing in her doorway smiles, and we strike up a conversation about the goings-on. A man with a pot of stone-coloured paint is busy splashing it over the yellow anti-parking lines. They are obliterating all such modern sights in order to shoot *Venus Peter*, a film set in an old Fife fisher town. No doubt they will be happy enough to leave Raymie Manson's antique salt ling hanging where it is.

But my friendly Sromnessian has now invited me in to see her house where she lives alone, a neat trim little place, narrow in width but three storeyed with deep-set windows and photos everywhere of her family, all living in Canada. She makes tea and we talk about – yes – salt fish, mealy potatoes and Orkney butter.

I should be able to get Golden Wonders at the butcher's round the corner, but the golden butter may be more difficult. How does she cook fresh fish, I ask. Very lightly poached, it seems, in a little water, with lots of butter, which mixes with the water to make a sauce, a fine buttery sauce, as she describes it. No, she doesn't much care for it fried. There is obviously something about this fish-butter thing among these well-practised Stromnessian fish-eaters.

There is no butter at the butcher's, as she had suspected, but Golden Wonders in plenty – salt fish and potatoes will keep. Besides, there will be trips back to these friendly out-going people to see and taste many more Stromness food attractions, to talk to the Orkney fishermen boiling their crabs at the crack of dawn, to investigate the dark blue orange-speckled lobsters waiting in tanks, to visit George Robertson and taste his famous Orkney fudge, to glimpse at the production of the half million Stockan oatcakes which are made here every week, to talk with Ken Sutherland about Orkney farmed salmon and the success of his Marinated Orkney Herring. But above all to wander The Street and seek out the curiosities that are only yet glimpsed: a Birsay loaf, the Westray biscuits, yellow rounds of cheese in butchers' windows, grey-brown bannocks and strange-looking teabreads.

Except for some hills on Hoy, the Orkney islands are all fairly flat. Not an extension of Highland glens and mountains, but mostly covered with a carpet of green fertile land. The Orcadians who live here, principally farmers, do a bit of fishing on the side.

It is in one of the old well-lived-in, single storeyed and one room thick farmhouses that I have come to stay. New farmhouses there are, to be sure, modern bungalow-type houses, though, and quite unlike the old style where each room leads into another in a long corridor of rooms which goes from human living and sleeping quarters through to byre, stable, barn and sometimes a kiln at the very end – a sensible arrangement for people can tend animals and do farmwork in the winter without stepping out into icy blasts. It gives a cosy feeling too with everything under one roof. Round the peat burning Raeburn at night with my hosts we drink the local Highland Park whisky and I learn more of the lives of these hospitable and characterful people. As it turns out this is a beef farm and to track down the elusive butter, and hopefully some farm-house cheese too, I must make for the rich farmlands on the isle of Shapinsay the next day.

I had been to Shapinsay before, a few years ago, for one brief night at the commanding Balfour Castle as a paying guest of the enterprising Scots-Polish Zawadzki family who provide the interesting contrast of living in the grandeur of a mid-Victorian turreted and four-poster-bedded castle, along with some of the pleasures of remote island life.

Like the lobster-fishing trip which Christopher Zawadzki took us on when we found ourselves pulling up creels and their precious contents, then sailing close to a beach covered in basking seals, and later into the darkly mysterious caves round cliffs when we thought of the Norse King Haakon who sheltered his magnificent war galleys here as he paused before taking off for the Battle of Largs in 1263.

Dinner in the castle dining room was a reminder of old-fashioned private Highland hospitality where guests and hosts sit down together to share the plenty of the land.

There was good broth to start, and a whole leg of sweet-tasting roast pork from a Shapinsay born and bred pig from their own farm. The whole joint was brought to the table and carved by the host. Crunchy crackling and rich gravy along with some creamy mashed potatoes and fresh green cabbage: this was the best island eating we had come across so far. And we finished with two of their own cheeses with thin crisp Orkney oatcakes. One cheese was crumbly, but the other was much richer, a deep golden, more Brie-like in texture. Highland Park took care of the rest of the evening and in the best traditions of Scottish hospitality we drank with the family and no tally made on the amount. We were off the next day on a tight schedule and with no more time to explore the island. But this visit now among the farmers and the ladies of the cheese and butter-making was to be quite different.

The island farmers rear mostly beef though many of the farms, keeping traditions alive, have one cow which they use for the cheese and butter they sell locally. If they have more cows and sell the cheese and butter commercially further afield then they lose their beef subsidy – 'Red Tape' they call it, but a bad system, it seems to me, which stifles a worth-while local cheesemaking industry on the island. It accounts for the reason why the precious butter is so hard to come by and the cheeses mostly unavailable beyond the 'Mainland' shops. My helpful farmer, Kenny Meason, who met me at the pier, explained all this as we toured the island. The first visit was to Jean Wallace at Girnigoe farm. Because her husband has been invalided out of farming and they have no beef cattle she is able to keep five milking cows on their farm and has built up a reputation selling to specialist cheese shops on the mainland and in England. A visit from farmhouse-cheese-campaigner, Patrick Rance, some years ago gave her the confidence, initially, to sell beyond the islands, but she has no ambitions to increase her output to more than she can cope with herself.

The ladies of the milk graze in lush grassy fields: Nessie is a doe-eyed aristocratic Jersey; Florrie a more common-looking black and white Ayrshire; Kitty and Agnes are both straightforward Friesians; but Selina is a handsome mixture of Jersey and Limousin. Between them they produce the milk which makes the special cheese – along with the grass they eat which has as much to do with it as their own inbred ability to make good milk.

Inside the farmhouse Jean's little dairy is a lean-to that has been extended. Cheese-laden shelves are round all the walls. Low down are daffodil-yellow, sharp edged young cheeses, and further up the middle-aged and mouldy old characters, their sides sagging with age. As she explains, not all cheeses develop this white mould, but when they do it is the sign of a well-flavoured cheese. The Kirkwall shops like a very new 'squeaky' cheese and most island cheesemakers do not mature their cheese for longer than a week or two. Cheeses which she sends further afield are more mature – about three to six months old. She makes her best cheese from spring and summer milk between May and October.

Hanging from one shelf are two huge bags of curd dripping into a bowl, and today's milk – a gallon from each cow – is waiting to be heated up with some rennet. It goes on the cooker behind the door and she uses her hand (a well sterilized one) to mix the milk. This is the method she teaches new cheesemakers; it is the old way of doing, before thermometers. The experienced clean hand is a more accurate tool. The milk separates in about ten to fifteen minutes and then the curd is put into the bag to drip for a day. Once it has dripped she mixes in some salt and packs it into a muslin-lined mould which is pressed for another few days.

It is a simple enough process but with so many variables. Even the weather, for cheese will not mature properly if the day is humid: 'running' instead of drying-out. A cool breezy day is best, not much of a problem on these windy islands where the pure sea breezes blast through the open window of this dairy, adding yet another dimension to this unique cheese. Along with the ladies of the milk and what they eat and the lady of the cheesemaking and what she does, they make up its character. We eat some for lunch with bannocks, vegetable broth, cold Shapinsay brown trout, and – worth waiting for – the golden and delectable Orkney butter!

Shapinsay is shaped something like a Viking helmet six miles long and about five wide at the narrowest part; we are now on the westerly horn not far from the Iron Age broch of Burroughston and visiting the farm of Hillside. We have passed through fields spotted with harvested stooks and old-fashioned cottage-like haystacks. The land slopes downwards towards sea cliffs and distant islands of sleeping whales beyond.

Inside, the ceiling of the kitchen where we sit is covered with hooks; there are hooks too on the outside wall of this single-storeyed traditional Orkney farmhouse. They are a clue to the customs of Robert and Mary Leslie, farmer-fisherfolk who, with characteristic Orkney enthusiasm, continue their old ways.

'Ah, but you wouldn't like the way we do with fish. Take guffan skate now, you wouldn't be able to eat that.'

They didn't have any so I couldn't try, but when they explained that it was a wing of skate which they hung outside till it stank so highly, accounting for the guff (smell) that even the bluebottles were frightened off, I began to see what they meant.

'What about other fish then? What do you hang on those hooks up there?'

They were empty now but soon to be filled with salted cuithes which would dry out slowly till the moisture was all gone. This is a special cure for these young saithe, also known as coalfish or coley. A cuithe is the Orkney name for the year-old fish about 8 to 10 inches long; the younger ones around 4 inches long they call sillocks.

So what makes the special cure? First we must go to the byre and have a look at the barrel in the corner which is half full of the little black fish from last year's curing. Layered in straw, they are as hard as rock, salt encrusted and headless. Mary puts four into a bag and we go back to the kitchen. She takes a knife and cuts a thin sliver from the edge of the back and belly, removing the fins. Now she strips off the papery skin. There you are, ready for cooking. No soaking? But they are not salty enough it seems, and soaking would remove too much flavour.

Robert describes the process: gutting and heading first, then layering in salt. The salt they use now is common table salt but the coarse salt they used in the past made the fish much saltier. They like them better now with less of a salty taste. Each layer of fish is covered with salt until, as he describes it, 'the fish are nearly taken out of sight'. Then they are left for about five days before being taken out, washed, and pressed with stones to get out some of the moisture. The final stage is drying them out. Tails tied together, the fish are hung out to dry like washing on the line when it's bonny dry weather; when it rains brought inside to the hooks in the ceiling.

And how do you cook and eat them? Yes, of course with potatoes! – their own grown Records, Sharps Express or Keppleton Kidneys. The fish are simmered in water for about twenty minutes and then eaten with some good melted dripping and the mealy potatoes.

Mary gives me a bag of Keppleton Kidneys and half a dozen cuithes and I eat them later, their strange sourish fishy taste an intriguing and not unpleasant adjunct to the full-flavoured potatoes; more of a relish in a way. And when you think of it, not a dissimilar idea to the dried fish known as Bombay Duck which Indians sometimes eat as an accompaniment to curries.

At Fruistigarth, Kenny Meason's farm, I taste yet more cheese. It is young, only a fortnight old and still very 'squeaky'. It tastes buttery and a little bland, but not unpleasantly so, a good match for the earthy-tasting bere, pronounced 'bare' (barley), bannocks which we eat – everyone eats – with the Orkney farmhouse.

The survival of this special northern form of barley which makes the distinctive bere bannocks is due to Fergus Morrison at the Boardhouse Mill. He grows all the bere on the island and, though a Borderer by birth, has learnt from the previous miller in Birsay the secrets of milling this very ancient and flavourful grain.

Now it is back in the ferry to the busy harbour at Kirkwall – ships always on the move, ferries, freighters, fishing boats, crammed together as we sail in. The Shapinsay ferry is laden with good produce from the island and home-baking donated by farmers' wives for a sale of Shapinsay produce to be held the next day in the St Magnus Church Hall to raise island funds. 'You must get there early,' warned Kenny, as I left him at the pier. 'Everything goes very quickly.'

And I do, but the Kirkwall folk know a good thing when they find it and the hall is packed, the Shapinsay produce disappearing like knockdown bargains at a closing-down sale. The ladies of the cheese are there with their cheeses. Scones, cakes, bannocks and oatcakes are nearly gone so I make for Kenny at the vegetable stall. There are big cabbages, good-looking turnips, bunches of herbs, and many different varieties of potatoes also catch my eye.

'But what would you do with these?' Kenny asks.

'These' are some fat bulbs of fennel which an enterprising islander has grown. While we discuss how they might be cooked an eager Kirkwallian swipes them from under our noses and they are gone. Get on with the buying and never mind worrying about how to cook seems to be the message.

Kenny is upset. But I am quite happy, instead, with a week's supply of Sharps Express and some Records and a large yellow turnip. A much better idea than the fennel for these, after all, are the islands which have made clapshot, the special combination of mashed potato and turnip, into a universal Scottish favourite.

As Orkney's most celebrated living writer, George Mackay Brown, says: 'Clapshot is one of the best things to come out of Orkney, together with Highland Park and Orkney fudge and Atlantic crabs.' (*Under Brinkie's Brae*, Gordon Wright 1979.) One of its advantages, as he points out, is that it goes with everything:

The other day, by way of a treat, I bought a piece of steak for grilling. Would clapshot go with grilled steak? No harm in trying. I peeled carefully the precious 'golden wonders' – and thought what a shame, in a way, 'golden wonders' being so delicious boiled in their thick dark jackets. And while the tatties and neeps were ramping away on top of the electric grill, it came into my mind that somewhere, a while back, I had read a recipe for clapshot that advised an onion to be added. (It may be in one of the books of F Marian McNeill, the Orkney-born connoisseur of food and ancient Scottish lore.)

In no time at all I had an onion stripped and chopped and delivered (my eyes weeping) among the neeps and tatties in the rampaging pot . . . Fifteen minutes later the probing fork told me that all was ready. Decant the water into the sink, set the pot on the kitchen floor on top of last week's *Radio Times*, add a golden chunk of butter and a dash of milk, then salt and plenty of pepper, and begin to mash . . .

Everything about clapshot is good, including the smell and the colour. I think this particular clapshot, with the onion in it, was about the best I've ever made. And it blended magnificently on the palate with the grilled steak. And it made a glow in the wintry stomach.

Everything good about clapshot? I have a certain reservation about the name. It sounds more like some kind of missile used in the Thirty Years' War than the name of a toothsome dish. And yet I've no doubt the roots of the word are ancient, worthy, and venerable. As soon as I've finished writing this I must dip into *The Orkney Norm*.

Beautiful Orkney, historic land of special foods, continue to resist the tide of uniformity, continue to use your powers of common sense to treat progress with the caution it deserves, and continue to provide for the rest of Scotland the taste and flavour of foods which have emerged from your distinctive mould.

A FINAL NOTE

I do not want to end this part giving the impression that the only area of Scotland with distinctive food traditions is Orkney. The rest of the country deserves much more attention, but not within the scope of this book.

Gesturing a march of time through the three centuries from 1690 to 1990, investigating some of the facts, seeing in occasional snapshots the pictures of a time both past and present, I have tried to avoid the well-worn personal opinions and descriptions which have so often embroidered the picture of Scottish food.

There are so many quotations which have been on the go for so long, of this or that person's idea of Scottish food, that they have – rightly or wrongly – taken on the illusion of fact. If we are all to continue believing the opinion of the outrageously sarcastic English lexicographer who visited the country for a few months during a tour, over two hundred years ago, then we must settle for the truth that the Scots live on oatmeal, make bad suppers, mediocre dinners, but are nevertheless capable of producing quite excellent breakfasts.

The more you search, the fewer opinions you believe. For every quotation giving one angle you can find others modifying, some even contradicting. It is one of the hazards of writing about the food on the plate which is no longer there.

It may seem, in the recipes which follow, that it is limiting in this day and age not to talk of microwave ovens, not even to talk much of ordinary ovens. But whatever the sophistications of the modern kitchen, if there is to be an identity for Scottish cooking it must come from the deep-rooted cooking systems which have evolved from the old black pot hanging over a slow-burning peat fire, along with the iron girdle and the habit of mixing a meal in a deep wooden bowl.

It may be that such primitive cooking methods produce primitive food. But that depends on the cook and the raw materials. If the cooking Scots master the techniques and if they always stay with top quality raw materials, then it doesn't really matter if the food comes out of a primordial pot, is cooked on an old-fashioned iron girdle, or mixed with a horn spoon in an antique wooden bowl. Primitive cooking methods need not limit the capacity for culinary excellence and I can see no disadvantage in promoting these basic cooking styles which most clearly illustrate the essential elements of Scottish cooking.

They are our link with the past as we catch sight of the generations of living things which pass in a short time, but like runners hand on the torch of life.

They have handed on both the good things and the bad – these Scots of every generation. In their own distinctive way they have kept the flame burning. Will it burn more brightly in the years to come? What are the present generation of Scots likely to hand on to the next? You may look in the pages of this book for some of the clues, but only in their cooking pots will you find the answer.

RECIPES

WEIGHTS, MEASURES AND AMERICAN TERMS

Weights and measures

In all the recipes, imperial and metric weights and measures are given, as well as American measures. Do not mix measures: stick to one system throughout.

The main point to remember when using the American system is that they have actually retained the old British measure for 1 pint at 16 fl oz (UK = 20 fl oz), which was originally the same as the solid measure and which the British abandoned in 1825. American cups are graduated in fractions of 16 fl oz. Sets of cups are available (I use a set made by CUISENA). There are five sizes in the set – ⅛; ¼; ⅓; ½ and 1 cup.

American butter is packaged in 4 oz sticks, 4 to a box of 1 lb which makes for easy and quick measuring, especially since they are usually graduated on the wrapping paper.

American standard measuring spoons are the same as the metric measuring spoons now widely available in Britain.

All spoon measures are taken as level

For Liquids:

1 teaspoon	= 5 ml
1 tablespoon	= 15 ml
2 tablespoons	= ⅛ c = 1 fl oz = 25 ml (approx)
5 tablespoons	= ⅓ c = 2½ fl oz = 60 ml (approx)
8 tablespoons	= ½ c = 4 fl oz = 100 ml (approx)
1 tablespoon	= 3 teaspoons

American cooking vocabulary

British	*American*
COOKING TERMS	
Fry	Pan broil (without fat)
	Pan fry (with fat)
Grate	Shred
Grill	Broil
Gut	Clean
Knock back	Punch down
Prove	Rise
Sieve	Sift

COMMODITIES

Anchovy essence	Anchovy paste
Bannock	Flat, round cake
Bicarbonate of soda	Baking soda
Biscuits	Cookies or Crackers
Boiling fowl	Stewing fowl
Broad beans	Lima beans
Cake mixture	Cake batter
Castor sugar	Granulated sugar
Cornflour	Cornstarch
Desiccated coconut	Flaked coconut
Double cream	Whipping cream
Dripping	Meat dripping
Essence	Extract
Flaked almonds	Slivered almonds
Haricot beans	Navy beans
Hough	Shank of beef
Icing	Frosting
Jam	Preserves
Jelly (sweet)	Gelatin dessert
Rasher	Slice
Roast potatoes	Oven browned potatoes
Scone	Shortcake, biscuit
Single cream	Light cream
Soft brown sugar	Light brown sugar
Spring onion	Green onion
Stewing steak	Braising beef
Sultanas	Seedless white raisins

COOKING EQUIPMENT

Ashet (Scottish)	Meat dish
Baking sheet or tray	Cookie sheet
Frying pan	Skillet
Greaseproof paper	Waxed paper
Stew pan or pan	Kettle
Large pot	Dutch oven or deep cooking utensil with a tight fitting lid
Liquidiser	Electric blender
Roasting tin	Roasting pan with rack
Sandwich tins	Round-layer pans

I THE POT ON THE FIRE

II THE GIRDLE ON THE HOOK

III THE MEAL IN A BOWL

I

The Pot on the Fire

'A sort of soup, or broth, or brew . . .'

William Thackery
The Ballad of Bouillabaisse

STOCK POT BROTH ('Strong broth')

If there is a taking-off point in Scottish cooking it is here: the elemental extraction of flavour from food into a liquid producing the 'strong broth' which historically has formed the basis of the cookery, the working tool. Original, and characteristic of the country because of nationally distinctive foods, it gives cooks the versatility to sally forth into their own individual style, creating personal concoctions while remaining within the idiom. Without strong broth, as Escoffier once said, nothing can be achieved.

It is not a complicated or difficult procedure, not even an expensive one, but a classic ground rule in the professional kitchen where it has been most extensively refined and developed. Something to do with quantity, it lends itself to large-scale catering operations. Huge stock pots sitting permanently on the hob, bubbling receptacles. There is no good reason why it should not also translate into the domestic kitchen, on a smaller scale, but without the complications of clarification and reduction, the unnecessary and off-putting tricks of the trade. With careful skimming and gentle simmering there should be no need to clarify stocks to a whisky-clear state, at the same time removing flavour with the egg white carry-on. No need to reduce *ad nauseam* till you have such a concentrated essence of meat flavourings that it overpowers the flavour of the meat it accompanies.

But there are particular advantages, it seems to me, in following the idea for it not only provides in the first instance clear, light, aromatic soups (fat and sodium-free if necessary) but there is also a spin-off in the cooked meats which can be dealt with in a series of endless permutations to cope with several days' meals. Cook a stock pot broth today – it will take time to cook, yes, but no great effort, and in the process, what to eat in the next few days is solved.

Let's say it's Friday. You cook a large piece of beef, about 4–5 lb (2–2½ kg) of silverside. Tonight it can be eaten hot, surrounded by its vegetables, and perhaps some dumplings and the broth liquid with plenty of chopped parsley or chives. Saturday, you have a cold platter of meat garnished with cold boiled new potatoes, and some salad vegetables which have been marinating in an oniony vinaigrette – say, sliced mushrooms, sliced tomatoes and grated courgettes, perhaps a delicate nasturtium salad. On Sunday you slice the beef thinly, melt some oil in a pan and thoroughly brown a couple of sliced large Spanish onions, add some of the broth liquid and the sliced meat and just heat it through. Serve it hot with plain boiled potatoes – and there is still stock left for soup on Monday.

Method

The stock pot broth is the first stage in the broth-making process where bones, carcasses, tough, flavourful and gelatinous meats are gently cooked along with aromatic vegetables and herbs to extract the maximum flavour. At the end of the cooking they have surrendered everything to the liquid, their flavour exhausted. (Large pieces of meat or fish or whole vegetables can be added to this and cooked for the appropriate time and then removed.)

This liquid, call it what you will, though it is used in the professional kitchen as the foundation for sauces, stews, etc., is now also a broth in its own right and may be served simply with some herbs, chopped salad vegetables, chopped meat garnish, or lightly cooked vegetables. Or it can be used as stock in other dishes.

General rules

1 A large cooking pot or stock pot is essential for cooking ahead for two or three meals. Tall and narrow is the shape used in professional kitchens so that the liquid bubbles up through the layers of meat and vegetables to create a flavoursome broth. It is a great thing to have a proper stock pot, but just as good broth can be made in pots designed for other jobs. I have a lightweight 14 pt (7 l) enamelled stock pot and a large 12 pt (6 l) enamelled pot and both of them have been used for the quantities in the recipes. If you are puzzled about the relationship of the pot size to the amount of liquid in the recipes [usually 6 pints (3 l)] the extra space is required for bones and vegetables which will take up much of the bulk, the liquid being only part of the volume.

2 Though heavy-duty aluminium pots are hard wearing, some foods cooked in them do absorb the aluminium and there is some doubt, though as yet not conclusive, by scientists as to the safety of using aluminium pots. Stainless steel is another possibility though it does not conduct heat well. A good ironmonger will have a range of large pots or alternatively try a catering supplier who will have a more extensive range of larger pots.

3 It makes more sense to make up a large quantity since it will take almost the same amount of cooking heat as a smaller amount and the broth will store well in the fridge at 5°C for three or four days. Second and third day's broth will have a more mature, better developed flavour than the first day's. It can, of course, be deep-frozen though it will lose some of its fragrance.

4 A slow-cooker is ideal for making broth in small quantities.

5 Do not disturb by stirring during the cooking time.

6 Sweating vegetables (cooking gently in fat under cover to concentrate flavour), sautéing them (tossing in hot oil or fat till browned), and browning meat and bones are all a matter of preference but without these processes the flavour is blander and the colour paler. They are instinctive procedures in the professional kitchen.

   The smaller the vegetables are chopped the quicker they will release their flavour so if the broth has a short cooking time then the vegetables should be finely chopped. For longer cooking broths the vegetables need not be cut at all.

7 Pack the ingredients tightly into the pot. They should not float around, hence the advantages of narrow deep pots.

8 Always start with cold water.

9 Vegetables should be put in the base to prevent the meat sticking. Bring very slowly up to simmering. It could take up to an hour for a large potful. This allows the meats to precipitate albuminous proteins slowly. Do not skim too soon but wait till the scum rises in a sort of grey foam. Wipe round the sides of the pot if there is a crust of scum.

10 To release additional albumins add a cup of cold water.

11 Do not add any aromatic herbs till this process is complete.

12 At the barest simmer is how the broth should be cooked. There is no way of hurrying up the process of slow and gentle extraction of flavours. A rolling boil will break up solid ingredients and muddy the liquid. If necessary, leave the lid slightly askew to prevent the heat building up.

13 Straining is best done through a fine mesh conical strainer (*chinois*). With a sieve of this design with a long sturdy handle and a point which rests in the bowl it is easier to hold and press out, or sieve the liquid and vegetables. An ordinary sieve is convenient enough for straining off the liquid but not so good for pressing out and sieving from bones.

   Two layers of muslin may be used to line the strainer but this is a professional procedure to produce crystal clear stock.

14 If possible leave overnight in a cool place to let the fat solidify on top. Then it may be partly or completely removed, though the fat, of course, will contain some of the flavour.

15 No seasonings of salt or pepper should be added to a broth pot since the reduction of the liquid will concentrate the salt flavour. Pepper loses its aroma and has a bitter taste if cooked too long.

16 Do not use strong-tasting greens like cabbage or broccoli. Starchy foods, like potatoes, will cloud the broth.

17 If the broth is to be reduced further for using as a meat essence the reduction should be done after straining.
18 Make sure all the ingredients are the freshest and best quality you can afford.

MEAT BROTH

(14–16 SERVINGS, POSSIBLY 3–4 MEALS)

INGREDIENTS	3 tablespoons oil
	Any combination of the following:
	    Hough (beef shin)
	    Nineholes (beef flank)
	    Knuckle of veal or marrow bone
	    Shank (flank) or neck of lamb
	    Chicken carcass from roasting
	    Chicken giblets except liver
	Wine to rinse out pan (optional)
	1 onion, peeled and stuck with 8 whole cloves
	A few unpeeled cloves or whole unpeeled head of garlic
	1 large carrot
	Coarse green tops of leek
	Cold water
	Sprigs of fresh herbs: parsley, thyme, bay leaf
	Optional: piece of meat for eating separately, e.g. shoulder of lamb, leg of lamb, boiling chicken, silverside or brisket of beef

BROWNING	Heat the oil in a frying pan and sear the meats on all sides, or place them in a roasting tin, turn in the oil and leave in a very hot oven for about 40 minutes or till well browned. Pour off excess fat and swill out (déglacé) the frying pan or roasting tin with some water or wine, scraping to remove all the pan juices which should be added to the broth pot with the water.
SKIMMING	Put the vegetables in the base of the broth pot and pack all the meat and bones on top. Pour in the pan juices and enough cold water to barely cover. Heat up

very slowly and skim. Add a cup of cold water to release all the albumins from the meat before a final skimming.

COOKING

Add herbs and simmer gently for 5–6 hours. If, during this time, you are cooking a piece of meat for eating separately, keep it at the top and take care to remove it immediately it is tender.

STRAINING

Strain all the ingredients through a sieve. Remove any pieces of meat you want to keep, and the carrot, and discard the remaining bones and spent herbs and vegetables.

FINISHING AND SERVING

(a) Serve as a clear broth with fresh herbs added just before serving. Oniony chives are good with strong meat broth, as are parsley, watercress, and finely shredded fresh spinach. Add a glass of dry Madeira for a richer flavoured broth.

(b) Serve some as a gravy with the cooked meat. It may be reduced a little.

(c) Make **Potted hough** (beef shin): Remove any bone and gristle from the hough meat. Chop the meat finely. Leave the strained broth liquid to cool overnight. Next day the fat can be removed and you will see how firm the jellied broth is. If it is too wobbly it will need to be reduced a little. It should be the consistency of a setting jelly. To make the potted hough: put the chopped meat into a pan, add enough melted stock to just cover the meat, heat through and season with salt and freshly ground pepper. Pour into wetted moulds and leave to set. Unmould before serving and eat with hot mashed potatoes or buttered toast.

(d) Make a **Three-Day Series**:

Day 1: meat, vegetables, broth and herb dumplings.
Day 2: cold meat, cold potatoes, marinated vegetables and nasturtium or other salad.
Day 3: fried sliced meat with onions, and boiled potatoes.

Herb Dumplings: mix together 4 oz (125 g) self-raising flour (1 c), 2 oz (50 g) shredded beef or vegetable suet (½ c), 2 tablespoons freshly chopped chervil or parsley with some chives, 1 egg, salt. Add enough milk to make a soft dough. Divide into eight dumplings. Fill a wide pan with boiling salted water (the dumplings are best cooked in a separate pan as they would cloud the stock), drop in the dumplings and cook them for about 20 minutes with the lid on. Drain and serve one in each deep plate along with the meat, vegetables and broth.

Vinaigrette for the cold platter: mix into 8 tablespoons of the best olive oil you can afford: 3 tablespoons white wine vinegar, 1 tablespoon finely chopped chives, 1 tablespoon finely chopped parsley, 1 small clove of garlic, crushed, 1 tablespoon finely chopped spring onion, 1 teaspoon Dijon mustard, 1 teaspoon castor sugar, salt and freshly ground black pepper. Use to marinate cold boiled new potatoes, sliced mushrooms halved tomatoes and grated courgettes.

Nasturtium salad: 'Put a plate of flowers of the nasturtium in a salad bowl, with a tablespoonful of chopped chervil; sprinkle over with your fingers half a teaspoonful of salt, two or three tablespoonsful of olive oil, and the juice of a lemon; turn the salad in the bowl with a spoon and fork until well mixed and serve.' (From *The Turkish Cookery Book* by Turabi Efendi, 1864.)

GAME BROTH

INGREDIENTS   As for Meat broth, omitting all other meats and using the meat and/or carcasses and trimmings of furred or feathered game. A good robust red wine may be added to clean out (déglacé) the pan after browning, and some may be added to the finished broth.

METHOD   As for Meat Broth.

CHICKEN BROTH

(8–12 SERVINGS, POSSIBLY 2 MEALS)

INGREDIENTS

2 tablespoons oil
1 boiling fowl or carcass of roasted chicken
1 onion stuck with a few whole cloves
1 stick celery
A few unpeeled cloves or whole unpeeled head of garlic
1 large carrot
Cold water
Sprigs of fresh herbs: parsley, thyme, bay leaf
Tarragon, chervil or parsley to be added at the finishing stage

BROWNING

Heat the oil in the broth pot and brown the chicken on all sides. Remove and set aside. Leave the fat in the pot.

SKIMMING

Put vegetables in base of pot and sauté lightly for a few minutes. Place chicken on top, cover with cold water and bring slowly to a simmer. Skim when necessary.

COOKING

Add herbs and simmer till the chicken is tender, 2–3 hours depending on size.

STRAINING

Strain off liquid. Discard vegetables and herbs. Leave chicken to cool.

FINISHING AND SERVING

(a) Cut some of the best pieces of meat from the chicken and place in the centre of the broth plate. Add a few ladlefuls of the broth and finish with some whole leaves of tarragon or chervil, or some chopped parsley.
(b) Use some of the chicken broth as a soup and the remainder to make a tarragon-flavoured sauce to serve with the cooked chicken. This can be made by reducing the broth and adding some cream, or by making a traditional roux-based white sauce with 1 oz (25 g) flour (¼ c); 1 oz (25 g) butter (¼ stick); ¼ pt (150 ml) milk (¾ c); ½ pt (300 ml) broth (1¼ c); 2 tablespoons chopped tarragon. Melt the butter, add the flour, cook for a few minutes, stir in the milk and

broth gradually, bring to a simmer and cook for five minutes. Season and add tarragon.

(c) Reserve broth for use in other dishes.

VEGETABLE BROTH

(6–8 SERVINGS)

INGREDIENTS	2 tablespoons oil
	Vegetables very finely chopped:
	    1 onion
	    1 leek
	    1 fennel bulb
	    Half head of celery
	Clove of garlic, peeled
	Cold water
	1 tablespoon blanched Autumn dulse, finely chopped
	2 tablespoons of chopped mixed herbs:
	tarragon, chervil, or to taste

SWEATING AND COOKING	Heat the oil in the broth pot and sweat the vegetables gently for 5–10 minutes on a low heat without browning. Stir once or twice. Just cover with water, and add the dulse. Bring up to a gentle simmer and cook for 10 minutes. Add the herbs and cook for another 10 minutes. All flavour will have been extracted by this time.
FINISHING AND SERVING	(a) Season and serve as it is, or strain and serve with a herb garnish. (b) Remove the herbs, purée the cooked vegetables and return to the broth. (c) Reserve for use with other dishes.

FISH BROTH

(6–8 SERVINGS)

INGREDIENTS
White fish bones and heads: whiting, sole, turbot, etc.
1 tablespoon oil
1 onion, finely sliced
1 leek, finely chopped
1 carrot, finely chopped
Sprigs of fresh herbs: parsley, fennel stalks
Cold water to just cover
Optional: whole fish or large cut to be cooked and served separately.

PREPARATION
Wash the bones well, removing any traces of blood. Heads should have the gills removed.

SWEATING AND COOKING
Heat the oil in the broth pot, add the onion, leek and carrot, and sweat for a few minutes without browning. Add the well-washed bones and heads and sweat for another few minutes. If you want to cook a whole fish or cut to be served separately, lay it on top and just cover with water. Bring to a low simmer and remove the fish or cut immediately it is cooked. It may only take a few minutes depending on size and shape. Gently insert a sharp-pointed knife between the flakes and down to the bone to check if the fish is cooked; if it is the flesh will be opaque; if the flesh is still transparent cook for a few minutes longer. Alternatively the fish can be added towards the end of the fish broth cooking time. The broth should cook for about 15–20 minutes. By this time all flavour should have been extracted. Strain and discard bones and vegetables.

FINISHING AND SERVING
(a) Use clear broth as a soup with a simple garnish such as anise-flavoured fennel and/or some flaked fish.
(b) Reduce the broth a little to serve as a sauce with some chopped fennel for the cooked fish.
(c) Use for making a **Butter sauce**: put into a pan 3 tablespoons of the broth, 2 tablespoons white wine vinegar, 2–3 very finely chopped shallots, and bring to a simmer. Cook to reduce till there is a moist mushy

mixture of shallots in the base of the pan. In a wide pan it will only take a few minutes to reduce. Add 2 tablespoons of cold water, reduce the heat to the lowest possible and then whisk in gradually 6 oz (175 g, 1½ sticks) unsalted butter (slightly softened), removing the pan from the heat after half the butter has been beaten in, whisking all the time. Season with salt and pepper and sharpen with lemon juice. Serve immediately.

(d) Reserve stock for use with other dishes.

SCOTCH BROTHS (Meals in a pot)

Make a light Stock pot broth one day (the starter to a substantial meal). The next day turn the stock into a more substantial Scotch broth (a meal in itself).

It is an affront to gastronomy to serve a sustaining broth, traditionally eaten as the focal point of the meal, as the opener to three courses: but it happens. It is also an affront to use some kind of commercial stock cube, tasting mostly of salt, monosodium glutamate and flavour enhancers. But that's about convenience and saving time which you may, or may not, feel is a good enough reason. It seems to me that when women were released from the tyrrany of Victorian kitchens they had every right to welcome the advent of convenience foods, and to consider the preparation of a meal, without such help, as a betrayal of their hard-won liberation. We still have the right, of course, to choose not to cook, to depend on the conveniences of the modern food-processing industry which beckon so alluringly from supermarket shelves. No one should be denied freedom from kitchen slavery, least of all those – of whichever sex – who are thirled to the treadmill of daily chores. But at the risk of sounding like an unliberated cookaholic (which I decidedly am not) I am suggesting that those in the kitchen might leave aside the little square packets, just occasionally, and see their way to cooking up some of the fresher tastes to be found in a simple broth.

The stock cube cannot really substitute for real broth if the start of the meal, or the focal point in the middle, is to have the required impact. 'It breathes reassurance,' said the American Louis P De Gouy in *The Soup Book* (1949), 'it steams consolation; after a weary day it promotes sociability . . . there is nothing like a bowl of hot soup, its wisp of aromatic steam making the nostrils quiver with anticipation.'

Such a powerful restorative, this intrinsic quality was used for the name of the place where the Parisian vendor Boulanger (in 1765) sold his soups: 'La Ristorante'. Not called soups, though, for *la soupe* in those days was the crust of bread served with the liquid, *le potage*. In English there is a confusion since the 'sop' of bread and the 'broth' which was poured over it are now both described as liquids. To add to the terminology problems the French *consommé* has intruded into our language as a clear refined broth while the French for a simple clear broth, *bouillon*, is also frequently used, sometimes for stock cubes.

In England the word 'broth' quite often seems to imply just the clear liquid in which meat is cooked: the first stage which Scots originally called 'strong broth'. In Scotland (and the other Celtic countries within Britain) broths mean something more substantial and primordial and have always dominated over lighter soups.

In this versatile and varied cooking medium, remarkably free from rules and dictums, Scotch Broths take their colour from native ingredients and artists in the kitchen are inspired to paint some memorable pictures.

Native ingredients

This is by no means a definitive list, but rather a collection of the most common, along with one or two of the more unusual or less well-used, ingredients which you might like to consider whilst composing.

Meat and Fish

Beef   Fine-quality beef has been reared in Scotland since the nineteenth-century pioneers of cattle-breeding in Aberdeenshire and Angus produced the black cattle which have such outstanding characteristics of flavour and tenderness. Today cattle-breeding continues in the search for the finest beef. Well-matured and properly hung beef will have the richest flavour. The cuts for broth-making should be those from the harder-working parts of the carcass: leg, shin, shoulder, rump, brisket, flank. Bones on their own, of course, contain much flavour and, if cooked long enough, will release gelatine which gives body to a clear broth. Oxtails are also high in gelatine and flavour and make good additions.

Lamb or mature sheep   The tough cuts most suitable for broth are from mature sheep, over a year old, which are called mutton. They are difficult to buy since most butchers sell only lamb. Most of the tough flavoursome Scottish mutton is either made into pies or exported to Arab countries. In Shetland some butchers sell reested mutton which is mature sheep that has been salted and smoked (see Traditional Scottish Food Suppliers,

p. 243). Some butchers are willing to sell cuts of mature sheep (past its first birthday) and some will agree that this more mature meat has a better flavour. Neck, shoulder and flank are best for broths.

Chicken   Older and tougher boiling fowls which were used for cock-a-leekie are still sold by some fishmongers and butchers. If these are not available then packs of wings, thighs or legs can be had in supermarkets. (Turkey legs and thighs also make good broth.) Battery-produced roasting chickens will not survive the broth process – too bland in flavour, too delicate in texture – though once roasted, the carcasses are useful sources of chicken stock. Better flavoured free-range and properly hung roasting chickens can be used, but cooking time has to be watched carefully or they will disintegrate. With such chickens it is best to bone out the breasts and use carcasses and legs only for broths, keeping breast meat for other purposes.

Duck   Not a traditional bird for broths. Use free-range, roasting ducks, and, as for chicken, use boned-out carcasses and whole legs for making broths. Reserve breasts for other recipes.

Game birds   Tough old specimens are traditionally made into broth, adding to the richness with their more mature flavour. For a strong gamy flavour hang for at least a week. Remove the more tender breasts and use the rest for broths.

Venison   Well hung, mature wild venison is best for a gamy-flavoured broth. Young farmed venison is milder since the diet is mostly grass rather than mountain and moorland heather and rough grasses. Use the tougher cuts from lower ends of legs and neck, and flank and also the skinned head.

Fish   Fish broth was a staple item of diet in the fishing communities around the coast, the distinctive cullen skink using a smoky Finnan haddock for character. Oily fish are not suitable. Whole white fish of all kinds, and white fish bones and heads, make good broths, but cooking time for whole fish must be watched carefully. Sole provides a particularly good flavour. Fish heads have a large amount of gelatine which gives body and flavour; monkfish heads are very high in gelatine.

Shellfish   All Scottish shellfish is suitable for using in broths though the cooking times must be watched. The soft shells of crabs, lobsters and languoustines should be finely crushed and used to extract the maximum flavour.

Grains and beans

Oatmeal Less of a traditional thickener for broths because of its gummy water-soluble fibre which can be unpleasant if it is cooked for too long in a broth. Pinhead oatmeal will survive a longer cooking but medium or fine oatmeal should not be cooked for more than 10–15 minutes in a broth. It adds a sweet mealy flavour which can be very useful as a balance with sharp bitter tastes. Particularly good with kale. Coarse pinhead, lightly toasted, can be used as a garnish or in a thick grainy broth. Toasting the meal before use improves the flavour. (For buying oatmeal see p. 181.) Porridge oats are not suitable. Oats are rich in water-soluble fibre which reduces blood cholesterol, blood sugar and fats, and they contain more protein, fat, iron, B vitamins, calcium and calories than wheat.

Barley The most common thickener in Scottish broths, making a light smooth consistency. Pearl barley adds a mildly earthy flavour in a rich mix of vegetables and meat. Beremeal is earthier in flavour and should be used sparingly, and certainly not in a light delicate vegetable broth. High in Riboflavin, B vitamins, vitamin E, potassium and phosphorous.

Beans, peas and lentils All give body to broths, but because of their volume and blandness they absorb a lot of flavour from other ingredients. Bacon is the most traditional meat to be used with them. Pulses should not be used in delicate aromatic concoctions. High in proteins, potassium and iron.

Aromatic vegetables

Onions Highly esteemed and most widely used vegetable. There are hundreds of cultivated varieties which vary in size, colour, pungency and flavour. Most commonly available are the small, yellow globe onions which have a strong concentrated oniony flavour and should be used with strong competing flavours. The much larger yellow Spanish onions have a milder, sweeter flavour, better in broths which need their substance and comparative gentleness. The red Italian onion has a gentleness similar to the Spanish onion and is most commonly used in salads because of its attractive colour which is lost in a broth. An onion still in its skin will add yellow colour. To make a darker broth with more intense flavour onions should be finely chopped and browned lightly in oil. High in minerals, low in calories (38 cals in one medium-sized onion), rich in potassium and phosphorous.

Leeks   Onion family. A winter vegetable, sweeter and more delicate in flavour than the onion and often described as 'king of the soup onions'. Scottish leeks have a longer white part and shorter green since they are more used in broths than as a separate vegetable. Young, small to medium-sized leeks have the sweetest flavour; by March and April the older winter leeks become tougher and more bitter, and those that have 'shot' (i.e. have the shoot of the flower growing up the centre) are well past their best. Originally a winter vegetable, they are now being produced all year round. Browning the whites of leeks destroys their delicate flavour since they are not so robust as onions. The best inner parts of the green, finely chopped, make good garnish cooked for a minute before serving. The green will lose colour and freshness if cooked for much longer. Cooking leeks for excessive time makes them unpalatably slimy. Leeks are difficult to clean, the most efficient method being to insert a sharp knife about half an inch (1 cm) from the base of the root end and slice the whole leek lengthwise in two. Then make another slice at right angles to the first so the leek is in quarter strips joined at the root. Now it can be opened out and the inner leaves rinsed thoroughly. Outer coarse leaves are ideal for wrapping up herbs when making a bundle of aromatics for flavouring. Rich in vitamin A, potassium, phosphorous, calcium and vitamin C.

Shallots   Variety of the onion species. Grows in clusters of small bulbs and has an intense, but not pungent, flavour. More subtle than ordinary onions, it is better used as a final distinctive flavouring to a broth. Browning them causes a bitterness and the character is lost. Food value as for leeks.

Spring onions (syboes)   Onion family. Like miniature leeks, a mild and delicate flavour which will not stand long cooking or browning. Best used as a final flavouring to broths, either raw or cooked lightly in butter. Food value as for leeks.

Carrots   Their sweet flavour is an important ingredient in broths. Mature medium-sized carrots have more flavour and will stand up to longer cooking than younger smaller ones which are more suitable in a delicate combination of vegetables. Old and woody-centred carrots at the end of winter have lost most of their flavour: use only the outer part and throw away the central core. Too many can overwhelm with their sweetness. Contain more natural sugar than any other vegetable except for sugar-beet. Very high levels of vitamin A along with potassium, calcium and phosphorous.

Parsnips   Carrot family. Similar sweetness to carrots but blander. They soften more quickly than carrots and do not hold their shape well, though they can be used as a thickener. Not suitable for clear broths. Their mild sweetness makes a good foil for delicate spicing such as nutmeg, cumin or coriander. High in potassium, phosphorous, vitamin C and vitamin E.

Turnips   The yellow swede (*Brassica campestris*) is the Scottish turnip; it has a nutty sweetness, but is not as sweet as the carrot. The two are inseparable in traditional Scottish broths. The smaller white turnip (*Brassica kapa*) is not so common in broths though it may be used in a spring vegetable broth for its light aromatic, peppery flavour. There is a thick fibrous layer on the Scottish turnip which must be thoroughly removed before cooking. Medium-sized young and mature turnips have the best flavour, large old ones should be avoided, as they are not only coarse in texture, but their flavour is gone. Scottish yellow turnip has traces of all essential vitamins but is also high in potassium, calcium, phosphorous, vitamin C and vitamin A.

Celery   Its dominating flavour adds character to a broth provided it is used in moderation. The outer leaves are more pungent than the inner ones which are best used in light broths or salads. Celery seeds may be used in thick broths instead of celery. Lovage is a good substitute for celery. High in potassium, calcium and vitamin C.

Celeriac   The starch-storing lower stem of a special variety of celery. It is an interesting addition to broths, particularly good with game. When being prepared, it should be put into acidulated water after peeling to prevent discoloration. Food value as for celery.

Kale   An important Scottish vegetable. Because of its extensive use in the diet in broth and brose it became the generic term for a meal. The eighteenth-century St Giles Bell which rang out at two o'clock for dinner was known as the Kail Bell. A winter vegetable, best after a frost which seems to intensify its spicy character. A dominating vegetable in a broth so it must be combined carefully; oatmeal and barley were commonly used with it in the past and provide a good balance. Very high in vitamin C, iron, calcium and potassium.

Potatoes   The starchy flesh will thicken a broth, therefore not suitable for a clear broth. Some varieties have a subtle earthy taste, others bland

and uninteresting. Main crop mealy potatoes like Golden Wonder will break down and thicken more easily while young new potatoes and waxy varieties will hold their shape. A good all-round source of nutrients in dry weight terms: 66 per cent starch, 9 per cent protein, 4 per cent sugars, 0.5 per cent assorted vitamins, high in vitamin B. Vitamin C content deteriorates on storing from 30 mg per 100 g when freshly dug to 8 mg after 8–9 months.

Mushrooms   Tightly closed commercial ones will not deliver a great deal of flavour. Larger, older ones have more flavour but wild mushrooms have the best woodsy flavour. Though a total of 1,200 varieties are edible, about 30 may cause indigestion and about another 30, if eaten, will kill. There is also the problem of mushrooms from fields which have been sprayed by man-made chemicals and mineral pollutants which mushrooms absorb. Like brambles, mushrooms which are growing near main roads are always heavily contaminated with lead.

For identification: use a reliable field guide which has colour pictures of each variety in all its stages from early youth through to maturity and old age. If in doubt, always avoid the very young and very old which may not have enough distinguishing characteristics. *Mushrooms: and other fungi of Great Britain and Europe* by Roger Phillips (Pan) has 900 full colour plates which show up to ten different shapes and sizes as well as all the stages of ageing of each variety both edible and poisonous plus full scientific details of identification. The British Mycological Society, which can usually be contacted through the botany department of a university, is open to all interested in mycology. In the autumn, 'fungal forays' are held, often in conjunction with a local natural history society.

To begin with it is best to stick to easily recognizable *ceps, chanterelles* and shaggy ink caps which can be found in quantity in some areas: they add not only their distinctive flavours to a broth but also new textures. It is best to sauté them gently in butter before adding, to concentrate the flavour. Mature specimens can be dried in a warm dry place. They are also available dried in specialist food shops; these must be soaked first and the soaking liquid used in the broth. Though expensive they are highly concentrated and ¼ oz (6 g) will be enough for a large pot of broth. High in potassium and phosphorous, with a small amount of iron.

Lettuce   Although the leaves are fragile and delicate some varieties have sharpness which can balance a sweetish broth and give it more depth. The long-leaved Cos is a tall vigorous plant with a nutty flavour. There are a number of varieties of the round cabbage lettuce, such as the Butterhead, Web's Wonder and Iceberg, but their flavour is less distinct. Other lettuces which are worth using for both their flavour and attractive leaves are Lolla Rossa, Red and Green Oak Leaf and Quattro Stagioni. The flavour and freshness will be lost if cooked at all; their leaves should be torn into small pieces or shredded finely and added just before serving. A very popular vegetable in many old broth recipes though invariably cooked for too long. High in vitamin C and vitamin A.

Tomatoes Provide acidity in a broth and sharpen up flavours. If the acidity is too dominating some sugar can be added to correct the balance. They must be ripe and full flavoured. Bland-tasting or unripe tomatoes will add nothing and it is much better to use good tinned Italian plum tomatoes instead. High in potassium, phosphorous and calcium, vitamin C and vitamin E.

Fennel bulb Aniseed flavour which will dominate unless used with care. The delicate flavour goes well with fish. The finer inner leaves are milder and best for broths.

Avoid: *Broccoli*, *Cabbage*, *Cauliflower* and *Brussels Sprouts*, dominating vegetables which can disturb the balance of a broth. Their flavour (also their smell) becomes unattractive when cooked for too long.

Aromatic herbs and flavourings

Parsley A deep flavour which gives body to a broth. It can be used in large quantities. The flat-leaved variety has a more intense flavour than the curly variety though, as with all herbs, the nature of the soil and the climate are also important factors in the flavour.

Thyme Gives depth of flavour which is necessary with sweet light tasting vegetables. Lemon Thyme is good with fish and lamb.

Bay leaf The third member of the classic trio (parsley, thyme and bay leaf) which give so much character to broths. A strong dominating herb compared with the other two, so should not be used in quantity.

Chives Very mild oniony flavour. A hardy pot-herb for growing on a window sill, they are frost resistant. Their leaves may be snipped throughout the year, if they are grown indoors, without the plants coming to any harm. They should not be cut too near the ground which might damage the growth centre. They do not withstand cooking and should be added to the broth just before serving. The flower has a special pungency and is sometimes sold with the leaves in herb packs. Use only a few of the florets to flavour – they are pungent, a whole head would be overpowering.

Garlic   The sharp, pungent flavour of cultivated garlic sweetens when cooked for a length of time. Peeled, it will disintegrate and cloud a clear broth; unpeeled it will release just as much flavour.

Nettles   Picked when young in the spring (before mid-June) they have a deep earthy flavour and a good green colour. Later they are tough and bitter and not suitable for cooking. Pick with leather gloves and scissors. Widely used by Highlanders in the past in Nettle kail (see p. 215). Three platefuls of this during the month of March was said to restore the body to good health after a winter deprived of fresh meat and vegetables. Very good as a garnish for potato broth.

Sorrel   Known in Scotland as sourocks for its sour taste. Children chew the leaves raw for the mouth-puckering sensation when the sharp juice is released. A delicious herb, widely used for its lemony acid flavour to off-set rich food. It will lose flavour if cooked for any length of time and is best added, chopped, in the later stages of broth-making. The young leaves can be floated in a clear broth. Do not cook in an iron pan; the sorrel takes on a metallic taste.

Lovage   The species *Ligusticum scoticum* is known as sea lovage or Scottish lovage in America where it grows wild on the north Atlantic coast. In Scotland it was much used in the past with the common name of shunis. A powerfully scented herb, something like celery but with a musky lemon scent, its leaves are large and a few can be used instead of celery. It can be used either blanched or unblanched in salads, the stems can be candied like angelica and the seeds used on cheese biscuits, but its most successful use is the unusual flavouring which it imparts to broths, clear or thick. A neglected old-fashioned herb which could be more widely used. (A bunch held under the bath tap makes an aromatic relaxing herbal bath.)

Borage   Grown mostly for the decorative flowers tasting of milk chocolate and used to decorate sweets and puddings. Though coarser, the prickly leaves can be used instead of parsley in a bundle of aromatics for their deep cucumber flavour. Good also to float in a clear broth but they must be finely chopped because of their hairy texture.

Summer savoury   Something akin to thyme in flavour but more biting and quite distinct. It is better before it flowers than after; the flowers have no flavour. It can be used in a bundle of aromatics but not in quantity. Overdone, it is a mistake.

Chervil   One of the most delicate herbs with a fresh tasting astringency slightly reminiscent of anise. Attractive lacy leaves. Not as robust as parsley so should be added just before serving.

Chickweed   (*Stellaria media*) A common herb with heart-shaped leaves and tiny white flowers which grows wild in waste places though it may also be cultivated. (Not to be confused with Greater chickweed (*Stellaria neglecta*) which is larger, up to 3 feet (1 m) tall, and found on hedge banks rather than wild places.) Best in the late summer and early autumn, it is most used as a salad herb but is useful in light aromatic vegetable broths and potato broth. Remove the tough stems and add just before serving. Gather using scissors rather than pulling up by the root.

Purslane   A wild or cultivated plant which was very popular in the Middle Ages when it was used in salads but also cooked and eaten as spinach. Its leaves have a delicate flavour and should be finely chopped and added just before serving.

Rock samphire   Grows wild at the sea coasts, where clumps hang in tassels from rocks or in the sand. It has a strong aromatic salty taste. The leaves are best picked in spring or early summer before the flowers appear. Remove any hard parts of the stalk or slimy leaves and cook lightly in the broth for the last 10–15 minutes.

Sage, rosemary   Pungent flavours which are generally too strong in broths.

Sprigs of fresh herbs (Bundle of aromatics)   Essential for good broth-making. The herbs which are normally present are parsley, thyme and the European bay leaf. Fresh herbs give a better flavour. If dried slowly the flavour will still be good but dried thyme can become bitter if cooked too long or left in the broth after it is cooked. The proportion of fresh herbs is usually three sprigs of parsley to one of thyme and one of bay leaf. The size of the bundle will depend on the length of the cooking time and the quantity of the broth. Short-cooked broths will need less, longer-cooked more. The longer they are cooked the less aggressive their flavours become, blending and softening so that individual definitions disappear in a fusion of flavours. Put the herbs, fresh or dried, inside a couple of celery stalks or the tough green outer leaves of a leek about 3–4 inches (7–10 cm) long; the bundle should be about the thickness of a small banana for a 6 pt (3 l) quantity of robust broth. Tie with string or wind round some white cotton thread to hold herbs in place. For smaller quantities, herbs may be put into a muslin bag or other receptacle rather than tied up. If the broth starts off with a stock pot where everything is strained at the end of the cooking then there is no need to tie up at all. Do not stick to the classic three all the time: lemon thyme, sweet marjoram, winter savoury, basil, a blade of mace are worth experimenting with, as are many others. This is an area for original blending to create individual flavours.

Lemon and orange   The thinly-pared rind of a Seville orange was added to broths in the past and frequently lemons were used as a final garnish, especially for their sharpness with rich gamy broths.

Sea vegetables

Gaelic names for different types of sea vegetables number twenty-two! There are another nine in Orcadian English and probably five in modern English vernacular. (My authority on the subject is Julian Clokie, biologist, seaweed collector, drier and wholesaler for the Sea Vegetable Company, see Traditional Scottish Food Suppliers, p. 253.) Though there is some evidence of the extent to which the Highlanders incorporated them into their diet, the fact that they had so many common names suggests that they were an everyday part of the diet, widely used in all communities on the coast. Some of the Gaelic names are given in parentheses in the list below.

To get the best flavour from seaweed the season is important. In the growing cycle there is a time when the quality of the new growth is at its best. This time may be quite short, which makes harvesting difficult. Unlike herbs which lose flavour when dried, seaweeds are improved by careful drying.

Sea vegetables are invaluable in flavouring broths, a fact which our Gaelic ancestors clearly learnt by experience. Their high content of strongly flavoured amino acids deepens the flavour of broths considerably. They should be added to broths about 20 minutes before serving.

Some – sugar ware, grockle, dulse and *nori* – can be crisped very lightly under the grill and served in small dishes to accompany the broth. They become very brittle and crumbly, the flavour intensified, and make a pleasant addition to any kind of broth or soup, particularly fishy concoctions. They can also be served in this way as appetizers.

Sea vegetables are low in carbohydrates and fat, rich in vitamins A, B1, B6, B12, E, K, panththenic acid and folic acids; all these are especially high in dulse and purple *nori* – as high as or higher than in liver and spinach. They accumulate many trace elements from the sea: calcium, iron, copper, manganese, iodine and phosphorous salts. Fresh from the sea they must be thoroughly rinsed of marine organisms.

Dabberlocks (Gruaigean) Delicate, slightly astringent taste, with a variety in texture from thicker central stalk to papery wing. Related to the popular Japanese *wakame*, it is good in all cooked dishes. Boil for 5 minutes, chop, and add with cooking liquid to the dish to be cooked. For salads boil for 10 minutes, drain and chop.

Dulse (Duileasg) Strong flavoured sea vegetable, with a salty iodine aroma. It has a soft texture which breaks down and mingles with other ingredients on cooking. Particularly good in thick meaty broths where the flavour blends well with other ingredients. For salads boil for 10 minutes, drain and chop. For other uses scald in boiling water and drain.

Autumn dulse Treat as for Dulse. Its colour is a much deeper more intense purple, its flavour slightly more astringent. Gives more flavour and colour to traditional broths than summer dulse. An exotic colour and shape.

Finger ware (Bragair) Thicker and tougher in texture, used as an alternative to pasta in such dishes as *lasagne*. It can be used as a vegetable in salads and added as a flavouring to be removed in a stock pot broth. Not suitable for adding to the finished broth. Boil for 45 minutes when using as a pasta. Use the cooking liquor cautiously, according to taste.

Grockle (Sgrothach) Earthy, salty flavour and stringy texture, but tender. It can be chopped finely and added to broths 20 minutes before serving.

Purple nori (Slabhagan) Closely related to the traditional Japanese *nori*, the universal sea vegetable in Japan. Not a strongly flavoured vegetable, it has a light oystery nuttiness and a very delicate texture. It need not be cooked for any length of time. May be dipped in *tempura* batter (Japanese coating batter for deep-frying), mixed into a stir fry of vegetables, added to casseroles and stews, and both delicate and robust broths. Chop finely and add direct to the soup just before serving. The richest in food value of all the sea vegetables. Very long boiling produces a paste: laverbread in Devon and Wales, *nori-tskudani* in Japanese.

Sugar ware (Smeartan) Delicate flavoured version of the Japanese *kombu*. Its sweetish flavour is useful in broths. It should be chopped finely before adding to the broth. Boil for 5 minutes and drain when adding to salads. When adding to stocks it can be boiled in water for 3 minutes and then drained to get rid of the debris. Use the liquor cautiously, according to taste for stock or for poaching fish.

Flowers

Not so long ago eating flowers was a much more common idea. Cowslip cream, violet soufflé, daffodil pie, marigold and mutton broth, salmon garnished with violets, nasturtium salad, fennel and mimosa salad were just a few of the flowery concoctions which enlivened the scent, taste and appearance of the Victorian dinner table.

Also full of references to flowers, mostly roses and violets, was classical Roman cookery. Today, in Japan, lily buds and jasmine are floated in soups, tea is scented with lotus; marigolds, narcissi and peonies, and chrysanthemums are fried in batter. Middle Eastern dishes, from pastry to ice cream, are flavoured with orange flowers and roses. In old recipes, carnations, chrysanthemums, dandelions, elderflowers, marigolds, nasturtiums, roses and violets are the most favoured for their subtle scent and flavour. Mediterranean countries sell masses of courgette flowers every summer, just for the eating.

Though Scotland may be the colder north, there seems no good reason why we should not float the odd flower in a clear, lightly flavoured broth, making more use of these delicate attractions and fleeting flavours, for our ancestors certainly did.

Pot marigold   A favourite garden flower because the flowering period is spread over summer and well into autumn. The petals were used in Roman times by the poor who could not afford the more expensive saffron. Its colouring (calendulin) is soluble in fats and was used particularly in soups, but also in butter and cheese. The flowers can be dried in a dark well-ventilated place and kept in airtight containers.

Primrose   The flowers were used in salads and were made into tea and wine. They were also ground with rice, almonds, honey and saffron to form a primrose pottage. The leaves were used as a salad and for flavouring as a pot herb. Whole flowers may be floated in soup on the point of serving. Flowers do not dry well.

Nasturtium   A hardy garden annual with its orange-yellow trumpet-like flowers. Regarded as one of the best-tasting flowers, it has a piquant and faintly spicy flavour. Its leaves have a cress-like flavour and can also be used in broths and salads.

BEEF AND BARLEY

(12–14 SERVINGS, POSSIBLY 3–4 MEALS)

INGREDIENTS

3 lb (1.5 kg) brisket, hough (beef shin), nineholes (beef flank), or other meat suitable for long cooking
1 marrow bone
6 pt (3 l) cold water
2 oz (50 g) pearl barley, washed (⅓ c)
2 oz (50 g) dried peas, soaked overnight (⅓ c)
1 whole onion stuck with cloves
Sprigs of fresh herbs: parsley, thyme and bay leaf tied together in a bundle with celery or leek
1 large onion, finely chopped
3 medium carrots, finely diced
Quarter turnip (swede), finely chopped
1 head of celery, chopped
2 leeks, finely chopped, white and green separated
1 teaspoon sugar
Seasonings: salt and pepper
Garnish: chopped parsley, marigold petals

COOKING THE BEEF

Put the meat and bones into a 12–14 pt (7–8 l) pot, add the water, barley, peas and studded onion. Bring slowly to a simmer and skim. Turn down the heat, add the herbs and cook very slowly till the meat is tender. Remove the meat and set aside. Discard the bones.

COOKING THE VEGETABLES

Add the onions, carrots, turnip, celery, white of leek and sugar, and cook slowly till the vegetables are just tender.

FINISHING AND SERVING

Remove the bundle of herbs and just before serving season and add the green leek, parsley and marigold petals. Slice some of the meat thinly into bite-size pieces and put in the centre of the plate or serve separately.

HOUGH AND KIDNEY*

(12–14 SERVINGS, POSSIBLY 3–4 MEALS)

INGREDIENTS

2 tablespoons oil
1 large onion, finely chopped
1 lb (500 g) hough (beef shin)
1 lb (500 g) ox or lambs' kidney
6 pt (3 l) cold water
Sprigs of fresh herbs: parsley, thyme and bay leaf tied together in a bundle with celery or leek
4 medium carrots, diced
Half a medium turnip, diced
3 stalks of celery, diced
2 leeks, sliced, white and green separated
Seasonings: salt and pepper
Garnish: chopped parsley or chervil

BROWNING

Heat the oil in a 12–14 pt (7–8 l) pot and sauté the onion till a good brown colour. Remove excess fat and gristle from the meat and core the kidneys. Chop both finely. Add to the pot and brown. Add the water and herbs and bring up to simmering point slowly. Skim.

COOKING

Simmer till the meat is almost tender, about 1 hour, and add all the vegetables except the green of the leeks. Simmer till all the vegetables are just cooked.

FINISHING AND
SERVING

Season, and garnish with the green leek, and parsley or chervil. Serve.

*A broth from the Borders served at Dolphinton House Hotel by Chef Roy Ellis – one of his mother's family recipes.

LAMB AND GREENS (Hotch potch)

(12–14 SERVINGS, POSSIBLY 3–4 MEALS)

INGREDIENTS

3 lb (1.5 kg) neck, shank or flank of lamb*
1 marrow bone
6 pt (3 l) cold water
Sprigs of fresh herbs: parsley, thyme and bay leaf tied together in a bundle with leek or celery
2 young carrots, grated
2–3 white turnips, grated
1 oz (25 g) dried Autumn dulse, blanched and chopped
1 teaspoon sugar
1 lb (500 g) peas, fresh or frozen
1 oak leaf lettuce, finely shredded
Chopped chervil
Seasonings: salt and pepper

COOKING THE MEAT

Put the meat and bones into a 12–14 pt (7–8 l) pot and add the water, bring up to simmering slowly, and skim. Add the herbs and cook till the meat is tender. Remove the meat and set aside.

COOKING THE VEGETABLES AND SERVING

Add the carrots, turnip, dulse and sugar and cook for a few minutes. Then add the peas, lettuce, and chervil and season. (If using fresh peas cook for 3 minutes before adding lettuce and chervil). Serve immediately with some of the sliced lamb in the centre of the plate, or serve the lamb separately.

*Use mature sheep or reested Shetland mutton (see p. 102).

CHICKEN AND LEEKS (Cock-a-leekie)

(12–14 SERVINGS, POSSIBLY 3–4 MEALS)

INGREDIENTS	1 boiling chicken (or 6 drumsticks, 6 wings or 6 thigh pieces)*
	6 pt (3 l) cold water or strong beef broth (see p. 95)
	Sprigs of fresh herbs: parsley, thyme and bay leaf tied together in a bundle with leek or celery
	2 lb (1 kg) leeks, finely chopped, white and green separated
	2 oz (50 g) long-grain brown rice or small pasta (pastaini) (⅓ c)
	8 soaked prunes or 1 teaspoon sugar**
	Seasonings: salt and pepper
	Garnish: chopped parsley
COOKING THE CHICKEN	Put the chicken into the water or stock and bring slowly to a simmer. Skim. Add the herbs and cook for 1 hour (half an hour if chicken pieces are used).
COOKING THE VEGETABLES AND RICE	Add the white of leek, rice, prunes or sugar and cook for another half hour. Remove the chicken when it is tender, and set aside.
FINISHING AND SERVING	Season, and add the chopped green of leek and parsley just before serving. Serve the broth with some of the chicken meat in the centre of the plate, or serve the chicken separately.

*Turkey legs, capon legs, giblets and trimmings from poultry may all be used either with the chicken or instead of it.
**Prunes were added to sweeten the broth – as raisins once were in beef broths. A teaspoonful of sugar works just as well, but black prunes add a distinction to the appearance of the broth and their sweet flavour, provided it is in moderation, is not unattractive with chicken and leeks – though there are those who detest the idea.

HAM AND LENTILS (Brochan buidh)

(12–14 SERVINGS, POSSIBLY 3–4 MEALS)

INGREDIENTS	2 tablespoons oil 2 carrots, finely diced Half a turnip (swede), finely diced 3 large potatoes, peeled and sliced thinly 2 onions, finely chopped 8 oz (250 g) red lentils, washed (1⅓ c) 2 teaspoons tomato purée 1 teaspoon black treacle or brown sugar Knuckle of ham 6 pt (3 l) cold water Sprigs of fresh herbs: parsley, thyme and bay leaf, tied together in a bundle with leek or celery *Seasonings*: salt and pepper, lemon juice to taste *Garnish*: 2–3 slices garlic salami, roughly diced, 1 tablespoon chopped parsley
SWEATING THE VEGETABLES	Heat the oil in a 12–14 pt (7–8 l) pot, add the vegetables and lentils and stir well. Cover and sweat for about 10 minutes, stirring occasionally to prevent sticking. Add the tomato purée and treacle or sugar.
COOKING	Add the ham, water and herbs, bring up slowly to a simmer, and skim. Cook slowly for 1–1½ hours.
FINISHING AND SERVING	Remove the ham bone. Cut off any meat, chop and return to the soup. Season. Garnish with garlic salami and parsley and serve.

GAME AND JUNIPER

(12–14 SERVINGS, POSSIBLY 3-4 MEALS)

INGREDIENTS

2 tablespoons oil
1 onion, finely chopped
2 rashers streaky bacon, chopped
Game bird carcasses, or venison, hare or rabbit bones
6 pt (3 l) cold water or strong beef broth (see p. 95)
Sprigs of fresh herbs: parsley, thyme and bay leaf tied together in a bundle with celery or leek
12 juniper berries
2 oz (50 g) butter (½ stick)
Slices of haunch of venison, slices from saddle of hare or rabbit, or breast meat from game birds
2 carrots, finely diced
1 head of celery, finely chopped
2 oz (50 g) fine oatmeal (½ c)
Juice of a lemon
8 oz (250 g) fresh spinach or a mixture of spinach and sorrel, very finely chopped
Sprigs of purslane
Seasonings: salt and pepper
Garnish: finely sliced lemon

BROWNING THE MEAT AND COOKING THE BROTH

Heat the oil in a 12–14 pt (7–8 l) pot and cook the onion and bacon till lightly coloured. Add the carasses or bones and brown well. Add the stock or water and bring slowly to a simmer. Skim. Add the herbs and juniper berries and cook slowly for 3–4 hours. Strain.

COOKING THE MEAT AND VEGETABLES

Melt the butter in a pan and sauté the meat till cooked but still pinkish in the middle. Remove and keep warm. Add the carrots and celery to the pan and sauté till lightly browned. Add the oatmeal and lemon juice. Now put the contents of the pan into the broth and cook till the vegetables are just tender. Add the spinach or spinach and sorrel to the broth and heat through. Season.

FINISHING AND SERVING

Place the slices of game in the middle of the serving plate and pour the broth round. Garnish with slices of lemon.

HARE AND POTATOES (Bawd bree)

(12–14 SERVINGS, POSSIBLY 3–4 MEALS)

INGREDIENTS

1 blue mountain hare (5–6 lb, 2.5–3 kg) hung and skinned, with blood reserved
4 tablespoons oil
1 onion, sliced
6 pt (3 l) cold water
Sprigs of fresh herbs: parsley, thyme and bay leaf tied together in a bundle with celery or leek
1 whole head of garlic, unpeeled
1 head of celery, finely chopped
2 carrots, finely chopped
1 onion, finely chopped
2 tablespoons flour
3–4 tablespoons port (optional)
Seasonings: salt and pepper, coarse sea salt
To serve: 6–8 medium-sized mealy potatoes (e.g. Golden Wonder, Records), boiled

BROWNING

Remove the best parts of the meat from the saddle and cut into small steaks. Set aside. Heat 2 tablespoons of the oil in a 12–14 pt (7–8 l) pot and thoroughly brown the onions and remains of the carcass. Add the water and bring to a gentle simmer. Skim.

COOKING

Add the herbs and garlic and cook gently for 2–3 hours. Strain broth into a bowl, pick the edible meat off the bones and discard the bones. Chop the meat finely and return to the broth. Heat the remaining 2 tablespoons of oil in the broth pot and brown the hare steaks lightly. Remove and set aside. Add the vegetables and sweat for 5–10 minutes. Sprinkle in flour and mix through the vegetables. Then add the broth and steaks and cook till just tender. The time will depend on the toughness of the hare. (There may be no need to cook the hare meat after the first browning: check for tenderness by tasting a slice before you proceed.)

FINISHING AND SERVING

Put the hare blood in a bowl and pour some of the hot broth over it. Pour the mixture back into the pot, being careful not to boil or the blood will curdle. Add the port, if using, and season. Pile some of the steaks in the centre of the plate with the potatoes, and pour the broth round, or serve the potatoes separately. Sprinkle with some coarse sea salt.

DUCK AND LIVER (*Pot-au-feu de canard et foie gras, son bouillon aux légumes de saison*, by Daniel Galmiche, see p. xviii)

(4 SERVINGS)

INGREDIENTS
2 × 2 lb (1 kg) Gressingham duck (young ones if possible)
1 carrot
1 leek
1 stick of celery
1 onion stuck with a clove
Whole black peppercorns
Sprigs of fresh herbs: thyme and bay leaf
4 oz (125 g) fresh parsley
Water or white stock pot broth (see p. 98)
8 baby carrots
8 baby turnips
8 baby fennel
4 baby leeks
1 head of celery, chopped
4 oz (125 g) *foie gras*
Seasonings: salt
Garnish: chopped chives mixed with coarse sea salt

PREPARATION
Bone out the ducks. Reserve the legs, but keep the rest of the duck meat for another recipe.

COOKING
Put the bones, carrot, leek, celery, onion, peppercorns, herbs and parsley into a pot and just cover with water or stock pot broth. Bring slowly to a simmer, skim, and cook for about 1½ hours to extract maximum flavour. Strain through a conical sieve, and season. Cook the duck legs in the stock now for about an hour. Remove and keep warm. Cook the baby vegetables and celery in the stock till just tender.
Prepare the *foie gras*: cut it into four equal portions, salt and pepper it and wrap up as for a parcel in

cling film. Cook lightly in a steamer for 3 minutes and unwrap gently.

SERVING   Serve in a deep wide plate, with a duck leg, a slice of *foie gras*, and some baby vegetables piled up in the middle, the plate filled with the clear stock pot broth. Sprinkle the chives and coarse sea salt on top and serve.

Wine: Meursault, Chablis, Monthélie Blanc. 'A good dish for wintertime . . . bon appétit.' (Daniel Galmiche)

FINNAN HADDOCK AND POTATOES (Cullen skink)

(4–6 SERVINGS)

INGREDIENTS   1 ½ lb (750 g) mealy potatoes (e.g. Golden Wonders, Records)*, peeled
1 onion, finely chopped
2 pt (1 l) water (5 c)
1 lb (500 g) Finnan haddock on the bone**
Milk
2 oz (50 g) butter (½ stick)
Seasonings: salt and pepper

COOKING   Put potatoes and onion into a large pot with the water and cook till the potatoes are almost soft. Lay Finnan on top, put the lid on the pan, and cook for about 5 minutes till the fish is just cooked. Remove the fish, skin, bone, and flake the flesh. Meanwhile mash the potatoes and onions into the liquid in the pan.

FINISHING AND SERVING   Return the flaked fish to the pan, mix through and add enough milk and butter to make the desired consistency – you may want a thickish stew-soup or a thinner soup. Season and serve.

* More potatoes may be used to make a thick stew-soup. Waxy potatoes are unsuitable.
** Though Cullen skink is traditionally made with Finnan haddock on the bone, which gives a special flavour to the soup, other smoked white fish may be used instead. The Aberdeen fillet – a smoked fillet of haddock with skin but no bone – may be used, but luridly dyed 'yellow fillets' are not suitable.

CRAB AND RICE (Partan bree)*

(8–10 SERVINGS)

INGREDIENTS

2 medium-sized (preferably live) crabs
4 pt (1.5 l) cold water
2 tablespoons oil
1 stick of celery, finely chopped
1 carrot, finely chopped
1 onion, finely chopped
4 oz (125 g) short-grain pudding rice (⅔ c)
½ pt (250 ml) double cream (1¼ c)
Seasonings: salt and pepper
Garnish: claw meat

COOKING THE CRABS

Bring the water to a rolling boil and plunge in the crabs. Cook for 10 minutes at a fast simmer. Remove crabs and leave to cool. Strain and reserve the cooking liquid.

COOKING THE STOCK

Heat the oil in a large pot, add the vegetables and sweat without colouring for about 10 minutes. Remove all the meat from the crabs (discard the dead men's fingers), keeping dark and white meat separate and claw meat and coral (if there is any) as whole as possible. Break up the softest parts of the crab shells, not the claws, with a cleaver; these softer bits may be puréed in a blender to break them down finely (this is optional but extracts maximum flavour – it was originally done in a pestle and mortar). Add all the crushed shells to the sweating vegetables. Sweat for a further 10 minutes, stirring to avoid sticking. Add the liquid the crabs were cooked in and bring slowly to a simmer. Skim. Simmer for about an hour till all the flavour is extracted. Strain through a sieve (preferably conical), pressing out all the liquid with a ladle.

FINISHING AND SERVING

Cook the rice in some of the stock till tender, put into a blender with the dark meat, and the coral if there is any. Purée, and add to the remaining stock. Heat through and add cream. Season and garnish with all the white meat, including the meat from the claws, in the centre of the plate.

* This recipe is a more refined version of the traditional and simply follows the well-established concept of extracting valuable flavour from shellfish shells.

MUSSELS AND ONIONS

(APPROX. 4 SERVINGS)

INGREDIENTS	3 lb (1.5 kg) mussels in their shells 1 pt (600 ml) water or dry white wine, or a mixture (2½ c) 1 oz (25 g) butter (¼ stick) 1 large onion, finely chopped 1 clove garlic (optional) 1 pt (600 ml) milk and/or single cream (2½ c) *Seasonings*: salt and pepper *Garnish*: chopped parsley or chives
COOKING THE MUSSELS	Scrub the mussels well and remove the beards. Discard any that are open (unless they shut when tapped). Put the water or wine into a wide deep pan and bring quickly to a simmer. Add the mussels, stir them about, put on a tight lid and cook quickly till all the shells are open. Turn them once again while they cook. They will only need 2 or 3 minutes. Overcooking will toughen them. Strain. Reserve the liquid and leave to settle. Taste for saltiness.
MAKING THE BROTH	Melt the butter in a pan, add the onion and cook without colouring till soft. Add the garlic, if using, and cook for a few minutes. Stir in the milk and/or cream and finally some of the cooking liquor judging the amount according to the saltiness. Season if necessary.
FINISHING AND SERVING	Return the mussels to the broth and let them just heat through without cooking. Serve with a pile of mussels in the centre of a deep plate and the broth round them. Garnish with parsley or chives.

Note The soup may be thickened with 1 tablespoonful of flour, if wished, added with the onion.

MONKFISH AND HERBS*

(APPROX. 8 SERVINGS)

INGREDIENTS

12 small new carrots, peeled, and 12 small new white turnips, peeled (all approx. the same size)
4 courgettes, sliced
4 oz (125 g) samphire, cleaned
2 oz (50 g) butter (½ stick)
1 lb (500 g) monkfish fillets, cut in 1 in (2.5 cm) dice
4 fl oz (125 ml) white wine (½ c)
5 tablespoons strong fish stock (see p. 100) – can be made from monkfish trimmings and head
1½ pt (900 ml) double cream (4 c)
1 lb (500 g) shelled mussels, cooked
1 oz (25 g) mixed fresh herbs: dill, chervil, parsley and chives
Seasonings: salt and pepper
Garnish: 8 sprigs of chervil, 8 *fleurons* (puff pastry decorative shapes)

COOKING THE
VEGETABLES
AND FISH

Boil vegetables till very lightly cooked. Melt the butter and sauté the monkfish till almost cooked. Remove and keep warm. Add the white wine and fish stock and reduce to a light syrup, about 2 tablespoonfuls. Add the cream. Add the mussels, the monkfish, and the cooked vegetables and finely chopped herbs to heat through for a few minutes.

FINISHING AND
SERVING

Season, ladle into large broth plates and garnish with the chervil and *fleurons* and serve.

* Ferrier Richardson's recipe which he serves as a main course in a deep soup plate at the October Restaurant in Glasgow.

SEAFOOD*

(APPROX. 6 SERVINGS)

INGREDIENTS	6 lb (3 kg) mixed fish on the bone
	12 mussels
	6 large langoustines
	1 tablespoon oil
	1 oz (25 g) butter (¼ stick)
	1 large onion, finely sliced
	1 leek, finely sliced
	2 pt (1 l) dry white wine
	3 pt (1½ l) water
	2–3 cloves of garlic, crushed
	Sprig of thyme
	1 bay leaf
	2 tablespoons tomato purée
	Pinch of saffron
	4 egg yolks
	5 tablespoons double cream
	Seasonings: salt and pepper
MAKING THE STOCK	Fillet the fish and set aside with the mussels and langoustines. Heat the oil and butter, add the onion and cook without colouring till soft. Add the leek and the fish trimmings, the wine and the water. Bring to a simmer, skim. Add the garlic, thyme, bay leaf and tomato purée. Simmer for about 1½ hours. Pass through a sieve (preferably conical) into a bowl.
COOKING THE FISH	Put the fish fillets into a pan, add the strained stock and saffron, and bring slowly to a simmer. Add the mussels and langoustines to cook through for a minute. Remove from the heat, cover and leave for 5 minutes.
FINISHING AND SERVING	Beat the egg yolks and cream together and put into a pan over hot water. Add the stock from the broth gradually and heat slowly till it thickens, beating with a whisk. Season. To serve, lay the fish in a deep plate, white fish first, then mussels and langoustines on top. Pour over creamy rich broth and serve.

* Peter Jukes serves this dish at the Cellar Restaurant in Anstruther which was once a thriving fishing port on the Fife coast. Round the corner from the restaurant is a

comprehensive fishing museum for the area. Fresh fish is still landed at Pittenweem and St Andrews. Peter Jukes serves this rich seafood broth in handsome hand-thrown white pottery bowls (about 2 pt (1 l) in size) with a seafood motif in the base of the bowl.

CARROTS AND OATMEAL (Orcadian oatmeal soup)

(6–8 SERVINGS)

INGREDIENTS	2 oz (50 g, ½ stick) butter (Orkney butter if you can get it) 2 leeks, finely chopped, white and green separated 4 medium carrots, grated Half a yellow turnip (swede), grated 2 oz (50 g) fine oatmeal (½ c) 2 pt (1 l) cold water or vegetable stock (5 c) Approx. 2 pt (1 l) milk *Seasonings*: salt and pepper *Garnish*: chopped parsley
SWEATING THE VEGETABLES	Melt the butter in a pot and add the vegetables, but only the white of the leek. Sweat without colouring for about 5 minutes, stirring occasionally. Add the oatmeal and mix in. Cook for another few minutes.
COOKING	Add the water or stock and bring slowly to a gentle simmer. Cook till the vegetables are just soft, 5–10 minutes at the most.
FINISHING AND SERVING	Add enough milk to make a fairly thick consistency, add the green leek, and heat through. Season and serve garnished with parsley.

POTATOES AND CHIVES

(6–8 SERVINGS)

INGREDIENTS	2 tablespoons oil 2 rashers of Ayrshire bacon, finely chopped 1 medium onion, finely chopped 3 stalks of celery, with leaves, finely chopped 6 medium-sized potatoes, peeled and diced 1 bay leaf 2 pt (1 l) water or vegetable stock 1 × 8 fl oz (250 ml) cup instant dried milk (1 c) *Seasonings*: salt and pepper *Garnish*: chopped parsley, chives, dill or nettles
SWEATING THE VEGETABLES	Heat the oil in a pot and add the bacon. Cook till crisp and add the onion and celery. Cook without colouring for about 10 minutes.
COOKING AND SERVING	Add the potatoes, bay leaf and water or stock. Cook till the potatoes are just tender. Gradually stir in the dried milk. Season and garnish with herbs. Serve with toasted cheese (cheese on toast).

MUSHROOMS AND BARLEY (Vegetarian)

(6–8 SERVINGS)

INGREDIENTS	2 oz (50 g) pearl barley (⅓ c) 2½ pt (1.5 l) cold water 2 tablespoons olive oil 1 large onion, finely chopped 1 lb (500 g) mushrooms (wild if possible), chopped 1 clove garlic, crushed 1 teaspoon celery seeds ½ pt (300 ml) claret *Seasonings*: salt and freshly ground black pepper
COOKING THE BARLEY	Cook the barley in ½ pt (300 ml, 1¼ c) of the water till soft, about half an hour.

SWEATING THE VEGETABLES	Heat the oil in a pan and brown the onion lightly. Add the mushrooms and sweat for 10 minutes to concentrate the flavour.
COOKING	Add the garlic and celery seeds. Pour in the claret and reduce slightly. Add the barley and its cooking liquor, plus remaining water, and bring to a slow simmer. Cook for half an hour.
FINISHING AND SERVING	Season and serve with crusty brown bread and a ripe farmhouse cheddar cheese.

SHAGGY INK CAP* (Vegetarian)

(4–6 SERVINGS)

INGREDIENTS	1 lb (500 g) shaggy ink cap mushrooms or other wild mushrooms 2 tablespoons oil 2 pt (1.2 l) chicken stock or water (5 c) ¼ pt (150 ml) double cream (¾ c) *Seasonings*: salt and pepper *Garnish*: a few chervil leaves
COOKING	Clean the ink caps, discarding the stems, and chop finely. Heat the oil in a pan and sauté for 5–10 minutes. Add the chicken stock, or water for vegetarians. Bring to a gentle simmer and cook for 10 minutes (you may purée the soup at this point for a smoother result but it is not necessary).
FINISHING AND SERVING	Finish with the cream, season and garnish with chervil.

* A delicious soup served at Auchendeanan Lodge in the Rothiemurcus forest area of the Grampian Highlands. The ink caps are picked in the forest by the proprietor Ian Kirk.

AUTUMN DULSE AND CELERY (Vegetarian)

(8–10 SERVINGS)

INGREDIENTS

2 tablespoons oil
1 onion, finely chopped
1 head celery, finely chopped
3 medium potatoes, diced
2 tablespoons tomato purée
2 teaspoons sugar
4 pt (2 l) water
1 oz (25 g) autumn dulse
Seasonings: salt and pepper

COOKING AND
SERVING

Heat the oil in a pot. Add the onion, celery and potato, cover and sweat gently for about 10 minutes, stirring occasionally. Add the tomato purée and sugar. Stir in and then add water. Simmer for 15–20 minutes or till the vegetables are just tender. Put the dulse into a bowl and pour over enough boiling water to just cover. Remove dulse and chop finely. Strain the liquid into the soup. Add the dulse, season and serve.

VEGETABLE* (Vegetarian)

(14–16 SERVINGS, POSSIBLY 2–4 MEALS)

INGREDIENTS

2 tablespoons oil
1 onion, finely chopped
Half head of celery, chopped
½ lb (250 g) mushrooms
6 pt (3 l) cold water
3 medium carrots, diced
4 medium tomatoes, finely chopped, or 1 tin Italian plum tomatoes and their juice
2 tablespoons nutritional yeast**
2 tablespoons soy sauce
4 oz (125 g) brown rice (⅔ c)
2 oz (50 g) bulgur wheat or whole wheat kernels (½ c)
8 oz (250 g) cooked black eye or other beans (2 c)

2 teaspoons celery seeds
1 heaped tablespoon miso (Japanese soy paste)
Seasonings: salt and pepper, pinch of cayenne
2 tablespoons mixed herbs: basil, tarragon, oregano,
summer savoury

METHOD

Heat the oil in a pot and add the onion, celery and mushrooms. Cover and sweat for 10 minutes. Add water, and all the other ingredients except miso and herbs. Bring up to a simmer and cook slowly till the grains are cooked. Put the miso into a bowl and blend to a smooth paste with a little of the soup. Add to the broth. Season, and add herbs just before serving.

* Adapted from the recipe for Hearty Vegetable Soup from *Diet for a Small Planet* by Frances Moore Lappe (1971).
** Nutritional yeast (not the same as baking yeast) is available in health food stores but varies greatly among brands and is not to everyone's taste. A strong flavour, it is best in fairly robust broths such as this one. A valuable source of vitamins, particularly rich in B vitamins, phosphorous, and iron.

STEWS

Though stews date back to medieval English recipes, it is surprising to find Meg Dods (1826) saying that the idea of a 'soup-and-stew' or 'mouthful soup', as she describes it, is a novel idea in Scotland. One can only assume that, because the broth pot dominated to such an extent, the idea of a thickened stew with bite-size pieces of meat was not common. Much more practical to keep the meat in one piece, separated from the liquid, and eaten cold as required.

This is not to say that the stew idea has no Scottish pedigree. Those antiquarian recipes which resemble stews are more of the lightly stewed collops-in-the-pan type, using a tender cut and making something of the concentrated pan juices by adding other flavourings and reducing to intensify the flavours – ideal tavern fare in the eighteenth century when they could be cooked to order.

The humble mince is one of these dishes. Made in the Scottish style with the best steak, minced, it requires no more than a really thorough browning of onions and mince, with a little water or stock to moisten, and no need for a long stew. Beef collops and pickled walnuts is another old combination which was a common tavern dish in the eighteenth century. Fillet of hare in port and Venison fillet in sloe jelly are modern adaptations which seem to me to combine the need to retain as much of the natural freshness and juiciness of the meat – an important modern concern – while at the same time extracting the maximum flavour from the carcass meat and bones.

Oven temperatures

Mark 1	275°F	140°C	very slow (cool)
2	300	150	slow
3	325	170	
4	350	180	moderate
5	375	190	
6	400	200	moderately hot
7	425	220	
8	450	230	hot
9	475	240	very hot

BROWN BEEF STEW WITH HERB DUMPLINGS

(4 SERVINGS)

INGREDIENTS

2 tablespoons oil
1 onion, finely chopped
1 lb (500 g) stewing beef, cut into approx. 1 inch (2.5 cm) dice
1 carrot, sliced
1 clove of garlic, crushed
1 tablespoon tomato purée
1 teaspoon sugar
1 tablespoon flour
Sprigs of fresh herbs: parsley, thyme and bay leaf, tied together in a bundle with leek or celery
Water to cover
Seasonings: salt and pepper
Herb dumplings (see p. 96)*

BROWNING

Heat the oil in a pan or flameproof casserole and brown the onion. Draw to the side and brown the meat. Add the carrot and garlic and continue browning, then stir in the tomato purée and sugar. Sprinkle the flour over and mix in.

COOKING AND SERVING

Add the herbs and enough water to cover, stir well and bring slowly to a simmer. Season. Cover and cook till the meat is almost tender. This is best done in the oven at a slow heat. Make up the herb dumpling mixture. Drop spoonfuls of the dumpling mixture on top of the stew. Cover and leave to steam for 10–15 minutes.

* Alternatively serve the beef stew with Skirlie (see p. 145).

BEEF COLLOPS AND ONIONS (Collops-in-the-pan)

(4 SERVINGS)

INGREDIENTS

2 tablespoons oil
1 large Spanish onion, sliced
1 lb (500 g) thinly cut tender or medium-tender beef
steak
1 tablespoon liquor from pickled walnuts (optional)
Seasonings: salt and pepper
Garnish: pickled walnuts, chopped (optional), and
chopped parsley

COOKING

Heat the oil in a pan or flameproof casserole, add the
onion and brown to a good colour. Draw to the side of
the pan, add the meat and brown on both sides. If you
are using tender steak, no further cooking will be
necessary. Otherwise cover tightly with a lid and leave
to cook very slowly, preferably in a slow oven, till the
meat is quite tender. Time will depend on the toughness of the steak. Remove the meat and add the
pickled walnut liquor, if using. Add a little boiling
water to the onion sauce if it is too thick.

FINISHING AND
SERVING

Serve the steaks on the onion sauce, garnished with
some chopped pickled walnuts and chopped parsley.

MINCE AND TATTIES

(4 SERVINGS)

INGREDIENTS

1 tablespoon oil
1 large Spanish onion, finely chopped
1 lb (500 g) steak, minced*
2 medium carrots, finely sliced
1 tablespoon pinhead oatmeal, toasted
Water to cover
Seasonings: salt and pepper
4 slices black pudding (optional)
To serve: Mashed potatoes and butter

BROWNING	Heat the oil in a pan and sauté the onion till a good dark brown. Draw to the side of the pan and add the mince. Break up with a fork and brown, mixing the onions through. For a good flavour the mince must be well browned – this stage can take 10–15 minutes.
COOKING	Add the carrots and oatmeal, mix well and pour in enough water to just cover. Season. Bring to a slow simmer, cover and cook for about 10–15 minutes or until the carrots are just tender.
FINISHING AND SERVING	Grill the black pudding and lay on top of the mince just before serving. Alternatively the black pudding can be added during the cooking in which case it will break up and mix in with the mince. Serve with well-mashed potatoes and butter.

* The best steak, cut from the rump and minced by the butcher, is how many Scottish housewives buy mince.

LAMB STEW WITH SPRING VEGETABLES

(4 SERVINGS)

INGREDIENTS
2 tablespoons oil
4 neck cutlets of lamb
1 lb (500 g) flank (breast) of lamb cut into neat pieces 2 in by 2 in (5 cm by 5 cm)
1 onion, finely chopped
1 carrot, finely chopped
1 stalk celery, finely chopped
1 tablespoon tomato purée
1 oz (25 g) flour (¼ c)
1 clove garlic, crushed
1 teaspoon sugar
Sprigs of fresh herbs: parsley, thyme and bay leaf tied together in a bundle with leek or celery
Seasonings: salt and pepper
Water to cover
Garnish: 4 oz (125 g) each of baby carrots, baby turnips (white), new potatoes, mangetout
1 oz (25 g) butter (¼ stick)

BROWNING AND COOKING	Heat the oil in a pan or flameproof casserole and sauté the meat till brown. Remove and set aside. Add the onion, carrots and celery and continue browning. Add the tomato purée, and sprinkle in the flour. Add the garlic, sugar and herbs. Return the meat to the pan, season and pour in enough water to cover. Bring to a slow simmer, cover tightly and cook very slowly, preferably in a slow oven, for about 1½ hours.
FINISHING AND SERVING	Season. Cook the vegetable garnish till just tender. Toss in butter and serve round the stew.

OXTAIL STEW

(4 SERVINGS)

INGREDIENTS	2 tablespoons oil 2 lb (500 g) oxtail, jointed 1 large Spanish onion, finely chopped 1 carrot, finely chopped 1 tablespoon tomato purée 1 tablespoon flour 1 teaspoon sugar Water to cover 4 oz (125 g) haricot beans, steeped (soaked) overnight (optional) *Seasonings*: salt and pepper
BROWNING	Heat the oil in a pan or flameproof casserole. Cut off any excess fat from the oxtail joints and brown them well. Remove. Add the onion and brown, then the carrot. Stir in the tomato purée. Return the meat to the pan. Sprinkle over the flour. Add the sugar.
COOKING	Add enough water to cover. If using the beans, drain them and add. Bring to a gentle simmer. Cook very slowly, preferably in a slow oven till the meat is tender, approximately 3 hours.
FINISHING AND SERVING	Season and serve in a large deep plates with mealy potatoes.

STUFFED HEARTS

(4 SERVINGS)

INGREDIENTS	*Herb stuffing*: 2 oz (50 g) breadcrumbs (½ c) ½ oz (12 g) butter, melted (⅛ stick) 2 teaspoons each of parsley, marjoram, thyme, finely chopped Zest of a lemon Salt and pepper 1 small egg Milk to mix *Hearts*: 4 × 4 oz (125 g) lambs' hearts 2 tablespoons oil 1 onion, finely chopped 1 carrot, finely chopped 1 stick of celery, finely chopped 1 tablespoon flour Water *Seasonings*: salt and pepper *Garnish*: 8 oz (250 g) sliced mushrooms sautéd in 2–3 tablespoons olive oil
PREPARING THE STUFFING AND THE HEARTS	Mix together all the ingredients for the stuffing. Wash the hearts well and remove any pipes and excess fat. Cut with scissors some of the inside membranes of the hearts to enlarge the cavities. Fill the cavities. Skewer with a cocktail stick or bind up with thread.
BROWNING	Heat the oil in a pan or flameproof casserole small enough to hold the hearts fairly tightly. Sauté the onion, carrot and celery till a good brown colour. Add the hearts and brown well. Dust with the flour and mix in.
COOKING	Add enough water to come about half-way up the hearts. Season, bring to a slow simmer, cover and cook, preferably in a slow oven, for about 1½ hours.
FINISHING AND SERVING	Remove hearts from sauce. Take out cocktail sticks or remove thread. Halve each heart lengthwise. Correct the seasoning in the sauce. Serve hearts surrounded with sauce and garnished with the mushrooms.

STEWED TRIPE AND ONIONS

(4 SERVINGS)

INGREDIENTS
1 lb (500 g) cooked tripe
½ pt (300 ml) milk (1 ¼ c), plus a little extra
2 large Spanish onions, finely sliced
1 oz (25 g) flour (¼ c)
Seasonings: salt and pepper
To serve: 4 slices hot buttered toast

COOKING
Cut up the tripe into bite-size pieces. Put into a pan with milk and onions. Bring to a slow simmer and cook for about an hour.

FINISHING AND SERVING
Put the flour into a cup and blend with some cold milk till smooth. Add some hot cooking liquor and mix in. Add to cooked tripe. Simmer till thick. Season and serve either with or on hot buttered toast.

RABBIT STEW WITH SPICED DUMPLINGS

(4 SERVINGS)

INGREDIENTS
Rabbit
2 tablespoons oil
1 onion, chopped
1 rabbit, jointed
2 tablespoons seasoned flour
1 cooking apple, chopped
2–3 whole cloves
Water to cover
Seasonings: salt and pepper
Spiced dumplings
8 tablespoons fresh breadcrumbs
1 teaspoon freshly ground cinnamon
¼ grated nutmeg (½ teaspoon ground)
1 teaspoon ground cumin
2 tablespoons melted butter
1 egg
Salt and pepper
To coat: 4 tablespoons fresh breadcrumbs
1 tablespoon oil

BROWNING THE RABBIT	Heat the oil in a pan or flameproof casserole and sauté the onion till a dark brown. Coat the joints of rabbit in seasoned flour and sauté till lightly browned. Sprinkle over any leftover flour.
COOKING	Add the apple and cloves and enough water to cover. Season and bring to a slow simmer. Cover and cook, preferably in a slow oven, till the rabbit is tender, approximately 1½ hours.
FINISHING AND SERVING	Just before it is ready, mix all the dumpling ingredients together and form into 12 small balls, coat in breadcrumbs and fry in oil till lightly brown. Serve with the stew.

JUGGED HARE

(6–8 SERVINGS)

INGREDIENTS	4 tablespoons oil 1 onion, chopped 1 young brown hare (approx. 6 lb, 3 kg), skinned, washed, and blood reserved 1 glass port 1 glass red wine 1 tablespoon redcurrant jelly 1 tablespoon flour 4 cloves 1 teaspoon black peppercorns Sprigs of fresh herbs: parsley, thyme and bay leaf tied together in a bundle with leek or celery Water to cover *Seasonings*: salt and pepper Juice of half a lemon (optional) *To serve*: 1 lb (500 g) mushrooms, sautéd
BROWNING	Heat the oil in a pan or flameproof casserole and brown the onion. Add the hare and brown on all sides.
COOKING	Add the port, red wine and redcurrant jelly, coat the meat well and reduce a little. Sprinkle in the flour, and add the cloves, peppercorns and herbs. Cover with water, season, and bring to a slow simmer. Cook till

the hare is tender, preferably in a slow oven, approximately 2–3 hours.

FINISHING AND SERVING   Remove the hare from the sauce and keep warm. Add the hare blood and heat through gently (do not allow the sauce to boil or the blood will curdle). Strain the sauce. Test for seasoning. If too bitter add more redcurrant jelly; if too sweet some lemon juice. Pour the sauce over the hare and serve with the sautéd mushrooms or Skirlie (see p. 145).

FILLET OF HARE WITH PORT*

(2 SERVINGS)

INGREDIENTS
1 saddle of moutain hare
Water to cover
2 tablespoons oil
3–4 tablespoons port
Seasonings: salt and pepper
1 oz (25 g) butter (¼ stick)

PREPARING THE STOCK   Bone out the two loins and put the bones into a pan. Cover with water, bring to the boil, skim and simmer for 1–2 hours till all the flavour is extracted from the bones. Strain.

COOKING THE MEAT   Heat the oil in a pan and fry the fillets at a high heat on all sides for a few minutes. The meat should be pink in the middle. Remove and keep warm. To finish the sauce add the stock to the pan and reduce to a quarter of the original quantity, add the port. Reduce a bit more and taste for flavour. Season if necessary.

FINISHING AND SERVING   Finish with the butter which will give the sauce shine and a little more body. Strain onto heated plates. Slice the hare at ½ in (1 cm) intervals and fan out on the plate in roughly the form of a question mark. Serve.

* A recipe by Ruth Hadley of the Cross Restaurant in Kingussie.

VENISON IN CLARET

(3–4 SERVINGS)

INGREDIENTS	1 lb (500 g) venison, shoulder, neck or slices from the haunch 2 level tablespoons flour seasoned with salt and pepper and ½ teaspoon freshly ground allspice 2 tablespoons oil 1 onion, finely chopped 1 pt (600 ml) robust claret (2½ c) 1 tablespoon rowan jelly, plus extra for serving *Seasonings*: salt and pepper
PREPARING AND BROWNING THE MEAT	Cut the meat up neatly into bite-size pieces and coat in seasoned flour. Heat the oil in a pan or flameproof casserole and brown the onion, then add the meat and brown well. Sprinkle in any leftover flour.
COOKING	Add the claret and rowan jelly. Bring to a slow simmer, cover and cook, preferably in a slow oven, till the meat is tender, about 1½ hours.
FINISHING AND SERVING	Season and serve with mealy potatoes and rowan jelly.

VENISON FILLET WITH SLOE JELLY*

(2 SERVINGS)

INGREDIENTS	2 × 4–6 oz (125–175 g) fillets of venison (or any tender, sinew-free meat from haunch or loin) 2 tablespoons oil 1 glass fairly robust red wine 2 tablespoons port 1 tablespoon Moniack Castle sloe jelly (redcurrant, rowan, bramble and blackcurrant are equally suitable) *Seasonings*: salt and pepper 1 oz (50 g) unsalted butter (¼ stick) (optional) *Garnish*: appropriate fruit in season Lemon juice to taste

COOKING THE MEAT	Heat the oil in a pan and sauté the meat at a high heat for about 2 minutes. Very tender meat should preferably be served pink in the middle to retain as much of the natural flavour as possible. Remove and keep warm.
MAKING THE SAUCE	Add the red wine to the pan juices and reduce by about half, scraping the residues from the bottom of the pan. Then add the port and reduce a little more. Add the sloe jelly and stir in, still reducing. Finally add a little lemon juice to balance the sweetness, tasting as you go. Season. Finish with the butter which will give the sauce shine and a little more body.
FINISHING AND SERVING	Strain the sauce onto heated serving plates. Place the meat on top and garnish with some fresh sharp soft fruits in season. Serve with celeriac purée.

* Adapted from a dish served by Ruth Hadley at the Cross Restaurant in Kingussie which she, in turn, adapted from Francatelli's recipe for Redcurrant Jelly-Sauce for Venison (see National and Historical Dishes, p. 210).

PARTRIDGES (OR PHEASANT) IN CREAM*

(APPROX. 2 SERVINGS)

INGREDIENTS	2 tablespoons oil 1 onion, finely chopped 1 carrot, finely chopped 2–3 stalks celery, chopped 2 medium partridges or 1 large pheasant 1 liqueur glass brandy 3 wine glasses Chablis Water to half cover birds 1 bay leaf ¼ pt (125 ml) double cream (¾ c) *Seasonings*: salt and pepper
BROWNING THE BIRDS	Heat the oil in a pan or flameproof casserole and sauté the onion, carrot and celery till brown. Truss (tie up) birds and add. Brown lightly on all sides.
COOKING	Pour in brandy and wine and reduce a little with the pan juices. Pour in enough water to come half way up

the birds. Add the bay leaf. Cover and simmer gently for about 10 minutes (a little longer for pheasant), depending on the toughness of the birds. Remove the birds from the sauce and keep warm.

FINISHING AND SERVING

Reduce the sauce a little to concentrate the flavour. Add cream and reduce further till a good consistency and flavour. Season. Pour the sauce over the birds and serve with a green salad and baked potatoes.

* Gabriel Tschumi's recipe, cooked for the royal household (see Chapter 6).

POTATOES AND ONIONS (Stovies)

(4 SERVINGS)

INGREDIENTS

2 oz (50 g) meat dripping with 2–3 tablespoons of gravy (sold by some Scottish butchers in little tubs specially for making stovies) or 2 tablespoons oil and water
2 large Spanish onions, finely chopped
2 lb (1 kg) main crop, mealy potatoes (e.g. Kerr's Pinks, King Edward or Golden Wonder), peeled
Seasonings: salt and pepper
Garnish: any leftover meat, chopped, and chopped parsley

COOKING

Melt the dripping (or heat the oil) in a large deep pot. Add the onion and cook till soft but not coloured. Slice the potatoes, some thin some thick, and add to the onions. Mix well, cover with a tight-fitting lid and cook gently for about 10 minutes, stirring occasionally to prevent sticking. Add the meat gravy or water. Season. Stir well and put back lid. Leave to cook *very* slowly till the thin potatoes are mushy and the larger ones soft – about 1 hour. For browned stovies turn up the heat and brown them turning frequently to avoid burning, mixing in the browned bits (as for American hashed browns).

FINISHING AND SERVING

Garnish with chopped leftover meat and chopped parsley and serve with oatcakes and a glass of milk.

POTATOES AND TURNIP (Orkney clapshot)

(4 SERVINGS)

INGREDIENTS	1 lb (500 g) mealy potatoes (e.g. Kerr's Pinks, King Edward or Golder Wonder) 1 lb (500 g) yellow turnip (swede) 1 onion, finely chopped* 1 tablespoonful chopped chives Butter (Orkney if possible) and milk for mashing *Seasonings*: salt and pepper
COOKING	Peel the potatoes and remove the coarse skin from the turnip. Cut them both into roughly the same sized pieces. Put into a pan with the onion. Add boiling water to cover and simmer gently till just soft. Drain off cooking liquor.
FINISHING AND SERVING	Mash everything thoroughly, adding chives and enough milk and butter to make a light consistency. Season well with salt and pepper. Serve with cheese as a meal, or with haggis. This versatile mix will happily accompany many stews or fried meats.

* Orcadian writer and poet, George Mackay Brown, suggests the onion (see Chapter 9, p. 81). He thinks the idea comes from F M McNeill but in fact she suggests chives: no reason why both should not be used.

POTATOES AND CABBAGE (Borders rumbledethumps*)

(4 SERVINGS)

INGREDIENTS	1 lb (500 g) mealy potatoes (e.g. Kerr's Pinks, King Edward or Golden Wonder) 2 oz (50 g) butter (½ stick) 1 onion, finely chopped 1 lb (500 g) cabbage, finely chopped 1 tablespoon chopped chives Milk to mix *Seasonings*: salt and pepper 4 oz (125 g) mature Scottish cheddar, grated (1 c)
COOKING	Peel the potatoes, put in pot with boiling water, and simmer till soft. Melt the butter in a pan and sauté the

onion and cabbage till just tender. Drain the potatoes and add to the cabbage and onions. Add the chives. Mash well together, mixing in a little milk if too stiff. Season and put into serving dish.

FINISHING AND
SERVING

Cover with the grated cheese, brown under the grill and serve.

* The name comes from the Scots words 'rumbled', meaning mashed, and 'thumped', meaning beaten down.

OATMEAL AND ONIONS (Skirlie)

(4 SERVINGS)

INGREDIENTS

4 oz (125 g) fat (traditionally good flavoured dripping, or beef suet) or 4 tablespoons oil
2 onions, finely chopped*
8 oz (250 g) medium oatmeal, lightly toasted
Seasonings: salt and pepper

COOKING

Melt the fat or heat the oil in a large frying pan. Add the onion and cook till soft and golden. Add the oatmeal and mix in well. Cook for about 5 minutes, turning frequently. Season well and serve with light creamy mashed potatoes. Alternatively skirlie may be used as a stuffing for any kind of game bird or poultry. It is also a very good accompaniment to rich meaty and gamy stews.

* I had always assumed that the onion was obligatory but Scottish author from the north-east, Jessie Kesson, does not remember an onion every being used in their Aberdeenshire skirlie – just suet and oatmeal.

SALMON AND WHITE WINE (Tweed kettle*)

(3–4 SERVINGS)

INGREDIENTS
2 lb (1 kg) fresh salmon
2 tablespoons oil
1 small onion, finely chopped
1 leek, finely chopped
Quarter celery stalk, sliced
1 carrot, finely chopped
1 lb (500 g) sole bones, thoroughly cleaned
½ pt (300 ml) dry white wine (1¼ c)
½ pt (300 ml) water (1¼ c)
1 oz (50 g) butter (¼ stick)
Seasonings: salt and pepper
Garnish: a few sprigs of dill

PREPARING
THE SALMON
Fillet the salmon and set aside. Reserve skin and bones for stock.

COOKING THE
STOCK
Heat the oil in a large pan and add all the vegetables. Sweat for 2–3 minutes without colouring. Add the salmon skin and bones along with the sole bones and sweat for another few minutes. Pour in the white wine and cook for a few minutes to drive off the alcohol. Add the water and cook for about 20 minutes. Strain through a conical sieve, pressing out all the liquid. Skim off any excess fat.

COOKING THE
FISH
Return the stock to the pan and bring to the boil. Cut the salmon into four steaks, add to the stock and bring up to a very gentle simmer. Cook for the minimum of time (a 1 in (2.5 cm) thick steak will need about 5 minutes). Remove the salmon and keep warm. Reduce sauce by a half and add the butter for a glazed finish. Season. Garnish with dill and serve.

* Traditionally served with chopped hardboiled egg and/or shrimps, and creamed potatoes. Known in eighteenth-century taverns as Tweed Kettle or Salmon Hash.

LOBSTER AND DRAMBUIE

(4 SERVINGS)

INGREDIENTS	2 live lobsters, approx. 2 lb (1 kg) each 1 oz (25 g) butter, melted (¼ stick) 3 tablespoons Drambuie ½ pt (300 ml) double cream (1¼ c) *Seasonings*: salt and pepper
PREPARING THE LOBSTERS	Plunge lobsters into boiling water to cover, and cook for about 15 minutes. Remove and split in half with a very sharp knife. Remove stomach sack from the head end. Discard the intestinal vein. Put the soft brain into a cup. Remove the meat from the tails, cut in ½ in (1 cm) pieces. Take out claw meat, trying to keep it in one piece. Remove the gills at the leg joints. Scrape out coagulated white in the shell and sieve with the brain and any roe. Reserve the shells to make a clear stock pot broth (see p. 100).
COOKING	Melt the butter in a frying pan and add the tail meat. Sauté for a few minutes and pour in the Drambuie. Set alight. When the flames have died down, remove the lobster meat and keep warm. Add the cream and the sieved soft parts of the lobster and reduce to a good flavour and consistency. Season.
FINISHING AND SERVING	Pour the sauce onto warmed plates. Place a whole claw on each plate and arrange the remaining tail meat in the form of a tail. Serve.
CONCLUSION	With the remainder in the Drambuie bottle: pour a generous amount over some creamy Italian vanilla ice cream for the next course and drink the rest (if any) with coffee and crisp buttery shortbread. Slàinte!

POT-ROASTS

Old cast-iron cooking pots on three legs became ovens when they were placed among the fire embers and covered with tightly fitting lids: this kind of roasting depended so much on keeping moisture in that the lid was wrapped in a cloth to make a secure fit (the modern alternative is aluminium foil). In the majority of Scottish homes in the eighteenth century – devoid of iron grates and built-in ovens – this was the nearest they came to roasting. A pot-roasted (stoved) chicken was one of the old standbys when unexpected visitors arrived – first catching it in the yard and, as they described it, depriving the bird of life and feathers. Though methods of acquiring chickens have changed, the cooking method survives. Besides the saving of fuel, it is a useful way of cooking 'in between' cuts: those not quite tough enough for the broth pot yet not quite tender enough for a hot fast roast. It is a particularly useful method for game, furred or feathered, of dubious vintage.

The basic method requires a casserole (preferably one that can be used in the oven and on the hob) just slightly larger than the meat: Place a layer of whole or large cut raw vegetables in the base with plenty of oil or fat, put the meat on top, butter it well, cover with a tight lid and cook on a slow heat or in a slow oven till the meat is just tender. It must be inspected, of course, every now and again to baste and turn the meat and check on the cooking. To finish, a reduced gravy can be made with the pan juices and wine or stock – a refinement. For every day, the natural cooking liquor with well-stewed vegetables suffices.

See oven temperatures, p. 132.

SILVERSIDE OF BEEF AND CARROTS

(6–8 SERVINGS)

INGREDIENTS	3 tablespoons oil
	3 lb (1.5 kg) silverside or brisket
	1 onion, chopped
	4 carrots, halved
	1 bay leaf
	1 sprig of thyme
	Seasonings: salt and pepper
COOKING	Heat the oil in a casserole which will just hold the meat and vegetables neatly. Add the meat and brown

lightly. Remove and add the vegetables, toss in the oil and replace the meat. Season and cover tightly, using aluminium foil if necessary to make a good seal. Cook very slowly, preferably in a slow oven, till the meat is tender, approximately 1½ hours. Turn the meat twice and baste with pan juices two or three times. If in the oven, remove the lid and turn up the heat to very hot for the last 10 minutes to brown the surface. Serve with the vegetables and pan juices.

SHOULDER OF LAMB WITH GARLIC, LEMON AND ROSEMARY

(4–6 SERVINGS)

INGREDIENTS

3 lb (1.5 kg) shoulder of lamb
2 cloves garlic, halved
4 sprigs of rosemary
2 tablespoons lemon juice
1 tablespoon olive oil
Seasonings: salt and pepper
2 tablespoons oil
1 onion, roughly sliced
1 lb (500 g) waxy potatoes, thickly sliced
1 bay leaf
2 strips of lemon rind

MARINATING THE MEAT IN GLASS OR EARTHEN-WARE DISH

Slide a sharp knife along the bones and insert the halved cloves of garlic, distributing them through the joint. Make some incisions in the surface fat and push the sprigs of rosemary through. Put into a deep bowl with the lemon juice and oil, season and cover. Leave to marinate for at least 12 hours, turning twice.

COOKING

Heat the oil in a casserole and cook the onion and potatoes for a few minutes without colouring. Add bay leaf and lemon rind, and lay the meat on top. Pour in the marinade. Cover tightly and cook slowly, preferably in a slow oven, till the meat is tender, approximately 1½ hours. The meat should not be turned, but baste occasionally.

149

FINISHING AND
SERVING

If it is being cooked in the oven, remove the lid and turn up the heat to very hot for the last 20 minutes to crisp and brown the surface fat on the meat. Remove the meat, carve, and serve with the potatoes and onions.

CHICKEN AND CELERY

(4–6 SERVINGS)

INGREDIENTS

3 tablespoons oil
4 lb (2 kg) chicken
2 small heads celery, chopped
1 onion, chopped
1 leek white, chopped
1 bay leaf
1 sprig of thyme
Seasonings: salt and pepper
2 carrots, cut into fine sticks

COOKING AND
SERVING

Heat the oil in a casserole and brown the chicken lightly on all sides. Remove. Add the celery, onion and leek and toss for a few minutes without colouring. Add the bay leaf, thyme and seasonings. Place the chicken on its side, on top of the vegetables. Cover tightly and cook on the hob or in a slow oven till the chicken is tender. Baste three times, at approximately half-hour intervals, each time turning the chicken, first onto its other side, then onto its breast and finally onto its back. Add carrots and mix through vegetables. If it is being cooked in the oven, remove the lid at this point and brown the breast for the last half hour at a very hot temperature. Serve with the vegetables.

PIGEON AND AYRSHIRE BACON

(4 SERVINGS)

INGREDIENTS
4 tablespoons oil
4 × 12 oz (350 g) pigeons, trussed
1 onion, chopped
1 carrot, chopped
1 stick of celery, chopped
1 bay leaf
1 sprig of thyme
Seasonings: salt and pepper
Garnish: 4 rashers Ayrshire bacon

COOKING
Heat the oil in a casserole and brown the pigeons lightly. Remove, add the vegetables and toss for a few minutes. Add the bay leaf and thyme, and put the pigeons on top, breast side down. Season. Cover and cook slowly, preferably in a slow oven. Baste throughout the cooking and turn the pigeons onto their backs half-way through the cooking. Leave the lid off for the last 20 minutes and turn up the heat to very hot to brown.

FINISHING AND
SERVING
Grill four rashers of Ayrshire bacon and serve with the pigeons.

PHEASANT WITH FRESH TARRAGON

(4 SERVINGS)

INGREDIENTS
2 × 2 lb (1 kg) pheasants
Bunch of fresh tarragon
3 tablespoons oil
1 onion, chopped
1 carrot, roughly chopped
1 stick of celery, chopped
Seasonings: salt and pepper
Garnish: chopped tarragon

COOKING AND SERVING	Stuff the breast cavities of the pheasants with tarragon. Heat the oil in a casserole and brown the pheasants lightly. Remove. Add the vegetables and cook for a few minutes. Replace the pheasants, season and cook on four sides (see Chicken and celery, p. 150). Turn the pheasants onto their backs for the final 20 minutes, removing the lid and turning up the oven heat to brown the birds. Serve with pan juices and vegetables. Garnish with chopped tarragon.

SHOULDER OF VENISON WITH JUNIPER BERRIES

(4–6 SERVINGS)

INGREDIENTS	3 tablespoons oil 3 lb (1.5 kg) boned and rolled shoulder of venison 1 head celeriac, sliced 1 onion, chopped 1 carrot, chopped 12 juniper berries, crushed Bunch of thyme 1 glass port *Seasonings*: salt and pepper
COOKING AND SERVING	Heat the oil in a casserole and brown the meat lightly. Remove. Add the vegetables, juniper and thyme, and toss for a few minutes. Then replace the meat, cover tightly and cook slowly, preferably in a slow oven, till the meat is tender. Baste and turn a couple of times. Remove meat, add port and reduce a little. Season and serve.

PUDDINGS IN THE POT

'Puddings', the colloquial term for the innards of an animal, was also used as the name of the mixture stuffed into them and cooked. The delightful sounding Pudding Lane in London, where the Great Fire started, should surely, one would imagine, have derived from the good tavern puddings sold there. Instead, it gets its name from the unsightly habits of the Eastcheap butchers who swilled their debris, puddings, etc., down the lane and into their dung-boats on the River Thames.

These early puddings cooked in stomach bags were first cousins to the haggis which was, until the late eighteenth century, a universal British dish. Etymologists differ on the derivation but Gillian Edwards in *Hogmanay and Tiffany* (1970) claims that: 'Some derive this word from the French *hachis*, which developed through the spellings *hache* and *hachy* into English hash, but except that haggis in Cumberland was called hash pudding, there seems no definite connexion. Another suggestion derives it from an old verb hag, to cut or chop, or the Anglo-Saxon *haecan*, to hack into pieces. Or again it may be related to the ancient name for a magpie, haggess.' Which, as she suggests, makes the connexion between the nature of the dish, as an accumulation of odds and ends, and the habits of the bird.

But the pudding story – whatever the obscurity of haggis – has moved on from just innards. First, to making puddings in a cloth: bag puddings in England and clootie dumplings in Scotland. The pudding-in-a-cloth was boiled, along with other things, in the universal pot. Then they were cooked separately in a pudding bowl and steamed rather than boiled, the bowl protecting the contents which could now be less robust, even delicate and soufflé-like.

Though a meal of broth and pudding stems from the original cooking pot we can be more flexible today: we may steam such puddings in a pot or bake them in the oven. The steamed ones are moister, the baked ones more cake-like in texture. The robust mixtures, of course, are still made to survive the rigours of the boiling pot either in animal 'puddings' or tied in a cloth. Aficionados maintain that they are 'not the same' cooked in a bowl and without proper beef suet for flavour. Certainly haggis is not haggis without its antique 'pudding' as a casing, nor dumplings 'clootie' without their skin.

Savoury

SHEEP'S HAGGIS

INGREDIENTS	1 sheep's pluck, liver, lights (lungs) and heart, washed* Cold water 1 sheep's stomach bag (optional) 1 lb (500 g) medium or coarse oatmeal, lightly toasted (4 c) 1–2 tablespoons salt Freshly ground black pepper 1 tablespoon freshly ground allspice 8 oz (250 g) suet (2 c) 4 onions, finely chopped
COOKING THE PLUCK	Place the pluck in a large pot and pour in enough cold water to cover. Hang the windpipe over the side with a bowl to catch the drips. Bring to a slow simmer and cook gently for about 2 hours or until tender. Leave to cool.
PREPARING THE BAGS	Wash the inside of the bag thoroughly. Leave for 8–10 hours in cold salted water. Alternatively the haggis may be cooked in a pudding bowl (see p. 158).
COOKING	Mince the pluck meat, or chop finely. It may be chopped in a blender but not too finely. Put into a large bowl with the oatmeal. Add about 1 pt (600 ml) of the cooking liquor to moisten. Add the seasonings. Taste for flavour and correct. Mix in the suet and onions. Fill stomach bags (or bowl if using), but not too full since the oatmeal will expand. Press out air and sew up. Prick with a fine needle to prevent bursting. Place in boiling water and simmer for about 3 hours.
SERVING	Serve with creamed potatoes flavoured with nutmeg, and mashed turnip flavoured with allspice, or Orkney clapshot (see p. 144).

* It is not necessary to use a whole pluck, just traditional. The liver, hearts and lungs can be bought separately from the butcher. There is much variation in texture and flavour in butchers' haggis since they use offal from other animals. Calves' liver is much liked for a stronger liver flavour. Pork fat is sometimes incorporated to give moistness. And of course seasonings vary enormously from highly spiced to mild and herby – it is all a matter of taste. But whatever the flavour, drams of whisky are poured down throats, *not* over the haggis!

SWEET HAGGIS*

(6–8 SERVINGS)

INGREDIENTS	Cotton or linen cloth, approx. 22 in (55 cm) square 8 oz (250 g) medium oatmeal (2 c) 4 oz (125 g) pinhead oatmeal (1 c) 4 oz (125 g) wholewheat flour (1 c) 12 oz (350 g) beef suet, finely chopped (3 c) 4 oz (125 g) soft brown sugar (½ c) 4 oz (125 g) currants (1 c) 4 oz (125 g) raisins (⅔ c) Salt and pepper Water to mix
PREPARING THE POT AND THE CLOTH	Fill a large pot with water, place a metal grid or upside down saucer in the base. Bring slowly to the boil. When it starts boiling put in cloth and boil for a few minutes. Lift out with tongs and spread out on table. Quickly sprinkle with about a tablespoonful of wholemeal flour and toss the flour to coat the main centre part of the cloth quite thickly. Alternatively, the haggis may be cooked in a pudding bowl (see p. 158).
MAKING THE MIXTURE	Put all the ingredients into a bowl and mix to a stiff consistency with water. Place in the centre of the cloth. Bring up edges and tie with a string leaving a little space for expansion of the meal. Hold the tied ends and pat the cloth into a good round shape.
COOKING	Place into the boiling liquid – it should come half-way up the pudding. Reduce to the lowest simmer, cover and cook for about 4 hours. Check occasionally and top up with boiling water if necessary.
FINISHING AND SERVING	Fill a bowl slightly larger than the one containing the pudding with cold water. Lift out the pudding and plunge into the cold water – this helps to release the cloth from the pudding skin. Keep in the cold water for one minute. Remove and put in another bowl about the same size as the pudding. Untie, open out the cloth and place a large plate or ashet on top and reverse. Remove the bowl and peel off the cloth. Put pudding into a hot oven, or leave at the side of the fire to dry off the skin. Serve hot, with grilled bacon.

Any leftover pudding may be sliced and fried for breakfast, or wrapped in foil and reheated in the oven.

* An old family recipe from Ayrshire which has been handed down through at least four generations.

SWEET MARAG*

(6–8 SERVINGS)

INGREDIENTS   8 oz (250 g) medium oatmeal (2 c)
8 oz (250 g) plain flour (2 c)
4 oz (125 g) beef suet, finely chopped (1 c)
2 oz (50 g) castor sugar (⅓ c)
1 teaspoon finely diced onion
2 oz (50 g) raisins (⅓ c)

PREPARING THE PUDDING, COOKING, FINISHING AND SERVING   As for Sweet haggis, p. 155, or cook in a pudding bowl, see p. 158.

* A variation of Sweet haggis, this recipe comes from Lewis and the result is much less mealy.

DEER HAGGIS

(6–8 SERVINGS)

INGREDIENTS   1 venison heart and 1 venison liver, simmered till tender, then chopped or minced
4 oz (125 g) chopped venison suet (1 c)
4 oz (125 g) pinhead oatmeal (1 c)
3 onions, finely chopped
Seasonings: salt and freshly ground black pepper

PREPARING THE HAGGIS, COOKING, FINISHING AND SERVING   As for Sweet haggis, p. 155, or cook in a pudding bowl, see p. 158.

Sweet

SPICED FRUIT DUMPLING (Clootie dumpling)

(8–10 SERVINGS)

INGREDIENTS

4 oz (125 g) wholemeal flour (1 c)
6 oz (175 g) fine brown breadcrumbs (1½ c)
4 oz (125 g) beef suet, finely chopped (1 c), or butter (1 stick)
1 teaspoon baking powder
1 teaspoon each freshly ground cinnamon, ginger, nutmeg and cumin
4 oz (125 g) sultanas (¾ c)
4 oz (125 g) currants (1 c)
2 oz (50 g) Californian raisins (½ c)
2 tablespoons black treacle
2 eggs
1 large cooking apple, grated
1 large carrot, grated
Juice and zest of a lemon
Fresh orange juice to mix

PREPARING THE PUDDING, COOKING, FINISHING AND SERVING   As for Sweet haggis, p. 155, or cook in a pudding bowl, see p. 158.

Note: When mixing the ingredients, the treacle should be stirred into the eggs before adding. The pudding mixture should be made slightly soft but not sloppy, and not too stiff. It will not hold together when turned out if it is too soft; on the other hand, too stiff a mixture will make for a heavy dumpling. Leave room for expansion since there is a raising agent in this mix. For a plainer mix cut out some of the spices and fruit, sometimes more palatable for children. Add silver coins wrapped in greaseproof paper for Christmas and New Year, charms for Hallowe'en: button, thimble, wishbone, horseshoe, ring, silver coin (see Cranachan, p. 185).

MARMALADE (Basic steamed sponge pudding)*

(6–8 SERVINGS)

INGREDIENTS

Pudding:
½ oz (12 g) butter, melted (⅛ stick)
1 tablespoon Seville orange marmalade
12 large Californian raisins
4 oz (125 g) unsalted butter (1 stick)
4 oz (125 g) castor sugar (½ c)
2 tablespoons Seville orange marmalade, finely chopped
Zest of a lemon
2 eggs
6 oz (175 g) self-raising flour (1½ c)
Milk to mix
Orange and lemon sauce:
1 tablespoon Seville orange marmalade
3 tablespoons fresh orange juice
1 tablespoon lemon juice

PREPARING THE COOKING POT AND PUDDING BOWL

Pour enough cold water into a large cooking pot to come half-way up a 2 pt (1 l, 5 c) pudding bowl. Place a grid in the base to keep the bottom of the bowl off the direct heat. A steamer may also be used – this has the advantage of holding the pudding above the boiling water and therefore preventing any water boiling over and into it.

Grease the bowl well with the melted butter. The bowl may have a lid but if not, prepare a lid of double-thickness foil with a pleat in the middle to allow for expansion. Grease it on the underside to prevent the pudding sticking to it. Have a piece of string for tying, or a rubber band. Put a tablespoonful of marmalade in the base of the pudding bowl, and sprinkle raisins on top.

MAKING THE PUDDING

Cream the butter and sugar together till light, mix in marmalade and lemon zest. Beat in the eggs gradually. Sieve in the flour and mix in lightly, adding some milk if necessary to make a soft dropping consistency. Put into the pudding bowl. Cover with lid or foil, and tie.

STEAMING	Put the pudding to steam for 1–1½ hours. The water should come about half-way up the bowl. Check water level occasionally and top up with boiling water if necessary.
MAKING THE SAUCE	Put marmalade into a blender with orange and lemon juice and blend till very smooth. Warm slightly.
FINISHING AND SERVING	Remove the lid or foil, loosen round the edge of the pudding with a knife and invert onto a round plate. Serve hot with the sauce. Alternatively serve with kumquats preserved in Cointreau, made according to the recipe for Preserved prunes (p. 187). Add some of the preserving liquor to the sauce.

* May also be baked in the oven (180°C, 350°F, Gas 4) in a greased 2 pt (1 l) pie dish or soufflé dish for 40–60 minutes.

URNEY PUDDING* (Sponge)

(6–8 SERVINGS)

INGREDIENTS	*Pudding*: ½ oz (12 g) butter, melted (⅛ stick) 4 oz (125 g) castor sugar (½ c) 4 oz (125 g) unsalted butter (1 stick) 3 tablespoons strawberry or raspberry jam Zest of a lemon 2 eggs 6 oz (175 g) self-raising flour (1½ c) *Fresh raspberry sauce*: 4 oz (125 g) fresh fruit 2 tablespoons Frangelica (wild hazelnut liqueur, Italian) or other liqueur is taste
PREPARING THE COOKING POT AND PUDDING BOWL, MAKING THE PUDDING, STEAMING OR BAKING, FINISHING AND SERVING	As for Marmalade pudding, p. 158.
MAKING THE SAUCE	Purée the fruit in a blender. Sieve. Stir in the Frangelica. Alternatively, heat 4 tablespoons strawberry or raspberry jam with a little water and sieve.

Note: Fresh raspberries, blackcurrants, redcurrants, brambles or blaeberries (6 oz, 175 g) can be used instead of jam: the result is a moister pudding because of the juice in the fruit and it is less sweet. Chopped cooking apples or chopped rhubarb may also be used. Serve with a sauce made with the fresh fruit as in the above recipe. Make it slightly sharp (use lemons if necessary) to balance the richness of the pudding. If using cooking apples or rhubarb, stew them first with some sugar before puréeing. Or serve with fresh whipped cream, or both!

* The origins of 'Urney' are obscure but F Marian McNeill claims the pudding as Victorian.

DATE PUDDING WITH STICKY TOFFEE SAUCE*
(Sponge)

(6–8 SERVINGS)

INGREDIENTS *Pudding*:
½ oz (12 g) butter, melted (⅛ stick)
6 oz (175 g) block of stoned dates
½ pt (300 ml) boiling water (1¼ c)
2 oz (50 g) butter (½ stick)
4 oz (125 g) sugar (½ c)
2 eggs
6 oz (175 g) self-raising flour (1½ c)
1 level teaspoon bicarbonate of soda
Sticky toffee sauce:
6 oz (175 g) demerara sugar (⅔ c)
4 oz (125 g) butter (1 stick)
¼ pt (150 ml) double cream (¾ c)
1 teaspoon vanilla essence

MAKING THE PUDDING Pour the water over the dates, mix well and leave to cool. Cream the butter and sugar till fluffy and beat in the eggs. Sift in the flour and bicarbonate of soda and fold in. Mix in the cooled dates.

PREPARING THE COOKING POT AND PUDDING BOWL, STEAMING, FINISHING As for Marmalade pudding, p. 158. It may also be baked in a greased shallow tin in the oven (180°C, 350°F, Gas 4 for 40–45 minutes).

MAKING THE SAUCE AND SERVING Put all the ingredients into a pan. Bring slowly to the boil, stirring to dissolve the sugar. Remove. Pour sauce over pudding when serving. Sauce will store well in the fridge for 2–3 weeks.

* A recipe by Alasdair Robertson of the Holly Tree Restaurant in Kentallen.

WALNUT AND COFFEE (Sponge)

(6–8 SERVINGS)

INGREDIENTS *Pudding*:
½ oz (12 g) butter, melted (⅛ stick)
4 oz (125 g) unsalted butter (1 stick)
4 oz (125 g) castor sugar (½ c)
2 eggs
6 oz (175 g) self-raising flour (1½ c)
2 tablespoons very strong coffee
2 oz (50 g) chopped walnuts (½ c)
Sticky Toffee Sauce: see p. 160

PREPARING THE COOKING POT AND PUDDING BOWL, MAKING THE PUDDING, STEAMING OR BAKING, FINISHING AND SERVING As for Marmalade pudding, p. 158. Serve with Sticky toffee sauce.

VANILLA (Basic pudding soufflé)*

(6–8 SERVINGS)

INGREDIENTS ½ oz (12 g) butter, melted (⅛ stick)
½ pint (300 ml) milk (1¼ c)
1 vanilla pod
2 oz (50 g) butter (½ stick)
2 oz (50 g) plain flour (½ c)
3 oz (175 g) sugar (½ c)
4 × size 3 eggs, separated

PREPARING THE COOKING POT AND PUDDING BOWL As for Marmalade pudding p. 158. Use a 3 pt (1.8 l) pudding bowl.

MAKING THE PUDDING Put the milk into a pan with the vanilla pod and heat gently. Leave to infuse for half an hour. Melt the butter in a pan, add flour and cook for a few minutes. Strain the milk into the butter and flour and stir in with the sugar, bring to a boil and cook till thick. Leave to cool. Beat in egg yolks. Beat whites stiffly and fold through carefully. Pour into pudding bowl and cover.

161

| STEAMING OR BAKING THE PUDDING | Steam for about 40 minutes. Serve immediately, in the bowl, or turn onto a plate. Alternatively heat the oven to 180°C, 350°F, Gas 4. Pour the mixture into a greased 2–3 pt (1–1.8 l) soufflé dish and bake for 30–45 minutes till firm. Serve immediately. |

* This basic pudding soufflé can be varied in a number of ways: add 2 tablespoons sweet liqueur (e.g. Drambuie or Glayva) to the above mixture. Serve a glass of the liqueur with the pudding.

LEMON (Soufflé)

(6–8 SERVINGS)

| INGREDIENTS | As for Vanilla pudding soufflé, p. 161. Omit vanilla pod and add zest and juice of two lemons. |
| METHOD | As for Vanilla pudding soufflé. |

CHOCOLATE (Soufflé)

(6–8 SERVINGS)

| INGREDIENTS | As for Vanilla pudding soufflé, p. 161. Add 3 oz (75 g) grated bitter chocolate (Meunier, or Terry's) to the milk and heat through to melt the chocolate. Add 3 oz (75 g) ground almonds. |
| METHOD | As for Vanilla pudding soufflé. Serve with Chocolate Sauce: melt 4 oz (125 g) bitter chocolate with 2–3 tablespoons double cream. |

II

The Girdle on the Hook

'In Scotland, amongst the rural population generally, the girdle until recent times took the place of the oven, the bannock of the loaf.'

F Marian McNeill
The Scots Kitchen

THE GIRDLE

There is a fire on a large flat stone. Now it dies down and the ashes are swept off, the hot stone ready for a 'girdle' baking.

More sophisticated methods use the flat cast-iron plates which were originally made in Scotland at Culross in Fife by the Company of Girdle-makers in the eighteenth century. These Culross girdles, of all shapes and sizes, which found their way to many parts of the country, were often huge. One baker describes his as being five feet (1.5 m) long! Normally they were made to fit the shape of the fire, some round, some rectangular, some oval. The thicker the better to conserve and distribute the heat – antique girdles (sometimes available at auction sales) can be up to half an inch (1 cm) thick.

Modern cast-iron girdles are available in a variety of sizes from 12 inches (30 cm) in diameter to around 14 inches (35 cm) from good ironmongers. The larger is a better buy since more can be cooked at one time thus saving fuel. They should all fit over a single gas or electric ring on a cooker or can be used over open fires or barbecues. There is also the square, lighter aluminium 'Elizabeth McKellar' girdle which has a plastic handle. It is not suitable for open fires or barbecues. (All girdles can be used for 'dry' grilling or griddling, when the raw food, steaks of meat or fish, hamburgers, bacon, sausages, etc., can be put onto a very hot dry girdle. The food will stick first, but as it cooks the fat and moisture loosen the surface, and the food can be cooked without fat. Wash well with a light detergent before using again for baking.)

Large heavy-duty or non-stick frying pans are good substitutes for girdles but if the sides are too deep it is a little more difficult to turn things like pancakes and crumpets. Some electric hot plates are also suitable but check with the cooker's instructions.

All the following recipes have been cooked on a 14 inch (35 cm) diameter girdle.

TURNING BAKING OR OTHER FOOD ON THE GIRDLE

To make lifting and turning easier the traditional implement was a bannock-spade, a long handled implement with a heart-shaped spade at the end. Modern spatulas tend to be thin and long and not a convenient shape, but a good quality paint-stripping knife with a supple blade of about four inches across is an ideal substitute.

SEASONING THE GIRDLE

A new girdle should be seasoned by covering the surface thinly with salt. Then it should be heated up slowly till scorching hot, left for about ten minutes, then cooled down before removing the salt.

Baking on a girdle is a satisfying occupation, the baking progress watched throughout and cared for more precisely than in oven baking. Attention, of course, is required: a dreaming King Alfred will not do.

USING THE GIRDLE

Never wash the girdle, but dust with a dry cloth after use. Once it has heated up, grease the surface lightly just before use and before each new batch is to be baked. A piece of suet wrapped in a muslin was used for this purpose, but an oil-impregnated cloth or piece of kitchen paper is just as good. Heat up slowly on a very low heat to give an even temperature. Once greased, dust with flour if the baking is a floury bannock or scone, or with oatmeal if the baking is oatcakes. To test the temperature: judge the heat with the palm of your hand held an inch from the surface of the girdle. It should feel comfortably, rather than fiercely, hot.

FLOURS

It is not necessary to use flours with a high gluten content (such as there is in strong flour) although there is no reason why a strong flour should not be used. A self-raising flour should not be used with buttermilk or treacle mixes since the acid balance would be wrong. Wholemeal, stoneground flours give the best flavour but because of the large amount of bran they will produce a much heavier result. White flour will give the best rise. Orkney beremeal is a much earthier taste than ordinary barley flour. For comments on oatmeal see p. 181.

RAISING AGENTS

Chemical raising agents were used first around the mid-nineteenth century. A mixture of an alkali and an acid with liquid gives off the gas which raises the dough. Bicarbonate of soda (alkali) and cream of tartar (acid) were first sold separately, but later produced as a 'baking powder', a mixture of the two along with some kind of starch to prevent the two agents reacting with one another before use. Apart from the convenience of measuring out one spoonful rather than two or three, there is no other advantage in buying baking powder since you pay for unnecessary extra starch.

To use bicarbonate of soda and cream of tartar separately they must be in the correct proportion: 1 part alkali (bicarbonate of soda) to 2 parts acid (cream of tartar). If the baking mixture already contains acid, such as buttermilk or treacle, the quantity of acid cream of tartar can be halved, or removed altogether if there is enough of the other ingredient. The raising agents should be thoroughly mixed and sieved with the flours to avoid any stray lumps. They give off their gas very quickly and once the mixture is made up it should be cooked as soon as possible. This is the reason for mixing only one girdleful at a time.

Methods of using raising agents:
For 8 oz (250 g) flour (2 c) using level
teaspoons
1. 1 teaspoon bicarbonate of soda
   2 teaspoons cream of tartar
   with fresh milk
2. 1 teaspoon bicarbonate of soda
   1 teaspoon cream of tartar
   with buttermilk
3. 2 teaspoons baking powder
   with fresh milk
4. Use only self-raising flour
   with fresh milk

In comparison with yeast-raised doughs these girdle baking specialities have the great advantage of being quick and easy to make but they do not keep well. Within twenty-four hours they are dry and getting hard. Though they may be toasted or fried, or deep-frozen, they are undoubtedly best served, still slightly warm, within an hour of baking.

BUTTERMILK

Buttermilk was originally the acidulous milk which remained after the butter had been churned but today cultured buttermilk is fairly widely available. With bicarbonate of soda it makes a moister scone. A recipe was published in *The Bakers ABC* (1927) and is referred to by Elizabeth David in *English Bread and Yeast Cookery* (1978): 'If about 3 oz of ordinary flour is carefully scalded with 1 qt. of boiling water, and about ½ oz malt flour and ½ pt fresh milk added when the scalded liquor cools, lactic fermentation starts spontaneously, and in two days, if the liquid has been kept warm, it is in the condition of an artificial buttermilk, answering all the purposes for scone-making, etc. A fresh mixing can be stocked with a quantity from a previous making, and a supply kept up, much in the same way as barm is made.'

MIXING DOUGH

When mixing the dough for soft light bannocks (large rounds) or scones (small rounds, or the triangles known as 'farls') the dough should be as soft and airy as possible. Handling is a challenge. Firmer dough may be easier to roll and shape but it will not make such a light end product.

Expert Scottish girdle-bakers begin by sifting the flour and dry ingredients straight onto the baking board (originally a rectangular board with edges like a tray which kept the ingredients together). When they are all mixed, a well is made in the centre for the liquid. The mixing is done by gradually drawing in the flour from the outsides with a round-bladed knife till there is a soft mass in the middle. This can also be done in a bowl. Then the dough is floured and lifted or tipped onto a floured girdle. The top is pressed lightly to make a round shape, and the bannock is cooked on both sides.

To make small scones rather than a large whole bannock, take small dessertspoonfuls of the mixture and toss them in a bowl of flour before putting them on the floured girdle. The surface is then pressed lightly and the scone cooked on both sides. Both these methods produce light bannocks or scones, rugged in appearance, a more rustic attraction.

Whether bannocks, scones or pancakes they should be allowed to cook three-quarters of the way through before turning so that they are properly set. If they are turned too soon they may be doughy in the middle. It is easy to see when to turn pancakes since they start to bubble when they are ready; scones and bannocks are more difficult to judge, but between five and ten minutes on the first side should be long enough. They need about the same time on the other side, though timing will always depend on the heat of the girdle.

COOLING

Wrap baking in a tea towel on a cooling rack to keep warm and moist.

OATCAKES

(MAKES 4 LARGE, 8 SMALL TRIANGLES)

INGREDIENTS	4 oz (125 g) medium oatmeal (1 c) 1 tablespoon melted meat dripping, bacon fat or oil Pinch of salt 2–3 tablespoons boiling water
PREPARING THE GIRDLE	Heat the girdle, sprinkle with oatmeal.
MIXING AND SHAPING	Sprinkle a baking board with medium oatmeal. Mix together the meal, dripping, salt and boiling water. Bring together into a ball and roll out quickly to a round about ⅓ in (½ cm) thick. Cut into four triangles. Repeat the process rather than make up double the quantity if you wish to make more. Each 4 oz (125 g, 1 c) quantity must be handled and rolled while still hot because the mixture becomes difficult to roll thinly when cold without breaking and cracking up.
COOKING AND SERVING	Put the oatcakes on the hot girdle and bake on one side only till the edges curl. To dry off, stand on end in a toast rack in front of the fire or in a hot dry place. Keep in an airtight tin and heat through before serving to dry off and sharpen up the flavour.

BARLEY BANNOCKS

(MAKES 6 MEDIUM)

INGREDIENTS	5 oz (150 g) barley flour or beremeal (1¼ c) 1 teaspoon baking powder 4 eggs 1 tablespoon sugar ½ pt (300 ml) milk 1 oz (25 g) butter, melted (¼ stick)
PREPARING THE GIRDLE	Heat the girdle and grease.

MIXING	Sift the flour and baking powder into a bowl. Make a well in the centre and add the eggs, sugar and milk. Whisk together. Mix in the melted butter to make a pouring consistency.
COOKING AND SERVING	Pour a ladleful onto the girdle, leaving space for spreading. Cook for a few minutes and turn. Cook for another few minutes. Remove. Wrap in cloth and keep warm. Serve slightly warm with butter and preserves.

BEREMEAL BANNOCKS (Orkney)

(MAKES 2 VERY LARGE OR 8 SMALL)

INGREDIENTS	6 oz (175 g) beremeal (1½ c), see p. 2 oz (50 g) plain flour (½ c) Pinch of salt 1 teaspoon bicarbonate of soda 1 teaspoon cream of tartar Approx. ¼ pt (150 ml) buttermilk (or fresh milk soured with lemon juice till it curdles)
PREPARING THE GIRDLE	Heat the girdle.
MIXING	Mix the dry ingredients in a bowl and make a well in the centre. Add the buttermilk and mix with a knife to a soft elastic dough. Divide into two and roll out on a floured board to make two 6 in (15 cm) rounds.
COOKING AND SERVING	Sprinkle the girdle with beremeal and bake bannocks on both sides till cooked. Alternatively small scones can be made by dropping tablespoonfuls of the mixture into a bowl of beremeal, coating and dropping on the floured girdle. Press down lightly and cook on both sides for about 5 minutes. Cool on a wire rack wrapped in a towel. Eat with Orkney butter and farmhouse cheese.

MEALIE BANNOCKS (Aberdeenshire)

(MAKES 10 MEDIUM)

INGREDIENTS
4 oz (125 g) fine oatmeal (1 c)
Pinch of salt
½ pt (300 ml) cold water (1¼ c scant)
2 eggs
4 oz (125 g) flour (1 c)
1 teaspoon baking powder
Milk to mix

STEEPING THE OATMEAL
Put the oatmeal and salt into a bowl and cover with water. Leave to steep (soak) for 1 hour or overnight, until the meal has absorbed most of the water.

PREPARING THE GIRDLE
Heat the girdle and grease.

MIXING
Add the eggs to the steeped oatmeal. Sift the flour and baking powder together and mix in. Add milk to make a thick creamy mixture.

COOKING AND SERVING
Drop spoonfuls of the mixture on to the girdle and turn when they bubble. Serve with butter and preserves.

BERE AND OATMEAL BREAD (Blaanda bread, Shetland*)

(MAKES 6 MEDIUM)

INGREDIENTS
1 oz (25 g) butter (¼ stick)
2 oz (50 g) beremeal (½ c)
2 oz (50 g) fine oatmeal (½ c)
Pinch of salt
1 teaspoon bicarbonate of soda
2 teaspoons cream of tartar
Milk to mix

PREPARING THE GIRDLE
Heat the girdle.

MIXING
Rub the butter into the meal mixture and salt, and sift in the raising agents. Add the milk gradually, mixing

170

with the right hand till a firm but not sticky dough. Shape into a round flat bannock.

COOKING Sprinkle girdle with beremeal and bake bannock slowly on both sides till cooked. Cool on a wire rack wrapped in a towel.

* From *A Shetland Cook Book* by Jenni Simmons (1978).

POTATO SCONES (Tattie scones)

(MAKES 8–12)

INGREDIENTS 2 oz (50 g) fine oatmeal or plain white flour (½ c)
1 level teaspoon salt
8 oz (250 g) cooked potatoes (1 c) mashed with 1 oz (25 g) butter (¼ stick)

PREPARING Heat the girdle and grease.
THE GIRDLE

MIXING Mix the oatmeal and salt into the mashed potatoes and knead with your hand to a firm pliable dough. Roll out very thinly into 6–8 in (15–20 cm) rounds, about ⅛–¼ in (¼–½ cm) thick on a floured board, prick with a fork and cut into triangles.

COOKING AND Bake on both sides till an uneven spotty brown. Cool
SERVING on a wire rack wrapped in a towel. Serve warm with butter and preserves, or cover with a thin layer of pickles and thick layer of grated cheddar cheese and brown under the grill.

MASHLAM SCONES (Mull*)

(MAKES 8 LARGE, 12 SMALL)

INGREDIENTS
4 oz (125 g) plain white flour (1 c)
1 teaspoon bicarbonate of soda
2 teaspoons cream of tartar
Pinch of salt
1 teaspoon sugar
4 oz (125 g) fine oatmeal (1 c)
1 oz (25 g) butter (¼ stick)
Milk to mix

PREPARING
THE GIRDLE
Heat the girdle and grease.

MIXING
Sift the dry ingredients, except the oatmeal, together. Mix in the oatmeal and rub in the butter. Make a well in the centre, add the milk and mix to a fairly soft dough. Dust with flour.

COOKING AND
SERVING
Sprinkle the girdle with flour. Turn the dough out onto it, press lightly on top and cut into four. Dust surface with flour. Cook on both sides. Cool on a wire rack wrapped in a towel. Serve with butter and cheese.

* From *A Mull Home Companion*, ed. Janet M Nelson (1977). Mashlam was the mix of meals which were grown in the fields and ground together.

BRUNNIES (Shetland)

(MAKES 8 LARGE, 12 SMALL)

INGREDIENTS
8 oz (250 g) wholemeal flour (2 c)
1 teaspoon salt
1 teaspoon bicarbonate of soda
1 teaspoon cream of tartar
Scant ½ pt (300 ml) buttermilk (1¼ c) (or fresh milk soured with lemon juice till it curdles)

PREPARING
THE GIRDLE
Heat the girdle and grease.

MIXING	Sift the flour, salt and raising agents into a bowl and mix in enough buttermilk to make a soft dough. Drop each tablespoonful of the dough into a bowl of wholemeal flour and toss till covered.
COOKING AND SERVING	Sprinkle the girdle with flour. Put scones onto it, press lightly on top and dust with flour. Bake on both sides till cooked. Cool on a wire rack wrapped in a towel. Serve warm.

SODA SCONES

(MAKES 4 LARGE, 6–8 SMALL)

INGREDIENTS	8 oz (250 g) plain white flour (2 c) 1 teaspoon bicarbonate of soda 1 teaspoon cream of tartar ½ teaspoon salt Scant ½ pt (300 ml) buttermilk (1¼ c) (or fresh milk soured with lemon juice till it curdles)
PREPARING THE GIRDLE	Heat the girdle.
MIXING	Sift all the dry ingredients together and mix to a light elastic dough with the buttermilk.
COOKING AND SERVING	Sprinkle girdle with flour. Turn out the dough onto the girdle, dust with flour and press out lightly to about 1 in (2.5 cm) thick. Cut into four or six triangles, or leave as a whole bannock. Bake about 10–15 minutes on the first side, 5 minutes on the second. Alternatively small scones can be made: drop spoonfuls of the dough into a bowl of flour, coat, drop onto the girdle, press down lightly and bake. Cool on a wire rack wrapped in a towel. Serve warm with butter and preserves or with cheese.

SWEET MILK SCONES

(MAKES 6 LARGE OR 8 SMALL)

INGREDIENTS	5 oz (150 g) self-raising flour (1¼ c) 1 tablespoon golden syrup 1 oz (25 g) butter, melted (¼ stick) 1 egg Milk to mix
PREPARING THE GIRDLE	Heat the girdle.
MIXING	Sift the flour. Put the syrup in a cup and stir in the melted butter, egg and a little milk. Stir into the flour and add enough milk to make a very soft dough. Put some flour into a small bowl. Drop tablespoonfuls of the mixture into the flour and toss to coat thoroughly.
COOKING AND SERVING	Sprinkle the girdle with flour and put on the scones. Press a little to flatten, and bake both sides till cooked. Cool on a wire rack wrapped in a towel. Serve warm (immediately if possible) with butter and preserves.

TREACLE SCONES

(MAKES 8 LARGE, 12 SMALL)

INGREDIENTS	8 oz (250 g) plain white flour (2 c) 1 level teaspoon bicarbonate of soda 1 level teaspoon freshly ground cinnamon 1 level teaspoon mixed spice 1 dessertspoon soft brown sugar Large pinch of salt 2 tablespoons black treacle 2 oz (50 g) butter (½ stick), melted 1 egg Milk to mix
PREPARING THE GIRDLE	Heat the girdle.

MIXING	Sift the flour and dry ingredients together. Put the treacle in a cup and stir in the melted butter, egg and a little milk. Stir into the dry ingredients and add enough milk to make a soft elastic dough. Fill a small bowl with flour, drop in tablespoonfuls of the mixture and toss to coat thoroughly.
COOKING AND SERVING	Sprinkle the girdle with flour and put on scones. Press down lightly, and bake on both sides till cooked. Cool on a wire rack wrapped in a towel. Serve warm (immediately if possible) with butter.

SCOTS PANCAKES (Dropped scones*)

(MAKES 12)

INGREDIENTS	8 oz (250 g) plain white flour (2 c) 1 teaspoon bicarbonate of soda 2 teaspoons cream of tartar Large pinch of salt 1 tablespoon golden syrup 2 oz (50 g) butter, melted (½ stick) or 2 tablespoons oil 1 large egg Milk to mix
PREPARING THE GIRDLE	Heat the girdle and grease.
MIXING	Sift all the dry ingredients into a bowl. Put the syrup in a cup and stir in the melted butter or oil, the egg and a little milk. Stir into the flour and add enough milk to make a thick creamy mixture, about the consistency of very thick double cream.
COOKING AND SERVING	Drop spoonfuls of the mixture onto the girdle and cook till they bubble on top. Turn and cook on the other side till golden brown. Cool on a wire rack wrapped in a towel. Serve warm (immediately if possible) with butter and preserves. Any leftover scones can be fried up with bacon for breakfast.

* The term dropped scone seems to have been adopted to distinguish between the thick Scots pancake and the thin French crêpe also known as a pancake. In England the term dropped scone seems to have been universally adopted, while in Scotland it is possible to come across both terms.

SCOTS CRUMPETS

INGREDIENTS AND PREPARING THE GIRDLE	As for Scots pancakes, p. 175
MIXING	As for Scots pancakes, except that the mixture should be thinned with more milk to make it runnier, about the consistency of single cream.
COOKING AND SERVING	Use a ladle to spoon some of the mixture onto the girdle – crumpets should spread to a thin large round about ¼ in (½ cm) thick and 6–8 in (15–20 cm) in diameter. Turn when the surface is covered with bubbles and cook for about a minute on the other side. Cool on a wire rack wrapped in a towel. Eat warm (immediately they are made), rolled up with butter and preserves.

GIRDLE SPONGES

(MAKES 4–6)

INGREDIENTS	1 tablespoon castor sugar 1 oz (25 g) butter (¼ stick) 2 eggs, separated 4 oz (125 g) self-raising flour (1 c) Pinch of salt Milk to mix
PREPARING THE GIRDLE	Heat the girdle and grease.
MIXING	Beat the sugar and butter till creamy, and beat in the egg yolks. Sift in the flour and salt and add enough milk (about 5 tablespoonfuls) to make a thick creamy mixture. Beat the whites to soft peak and fold in gently.
COOKING AND SERVING	Drop large ladlefuls of the mixture onto the girdle and turn when they start to bubble. Serve immediately with whipped cream and fresh raspberries or strawberries.

APPLE PANCAKES

(MAKES 6–8)

INGREDIENTS	4 fl oz (125 ml) *crème fraîche* or sour cream (¾ c) 2 eating apples, grated 4 oz (125 g) self-raising flour (1 c) 1 tablespoon honey 1 teaspoon cinnamon Half a nutmeg, grated, or ½ teaspoon ready grated nutmeg ½ teaspoon salt 4 eggs, separated
PREPARING THE GIRDLE	Heat the girdle and grease.
MIXING	Put all the ingredients (except the egg whites) into a bowl and mix to a soft dropping consistency. Beat the egg whites to soft peak stage and fold in carefully.
COOKING AND SERVING	Drop spoonfuls of the mixture onto the girdle and turn when they bubble. Cool on a wire rack wrapped in a towel. Serve warm with sour cream or *crème fraîche*, fresh fruits, honey and a dusting of cinnamon sugar.

III

The Meal in a Bowl

'. . . but it was my meat.'

*Old Aberdeenshire Ploughman's reply
when asked if he wasn't fed up with
eating brose three times a day.*

SCOTS BROSE

The 1970s saw the revival of a routine which had more or less sunk into oblivion with the demise of oatmeal as the core of the Scots peasant diet. A convenience food of the past, this simple brose-making by pouring water or milk onto oatmeal in a wooden bowl, now disguised in breakfast cereal packagery, and under a plethora of healthy-sounding names – as Muesli.

Why did Scotland fail to produce a campaigning Bircher-Benner with a clinic in the Highlands instead of Zurich? Why did Scots brose not take off as the panacea for urban health problems, returning to its position as a basic item of diet as it was in the healthier lifestyle of our rural ancestors? It's a classic convenience food: the answer to the haven't-got-time-to-cook problem.

MUESLI

In Switzerland, Birchermuesli was developed by Dr Max Bircher-Benner almost a hundred years ago, inspired by his visit to a mountain shepherd whose healthy way of life had greatly impressed him when he thought of the illnesses of his town patients. It was a mountain diet consisting of soaked oatmeal, dried fruit and nuts. Bircher-Benner, regarded as a complete crank by his contemporaries in the medical profession for suggesting that a simple change of diet could improve health, nevertheless continued feeding the mixture (muesli) to his clinic patients with such regularity that it became known as 'The Dish'.

He claimed that it was a 'perfect food'. Cereals containing vitamins A, E, B1, B2 and B12 and phosphorous, phospholipids, and protein. The milk providing vitamin B2, mineral salts, vitamins C and A and fats. The sugar or honey providing iron and carbohydrates. The apples containing potassium, vitamins C and B1, pectin and carbohydrates. The nuts containing protein, potassium, phosphorous, vitamins B1 and B2. Other fresh fruit may also be added and the lemon juice providing vitamin C and potassium.

'Muesli is a living food, and must therefore be eaten as soon as it has been prepared,' says Ruth Kunz-Bircher (Bircher-Benner's daughter) in *The Bircher-Benner Health Guide* (1977):

Any cereals may be used, though oatmeal is traditionally the favourite. For variety you can try mixing a teaspoon of oats with one of ground cereals (wheat, rice, barley, rye, millet, buckwheat, or soya), and mixing in some yeast flakes (vitamin B). The fruit should be entirely untreated, and only juicy and moderately sour apples chosen (do not use Golden

Delicious, the production of which is too industrialised, or excessively acid green apples.) Sweetened condensed milk, which keeps many of its biological qualities, is convenient, because you can use a little at a time and it keeps. Substitute raw milk, if you know a reliable supplier; or yoghourt. If sugar is used, it must be unrefined cane sugar; if honey, it must be pure, with no added sugar. Make sure the nuts added are fresh and in good condition.

It should be borne in mind that muesli is a light dish in which fruit predominates over whatever cereal is used.

BASIC MUESLI RECIPE

(FOR 1 SERVING)

8 g [1 level tablespoon] oats
3 tablespoons water
1 tablespoon lemon juice
1 tablespoon sweetened condensed milk
200 g (7 oz) apple
1 tablespoon grated hazelnuts or almonds
Soak the oats for 12 hours (If using flaked or rolled oats, do not soak, but add the same quantity of water.) Wash the apples and dry well with a clean towel. Remove the stalks, but leave the skins and cores. Grate directly into the mixture with a coarse grater (the apple must not be reduced to a mush). Stir continuously to prevent the apple going brown. Sprinkle the nuts on top just before serving.

As a healthy mix it is a great deal more attractive than some of the 'wholesome' and 'crunchy' jaw-exhausters which the £392 million breakfast cereal industry provides in the name of the original thing. Scots brose, to my mind, is also preferable, although not in the quantities consumed by the Scots peasantry in the eighteenth and nineteenth centuries when oatmeal became such a dominating feature of their diet.

BROSE

It is recorded in 1794 that single men, working on farms in the Carse of Gowrie and living in primitive bothies where they had to prepare and cook their own food, were given by the farmer, as part of their wages, a daily supply of food per person consisting of 2 lb 4 oz (1 kg, 9 c) oatmeal, 1 pt (600 ml, 2½ c) fresh milk, 2 pt (1 l, 5 c) buttermilk, and a little salt. It is just possible that they could have consumed a 12 oz (350 g, 3 c) bowlful of oats for each of their three meals! Given that the average cattlemen worked a ten and a half hour day, spread over the time from 5.30 a.m. to 8 p.m., it is not surprising that the meal mostly ended up in a bowl with water, sometimes heated, but often enough cold. Brose, three times a day, and in such quantities! No wonder they tired of it, no wonder the habit declined. For some, even today the idea of eating brose conjures up poverty and deprivation.

Of course, the attractions of processed food must also have had some bearing on its decline. It would have taken an extremely bold nutritionist to stick out for a return to eating humble brose as a solution to diet problems. But there is no doubt that it produced a hardy race of Scots who endured extremely long hours of physical labour. Also fuelled from the brose bowl were the academic labours of the legendary scholar-Scot. University students, with meagre resources, who survived principally on the sack of oatmeal they brought with them each term. (No evidence has been found that students made the trip home mid-term for more supplies, though the mid-term holiday is still termed Meal Monday at the University of St Andrews.)

Like Bircher-Benner, the brose-making Scots improvised on the theme; it was not all just water and oatmeal. Meals such as barley and pease were mixed together, and the meal was sometimes mixed with hot milk instead of water. Butter, cream, dried fruit, soft fruits when they were ripe on the bushes – they all found their way into the large wooden bowls. Good meaty ladlefuls of hot stock pot broth were poured over the meal too, and greens and chopped herbs added for flavour. No problem if you are catering just for one. No end to the variations. No difficulty in finding a mix which pleases, in this do-it-yourself meal in a bowl.

The texture and thickness is also entirely a matter of taste. Boiling water onto cold oatmeal, stirred with the shank end of a wooden spoon or spurtle (porridge stick) will produce the characteristic knotty tams ('knots' of oatmeal), small lumps which have a little raw oatmeal in the centre. They are not unpleasant, and not cumbersome to chew either – a simple variation in texture to add contrast.

OATMEAL

Thick or thin, knotty or smooth, the critical factor in brose is the quality of the oatmeal. A slow-ripening grain, peculiarly suitable to cool Scottish summers, good oatmeal has an attractive sweetish nuttiness. To the connoisseur there is a vast difference between slow-ripened Scottish oatmeal, kiln dried and ground in the traditional way between millstones, and fast-ripened, mechanically dried, roller-milled meal.

Much of the flavour of the oatmeal depends on the slow gentle warmth of the kiln drying, the nature of the fire – as with whisky – giving character to the grain. There are a number of revived and original mills in Scotland today producing kiln-dried and stoneground oatmeal (see Traditional Scottish Food Suppliers, p. 254). Though turning the grain involves more physical effort and skill, there is no doubt that good kiln-dried meal is far superior to meal dried by any other method. These traditional millers, though a minority, keep alive the taste and flavour of oatmeal as it used to be. My own choice for a year's supply of oatmeal would be from Montgarrie Mills in Alford, where the miller, Donald MacDonald, carries on the milling tradition which has been in his family for four generations.

Oatmeal, like coffee once it has been ground, should not be exposed to air. Pack the meal down tightly to exclude as much air as possible and keep it in airtight containers. In the past it was the children (feet cleaned first) who were put into the meal kist to tramp the air out of the meal which would be kept through till the following harvest. Before use it may be toasted in a warm oven to drive off excess moisture and increase the nuttiness of the flavour.

The grade of oatmeal used for brose – fine, medium or pinhead – is entirely a matter of preference. Rolled oats make a soft textured, more sloppy brose. Because of their heat-treatment some vitamins are lost and the flavour is less distinctive than that of nutty stoneground oatmeal.

FLAVOURINGS

When making brose, the flavours combined are purely a matter of taste: balancing sweetness and sourness, whilst taking care that the flavour of good oatmeal is not entirely overshadowed. Two particularly Scottish flavours – heather honey and whisky – are said to have a special effect when added to oatmeal, as the Eigth Duke of Atholl is reputed to have discovered during a contretemps when a rival clan was defeated because its men had become intoxicated with the Atholl mix. But there is yet plenty of scope for variations on such ambrosial themes.

Quantities

It is difficult to be accurate with these recipes since so much is a matter of personal taste and they will not fail if the exact quantity is not used. Tasting and trying is the best system.

Mixing and steeping (soaking)

When the meal is mixed with hot water or hot milk the brose is usually eaten immediately. If cold liquid is added to the meal, the meal is best left to swell before other flavours are mixed in.

Two handfuls (approximately 2 rounded tablespoons) of medium oatmeal mixed with ¼ pt (150 ml) of liquid should thicken up to a stiff consistency if left for a couple of hours, preferably longer, even overnight if possible, though it appears a very runny mixture when you first mix it.

The bowl

Original brose bowls were very large and deep, with a capacity of about 2 pt (1 l, 5 c). It is no use trying to make brose in a small bowl; you must have room for mixing. Making it in a large baking bowl means it has then to be transferred to individual serving bowls. A deep bowl (with a capacity of about 1 pt (600 ml, 2½ c) is the simplest method. Mix up the oatmeal and liquid in each bowl, leave to thicken and then place on the table with the selection of flavourings and additions. That way the cook is relieved of some effort and the eaters can adjust flavours to suit their personal tastes.

OATMEAL BROSE*

(1 SERVING)

INGREDIENTS	2–4 rounded tablespoons oatmeal, grade according to taste – fine, medium or pinhead Pinch of salt Piece of butter the size of a brazil nut (only if using boiling water or hot milk) Approx. ¼ pt (150 ml) boiling or cold water, or hot or cold milk (¾ c)
METHOD	Put the meal into a deep bowl, preferably a wooden one. Add the salt and butter (if using). Pour over enough liquid to cover the meal and make a thickish mixture. Stir with a spurtle (porridge stick) or the shank end of a wooden spoon if you like knots, but use the bowl end if you like it smooth. Sup the brose

183

with, for preference, a horn spoon, dipping each spoonful into a bowl of milk, cream or buttermilk.

* There is only the short step of putting the brose mix into a pot and cooking it to make porridge. The meal is best steeped (soaked) overnight and since it is cooked and thickens more, the proportion of liquid to meal is different: 2 oz (50 g, ½ c) medium oatmeal to a scant ½ pt (300 ml, 1¼ c) water. Put into a pan and cook gently, stirring with a spurtle or the shank end of a wooden spoon. 'Knots' are not attractive in cooked porridge so keep stirring to prevent lumps. I am not a great fan of the long, slow-cooked porridge: too glutinous, too gummy, too unpalatable a grey sticky pap. Shorter cooking, using medium oatmeal, perhaps with some coarse pinhead oatmeal or even some raw oatmeal thrown in just before serving, seems to me a more interesting texture. But it is a hotly disputed subject with contenders for and against rough or smooth, dry or sticky.

For a rough porridge with a pleasant chew, use about two-thirds pinhead oatmeal and one third whole wheat grains, steeped together overnight. Use medium oatmeal for a less coarse texture, fine oatmeal for (English) custard-like porridge.

PEASE BROSE

(1 SERVING)

INGREDIENTS
2–4 rounded tablespoons peasemeal
Pinch of salt
Piece of butter the size of a brazil nut
1 tablespoon sultanas or raisins
1 tablespoon honey
Approx. ¼ pt (150 ml) boiling water (¾ c)

METHOD
As for Oatmeal brose.

AIGAR* BROSE

(1 SERVING)

INGREDIENTS 1 rounded tablespoon oatmeal
1 rounded tablespoon peasemeal
1 rounded tablespoon beremeal
Pinch of salt
Piece of butter the size of a brazil nut
Approx. ¼ pt (150 ml) boiling water or hot milk (¾ c)

METHOD As for Oatmeal brose.

* This was the name of the brose mixed by beggars, aigar meaning a mixture of meals, which is what beggars collected in their bag (cf. mashlam, p. 172).

CRANACHAN* (Soft fruit brose)

(1 SERVING)

INGREDIENTS 2–4 rounded tablespoons medium oatmeal, toasted
5–8 tablespoon double cream (sour cream, *crème fraîche*, yogurt, or crowdie may be used with the cream according to taste)
Whisky to taste
Honey to taste
Soft fruit in season

METHOD Put the meal into the bowl, add the cream and leave to thicken for about 2 hours. (Alternatively, it can be mixed and eaten at once.) Flavour with whisky and honey, and sprinkle soft fruit on top or mix through.

* Cranachan was the traditional celebration, harvest-home dish. For a communal celebration round the table, the meal, fruit and cream were put onto the table and everyone made his own mix, lubricating it with whisky and honey. It was also eaten on other special occasions such as weddings, etc. In some parts of the country it was eaten in a slightly different form as a Hallowe'en dish, made up in a big pot without the fruit and whisky but with charms instead, the children dipping in with their spoons till they got a charm (not suitable for under-fives who may swallow charms in their enthusiasm). The button: batchelordom; the thimble: spinsterhood; the wishbone: the heart's desire; the horseshoe: good luck; the silver coin: riches.

ATHOLL BROSE*

(1 SERVING)

INGREDIENTS   2–4 rounded tablespoons medium oatmeal, toasted
2–4 fl oz (50–100 ml) double cream, stiffly beaten
1 glass malt whisky
1–2 tablespoons heather honey

METHOD   Put the oatmeal into the bowl, mix in the cream and leave to thicken. Pour in the whisky and add honey to taste. Serve.

* The Duke of Atholl's recipe involves steeping the oatmeal (6 oz (175 g, 1½ c) in (¾ pt (450 ml, 2 c) water first, and then pressing out the mealy liquid through a fine sieve. This liquid is then mixed with 4 tablespoons heather honey. The mixture is poured into a whisky bottle and filled up with malt whisky. It should be given a good shake before use.

CITRUS FRUIT BROSE

(2 SERVINGS)

INGREDIENTS   4 rounded tablespoons oatmeal
Approx. ¼ pt (150 ml) milk (¾ c)
Juice of 1 lemon
Juice of 1 orange
1 orange segmented
1 banana, sliced
1 apple, grated
A few blanched and roasted almonds

METHOD   Put the oatmeal into the bowl, add the milk and leave to thicken. Mix in the lemon and orange juice and the fruit, and sprinkle with almonds.

APPLE AND PRUNE BROSE

(1 SERVING)

INGREDIENTS
2–4 rounded tablespoons medium oatmeal, toasted
Approx. ¼ pt (150 ml) single cream or milk (¾ c)
1 large eating apple, grated
1 heaped tablespoon ground hazelnuts
2 tablespoons juice from preserved prunes*
3 preserved prunes, stoned and halved

METHOD
Put the oatmeal into the bowl, add the cream or milk and leave to thicken. Grate the apple on top of the meal, add the hazelnuts and prune juice. Mix through and put a few prunes on top.

* **Preserved prunes**: Cover 1 lb (500 g) large prunes with boiling water, leave for 5 minutes and drain. Put into a large jar to come about half-way up, and fill up with port. Cover tightly. The prunes will swell so leave room in the jar. Leave for at least three weeks, shaking the jar occasionally. The prunes will keep longer, at least a year. Alternatively use a mixture of port and claret, or brandy, rum or sweet sherry.

BLACKCURRANT AND REDCURRANT BROSE

(1 SERVING)

INGREDIENTS
2–4 rounded tablespoons medium oatmeal, toasted
Approx. ¼ pt (150 ml) single cream or milk (¾ c)
1 tablespoon rose flower water
1 tablespoon castor sugar
2 tablespoons ripe blackcurrants
2 tablespoons ripe redcurrants
Apple mint leaves

METHOD
Put the oatmeal into the bowl, add the cream or milk and leave to thicken. Mix in the rose flower water and sugar. Mix some of the berries through the brose and scatter the rest on top. Decorate with mint leaves.

GOOSEBERRY AND ELDERFLOWER BROSE

(2 SERVINGS)

INGREDIENTS
4 rounded tablespoons medium oatmeal, toasted
Approx. ¼ pt (150 ml) single cream or milk (¾ c)
8 oz (250 g) gooseberries, topped and tailed
1 tablespoon sugar
2–3 large elderflower heads in full bloom
4 tablespoons water
Garnish: 2 tablespoons thick Greek yogurt, *crème fraîche*, sour cream or whipped double cream
2 teaspoons heather honey
Some elderflower sprigs

METHOD
Put the oatmeal into the bowl, add the cream or milk and leave to thicken. Put the gooseberries into a pan with the sugar, elderflowers and water, and bring to a simmer. Cover and cook till the gooseberries are just soft. Remove the elderflower heads and beat the gooseberries to a rough pulp – there is no need to have them perfectly smooth; a slight roughness is better with the oatmeal. Leave to cool. Stir the cooled gooseberries into the meal. Add more sugar and adjust the consistency if neccesary. Serve topped with the yogurt or cream, a thin trail of runny heather honey (heat if necessary) and a sprig of elderflowers.

RHUBARB AND ORANGE BROSE

(2 SERVINGS)

INGREDIENTS
8 oz (250 g) rhubarb, sliced
2–3 tablespoons brown sugar
Juice and zest of 1 orange
1 teaspoon vanilla essence
4 rounded tablespoons medium oatmeal, toasted
¼ pt (150 ml) double cream (¾ c)
Orange flower water to taste
Garnish: 2 tablespoons thick Greek yogurt, *crème fraîche*, sour cream or whipped double cream
2 teaspoons heather honey

METHOD Put the rhubarb into the pan with the brown sugar, orange juice and zest. Cover and cook till the rhubarb is quite soft. Remove from the heat and beat to a rough pulp. Pour into a bowl, add the vanilla essence and leave to cool. When the rhubarb is cool, stir in the oatmeal and cream and leave to thicken. Stir in some orange flower water to taste. Serve topped with the yogurt or cream and a thin trail of runny heather honey (heat if necessary).

GINGER AND ATHOLL BROSE

(1 SERVING)

INGREDIENTS 2–4 rounded tablespoons medium oatmeal, toasted
Approx. ¼ pt (150 ml) Duke of Atholl's brose (see p. 186) (¾ c)
1 tablespoon ginger syrup
1–2 tablespoons crystallized ginger, roughly chopped
1 tablespoon Californian raisins, cooked prunes, or preserved prunes (see p. 187)
1 apple, grated
Garnish: a few slices crystallized ginger
1 tablespoon sour cream

METHOD Put the oatmeal into the bowl, add the Duke of Atholl's brose and leave to thicken. Add the ginger syrup and the ginger, raisins or prunes and apple. Top with the sour cream and a few slices of crystallized ginger and serve.

STRAWBERRY AND NECTARINE BROSE

(1 SERVING)

INGREDIENTS
2–4 rounded tablespoons medium oatmeal, toasted
Approx. ¼ pt (150 ml) single cream or milk (¾ c)
1 banana, mashed
Juice of half a lemon
1 tablespoon heather honey
1 nectarine, stoned and sliced
3–4 medium strawberries, sliced
Apple mint leaves

METHOD
Put the oatmeal into the bowl, add the cream or milk and leave to thicken. Mix in the banana, lemon juice, honey and nectarine. Pile the strawberries and mint leaves on top.

IV

National and Historical Dishes

'Mrs Dods has preserved the recipes of certain old dishes, which we should be loath should fall into oblivion in our day.'

Sir Walter Scott

THE RECIPES

The following recipes are a purely personal selection which I have used as the starting point or inspiration to experiment within the Scottish idiom.

Most of them are old dishes which have something worthwhile to say to modern cooks. They are sensible, practical ideas: some still firmly held to, some less so. Some are particular dishes belonging to a region of Scotland which may have no appeal to others in a different environment. But they are, nevertheless, the people's food, and for that reason alone are an important part of the Scottish food tapestry. In these circumstances, culinary excellence is relevant to the experience and the food expectations of the eaters. We may not all appreciate the attractions of Willie Fulton's cooked cormorant but he clearly enjoys both the ploy of catching and eating his fishy meal.

Just as there are local idiosyncrasies there are also bad habits. Overlong cooking times of certain foods, notably vegetables, is one black spot.

For the life of me I cannot see the virtue of cooking a lettuce in a pot of broth for three hours only to remove it at the end and throw it away – but they did. One of the problems with cooking times, at least with the Scottish peasant, was the system of putting the broth pot on in the early morning and leaving it for best part of the day while outside work was done. Food inevitably was cooked for longer than it ought.

Another factor which influenced vegetables in particular was the fashionable nineteenth-century fear of contamination from members of the onion family, which they considered 'tainted their breath'. The only way to prevent this was to cook all oniony dishes to death in order to kill off the smell and save the embarrassment. It was a whim which led to a bad cooking habit that has taken some time to eradicate. Even yet, the water-logged vegetable and over-cooked food makes for unpleasant eating.

Enlightened modern cooks must ignore such old ways. On the more positive side there is a knowledge in past generations of herbs and spices which is worth studying. Quantities are difficult to follow in some recipes, either because there is a lack of them or because different and confusing Scottish measures are used. Sometimes it is necessary to make an inspired guess. But what is important is their sensitive combining of flavours, colours and textures, some classic, others more novel: crusty bread, spread with a mint butter, floats in a pea soup; gingerbread is flavoured with caraway, coriander and oranges; oatmeal dishes are seasoned with wild garlic and mint; carrots and oranges flavour a pudding; mackerel is cooked with fennel; potted herring with sherry and lemon juice; apple pies are delicately spiced and garnished with crystallized orange and lemon . . .

What I particularly like about some of the eighteenth-century made-to-order dishes is the way cooks use the best cuts, but take the trimmings, whether they are gristle, sinew, bone or skin, and cook them up into a stock or gravy which is then incorporated into a sort of natural gravy sauce. This is how they make minced collops, the best steak thoroughly browned with some onion, then the gravy from the flavourful leftovers added. It is a concept developed more fully in recipes such as Fillet of hare with port (p. 140).

There is also the sensible idea of wrapping a rich fruit cake in a layer of plain bread dough (1736), now developed into a pastry crust and known as the Scotch Black Bun. Last summer I came across a yeasted fruit loaf wrapped in a puff pastry crust in a bakers in Thurso.

And, of course, there is the development of the Scots broth concept from an early sophistication in Scottish cooking whereby the first cooking of meat and vegetables was seen as the initial preparation of a good flavoured cooking liquor to be used for its intrinisic worth and its ability to poach large pieces of food, but also as the foundation for other dishes.

SOURCES

All the early Scottish cookery books are available in the National Library of Scotland in Edinburgh except for Mrs McLintock (the first published Scottish cookery book, 1736). There are only two copies of the original, both in Glasgow University Library, one in the John Ferguson Collection (which is bound separately), and one in the William Ewing Collection (which is bound with other works under the title *History of Adolphus*). The University of Strathclyde's Rare Books Department has a particularly fine collection of antiquarian cookery books, many collected by Professor John Fuller while he was Director of the University's Scottish Hotel School in the 1960s. It has two copies of Mrs Suzanna MacIver's *Cookery and Pastry*. The Rare Books Department of the Mitchell Library, Glasgow, has the original manuscript of Lady Castlehill's Recipes (a collection of about 400 dishes, 1712) in the Bogles of Daldowie Family Papers (possibly given to her daughter Anne who married George Bogle, a Glasgow tobacco merchant, in 1731). The manuscript recipes of Martha Brown were lent to me by Charles McGurk, librarian at Ayr and Cunningham District Library. Other books and manuscript recipes are from my own collection.

OLD SCOTTISH MEASURES

The first attempt to standardize measures in Scotland was when a commission in 1661 recommended that exemplars for national standards should to be kept in certain burghs: the ell for lineal measure in Edinburgh, the troy stone for weight in Lanark, the *jug* for liquid capacity in Stirling, the firlot for dry measure in Linlithgow. These recommendations were more or less kept to till the Act of 1824 when Imperial measures were statutorily established. Gradually they were conformed to, but it is not certain that recipes after 1824 necessarily kept to the new measures: just as metric and Imperial go hand in hand today and many continue with established systems. To confuse even further, they continued to use the old names such as firlot, forpet and lippie (still sometimes heard today in some rural areas) for fractions of the Imperial hundredweight.

Scottish liquid measures		Imperial
According to the standard of Stirling for JUG measure		
1 gill		.749 gill
4 gills	= 1 mutchkin	2.996 gills
2 mutchkins	= 1 chopin	1 pt 1.992 gills
2 chopins	= 1 pint	2 pts 3.984 gills
8 pints	= 1 gallon	3 gallons .25 gills

Scottish weights		Avoirdupois
1. According to the standard of Lanark for TROY weight		
1 drop		1.093 drams
16 drops	= 1 ounce	1 oz 1.5 drams
16 ounces	= 1 pound	1 lb 1 oz 8 drams
16 pounds	= 1 stone	17 lbs 8 oz

2. According to the standard of Edinburgh for TRON weight		
1 drop		1.378 drams
16 drops	= 1 ounce	1 oz 6 drams
16 ounces	= 1 pound	1 lb 6 oz 1 dram
16 pounds	= 1 stone	1 stone 8 lb 1 oz

Scottish dry measures		Imperial
According to the standard of Linlithgow for FIRLOT measure		
1. For wheat, peas, beans, meal, etc.		
1 lippie or forpet		.499 gallons
4 lippies	= 1 peck	1.996 gallons

4 pecks	= 1 firlot	3 pecks 1.986 gallons
4 firlots	= 1 boll	3 bushels 3 pecks 1.994 gallons
16 bolls	= 1 chalder	7 quarters 7 bushels 3 pecks 1.07 gallons

2. For barley, oats, malt

1 lippie or forpet		.728 gallons
4 lippies	= 1 peck	1 peck .912 gallons
4 pecks	= 1 firlot	1 bushel 1 peck 1.650 gallons
4 firlots	= 1 boll	5 bushels 3 pecks. 600 gallons
16 bolls	= 1 chalder	11 quarters 5 bushels 1.615 gallons.

THE EIGHTEENTH CENTURY

1710

Manuscript recipes by Martha Brown of Ayrshire.
A private collection held in Ayr and Cunningham Public Library.

To make Strong Broath
Take 12 quarts of water and 3 knuckles of veal and an hough of beef and two pair of calves feet and chickens and rabbits and a faggot of sweet herbs and 2 onions and some leimond peil and boile these together until it comes to 6 quarts and when this is strained it is fit for all Sauces and pottages.

To make a pottage
Take a leg of beef and boil it to a gillie and put to it a litle of baccon and 2 or 3 clives and 2 or 3 onions and a bunch of sweet herbs and stew these together and strain it through a cloathe and when it is cold take of the fatt then take 2 beef pallats [tongues] and boile them till that their skin cometh of then cut them very small. You take a buttock of beef and cut it in selyces and put it on a speet and half roast it and when this is done put it into a dish with some strong broath and an onion and a faggat of thime.

Rizzer [red currant] or Strawberrie Cream
Take your rizzers white or red or your strawberries and pick clean the[n] bruise them with a spoon and when they are bruised mix them with your boiling cream and sweeten with sugar.

A Churned Syllabub
Take a quart of cream and a pint of Spanish wine and sweeten it to your taste and shake it into a glass and churn it till it be very thick then put it into the

syllabub pott and let it stand a day before that you eat it and it will be the better.

Gingerbread
Take 4 quarts of fine flouer and a pound of sweet butter and half an ounce of ginger and as much pepper beaten and half a quarter a pint of rose water and as much seck [sherry] and 4 spoonfuls of Tryacle rub your butter into your flouer mix the rest and make it into a stiff paist when the Cakes are upon the mould prick them very thick Sweep the oven very clear Then cool the oven before you put them in and bake them drie you may mix your flouer at the first with carvie [caraway] and corriander seeds or oranges mix your flouer at the first.

Shortbread
Take 2 pound of butter and put it in a pan with water and let it be at the boiling then take a peck of flower and knead it up and roll your cake and see that you give it a soft oven and let them not stay in the oven till they be burnt.

1712

Manuscript recipes by Martha Lockhart, The Lady Castlehill
She lived at Cambusnethan House on the north bank of the Clyde near Wishaw. A quarter of the manuscript was published by Molindinar (1976) as *Lady Castlehill's Receipt Book*, edited by Hamish Whyte.

To make French Pottage of Pease
Take 2 legs of beef and boil them to a jelly. Put in one handful of thyme and marjoram and 2 whole onions and some whole onions some whole peppers cloves and mace and a race of ginger and when they are all boiled, strain the broth and some of the fat, then take a half a peck of pease and boil them very well, and strain them, then take the thickest of the peas broth and put it into the broth as it is boiling. Then put into it a quart of new milk and a pound and one half of bacon and in thin slices, and 2 lemons cut in halves and let them boil a quarter of one hour. Then squeeze out the lemons and take one handful of spinace one handfull of sorrel and boil in it. Put in half a pound of fresh butter a little before you dish it up. Toast some whole bread and lay it in the dish. Put half pint of gravy in it and so dish it up, you may have balls in it if you please.

To make Pease Pottage
Take a Legg of Veall, and a Pice of bacon, put them into cold water with your Pease, and boile your Veal to pices then straine your Broth: take a French Roll and sclice it, and put a good pice of Butter to it, and rub some dryed Mint into it, make some Balls of Veal and Suet and some Sweet Herbs, boile them in a little of the Broth and put them into the Dish.

For a Sallet
Take the top of sweet marjoram pick them leaf by leaf, being gathered in the heat of the day then dry them over the fire. Take some sugar and drye it, so put them into the Gally Glass or Pot, and put white wine vinegar to it when you use. This you may do with any herb or flower.

1730

Charles Carter, *The Complete Practical Cook*
Lately Cook to his Grace the Duke of Argyll, the Earl of Pontefract and the Lord Cornwallis. Facsimile published by Prospect Books (1984).

To make a STOCK of STRONG BROTH of FLESH
Take a Leg of Beef, a Knuckle of Veal, and a Neck of Mutton; wash all well: Put a large Pot on the Fire with fair Water, and then charge the Pot with your Meat: When it boils take care to scum it well; put in a Carrot or two and a Turnip, and a good Faggot of Sweet-Herbs, some whole Onions peeled, and season it with whole Pepper, Salt, some Blades of Mace, and some Cloves stuck in a Piece of Bacon; boil in it the Crust of a *French* Manchet, and when it is well boil'd, strain it out for Use.

Pottage of Venison
Take the Knuckles of your Haunches and Shoulders, and the Craig End [neck] of your Chine, and boil them for Broth; put in a French Manchet or two slic'd to help thicken your broth, or a little Oatmeal, for Venison makes but a very thin Broth of itself; season it as strong Broth of other Flesh, boil it out well, and strain it out for your Use; then take some of the Venison and cut it in Slices, and make good Gravy, season it well, and make it pretty thick; take some spinace and Sorrel, and Purslane and green Onions; pass them in a Pan, when cut a little, with brown Butter thicken'd; put in half Gravy half Broth, and then have in Readiness either the Head, that is the Cheeks of the Venison, or the thin Part of the Chine, ragou'd down very tender, and high seasoned, and then stove French Manchet in Gravy, and fill up the Dish with your Soup well stoved; lay over your Cheeks or Chine; garnish with some scalded Spinach and sliced Lemon, and serve it away hot.

1736

Mrs McLintock, *Receipts for Cookery and Pastry-Work*
The first published cookery book in Scotland; nothing is known of either the Glasgow publisher or the author. Facsimile published by Aberdeen University Press, Introduction by Iseabail Macleod (1986).

To make a Plumb Cake

Take a Peck of Flour, two Pound of Butter; rub the Butter among the Flour, till it be like flour again; take 12 Eggs, a lib. of Sugar, beat them well together; then take a Mutchkin of sweet Barm [brewer's yeast], half a Mutchkin of Brandy, then your Flour with the beaten Eggs and Sugar, and put in the Barm and Brandy, and work all well together; then take ten lib. of Currants, 2 lib. Cordecidron [lemon peel], 2 lib. of Orange-peil, 2 lib. of blanched Almonds cut, half an Ounce of Cinnamon, half an Ounce of Nutmeg and Cloves, half an Ounce of Carvey-seed [caraway]; take off the fourth Part of the Leaven for a Cover, and work the Fruits and Spices among the rest, then put on the cover, and send it to the Oven.

To make common Bisket

Take a lib. of Sugar, 8 Eggs, keep out two Whites, take a lib. of Flour, beat the Eggs and Sugar well together, till they be thick and white, mix in the Flour with a little Carvey-seed [caraway], and then mix them altogether, and drop them on a gray Paper, and glaze them with Sugar and a little Flour, and send them to the Oven.

To make a Soup

Make strong Broth of a Thigh of Beef, and a Nuckle of Veal cut in Pieces, put it in the Pot full of Water, and some hail Spice with a Blade of Mace, three great whole Onions, stuck with cloves, and a Bunch of Sweet Herbs, boil all together on a slow fire, till the Meat be all in Pieces, then strain the Broth thro' a callendar, and take some collops of Beef, dust them with flower, and fry them very brown, take the Fat off the strong Broth, then put in the collops among the Broth, and let them soke over a slow fire; and have ready some Pieces of tosted Bread for your Soup Dish, put in a Marrow Bone in the Middle, and pour in the Broth on the Bread, but keep out the collops, and serve it up.

1738

Hannah Glasse, *The Art of Cookery Made Plain and Easy* to which are added one hundred and fifty new recipes
Though Mrs Glasse was an English cookery writer she had this edition, the seventeenth, of her book published in Edinburgh and included a number of Scottish dishes. (17th edition)

To make Scots barley broth

Take a leg of beef, chop it all to pieces, boil it in three gallons of water with a piece of carrot and a crust of bread, till it is half boiled away; then strain it off, and put it into the pot again with half a pound of barley, four or five heads of celery washed clean and cut small, a large onion, a bundle of sweet herbs, a little parsley chopped small, and a few marigolds. Let this boil an hour. Take a cock or large fowl, clean picked and washed, and put into the pot; boil it till the broth be quite good, then season with salt, and send it to table with the fowl in the middle this broth is very good without the fowl. Take out the onion and sweet herbs, before you send it to table.

Some make this broth with a sheep's head instead of a leg of beef, and it is very good; but you must chop the head all to pieces. The thick flank (about six pounds to six quarts of water) makes good broth; then put the barley in with the meat, first skim it well, boil it an hour very softly, then put in the above ingredients, with turnips and carrots clean and scrape and pared, and cut in little pieces. Boil all together softly, till the broth is very good; then season it with salt, and send it to table, with the beef in the middle, turnips and carrots round, and pour the broth over all.

Beef Broth

Take a leg of beef, crack the bone in two or three parts, wash it clean, put it into a pot with a gallon of water, skim it well, then put in two or three blades of mace, a little bundle of parsley, and a good crust of bread. Let it boil till the beef is quite tender, and the sinews. Toast some bread and cut it in dice, and lay it in your dish; lay in the meat, and pour the soup in.

To dress Scots collops

Take veal, cut it thin, beat it well with the back of a knife or rolling-pin, and grate some nutmeg over them; dip them in the yolk of an egg, and fry them in a little butter till they are of a fine brown; then pour the butter from them, and have ready half a pint of gravy, a little piece of butter rolled in flour, a few mushrooms, a glass of white wine, the yolk of an egg, and a little cream mixed together. If it wants a little salt, put it in. Stir it all together, and, when it is of a fine thickness, dish it up. It does very well without the cream, if you have none, and very well without the gravy; brown; then pour the soup; then take a lib. and a half of White Pease, boil them in water till the skins come off then bruise them with a spoon, strain them thrugh a Callandar, put them into the soup, let them all soak together, put in a little spearmint and Marigold, and serve them up.

To make an eating Syllabub

Take a pint of White or Claret Wine, and as much sweet Cream, and sink it in the wine, put sugar and cinnamon on top of it and so eat it.

1755

Elizabeth Cleland, *A new and easy method of cookery* . . .
Chiefly intended for the benefit of the young ladies who attend her school, etc. Printed in Edinburgh. It was written as a manual of instruction for the cookery school which she ran in the city. Sir Walter Scott had a copy in his library at Abbotsford. (2nd edition, 1759)

Scots Barley Broth

Boil a Hough of Beef in 8 pts of water, and a pound of barley on a slow fire, let it boil to 4 pts then put in onions, pepper, salt and raisins if you like them, or you may put in greens and leeks. Neck and Breast of Mutton, cut it into pieces, put as much water as will cover it; when it boils skim it, put in barley, diced carrots, turnips, onions, a faggot of Thyme and parsley, pepper and salt, stove it all well together, you may put in a sheep's head, but first singe and scrape it, and soak it well in water, to make this green put beet leaves, broccoli and green onions all shred small.

1773

Suzanna MacIver, *Cookery and pastry. As taught and practised by Mrs MacIver, teacher of those arts in Edinburgh*
Printed in Edinburgh, it was written at her pupil's request. Though she began by selling jams, chutneys, pickles and cakes, she later ran a cookery school for the well-to-do. She sold the cookery book, costing 2s 6d (12p), privately to begin with from her house in Stephen Law's Close. (3rd edition, 1782)

A Good Scotch Haggies

Make the haggies-bag perfectly clean; parboil the draught; boil the liver very well, so as it will grate; dry the meal before the fire; mince the draught and a pretty large piece of beef very small; grate about half of the liver; mince plenty of suet, and some onions small; mix all these materials very well together, with a handful or two of the dried meal; spread them on the table, and season them properly with salt and mixed spices; take any of the scraps of beef that is left from mincing, and some of the water that boiled the draught, and make about a choppin of good stock of it: then put all the haggies-meat into the bag, and that broth in it: then sew up the bag; but be sure to put out all the wind before you sew it quite close. If you think the bag is thin, you may put it in a cloth. If it is large haggies, it will take at least two hours boiling.

To make minced Collops

Take a tender piece of beef, keep out all the skin and fat, mince it small, season it with salt and mixed spices; you may shread an onion small; and put in with it; spread the collops; and drudge flour on them; brown some butter in a frying-pan; put the collops in the pan, and continue beating with the beater till they suck up all the butter, and be a little brown. You may draw as much stock from the skins and tough pieces as will serve for the sauce; strain off the stock; set it on to boil, and put the collops in, and let them stew until they are enough. You may put in some pickles if you choose them. If you see any of the butter on the top, scum it.

To broil Beef-Steaks
Take the best bit of the beef for steaks off the rib-end of a sparerib; cut the steaks pretty thick; brade them with the flat side of the chopen knife; the gridiron must be very clean, the fire very clear, before you lay them on; keep turning them often. When enough salt them in the dish; strow pickles over them. Send them hot with a cover over them.

A Jugged Hare
Cut the hare in pieces; put a pretty large piece of butter in the bottom of a long jug; season it with salt and mixed spices; then pack in as many of the best pieces of the hare as the jug will hold; put in a faggot of sweet herbs, and two or three onions amongst them; take some of the water you washed the hare in and strain it through a searce; fill up the jug with it, and tie the mouth of it very close with several folds of paper; put it into a pot of cold water; the water must not come farther up than the neck of the jug, else it will boil into it; as the water boils in, you must put in more to keep it of an equal quantity. If it is an old hare, it will take three hours of doing; the butter will rise to the top; pour it clean off; take out the herbs and onions when you dish it, and pour the sauce over it; be sure to tie the jug to the handles of the pot.

An Apple Pie
Pair and quarter the apples, and core them; season them with sugar, beat cinnamon, and the grate of a lemon. If you would have a very rich apple pie, put in some ston'd raisins, blanch'd almonds, citron, and orange-peel cut down; cover them with puff'd paste. Don't be sparing of sugar to any fruit pie.

1791

Mrs Fraser, *The practice of cookery and pastry, pickling, preserving, containing . . . a full list of supper dishes . . . directions for choosing provisions: with two plates, showing the method of placing dishes upon a table. etc.*
Printed in Edinburgh, costing 3s (15 p). She was one of Mrs MacIver's assistants and took over after her death. (2nd edition, 1795)

Scotch Soup or Hotch Potch
Boil 4 lb of beef in 2 pts 1 gall water till the substance is out if it. Then take out the beef, and put in about 2 dozen turnips, neatly cut out with a nip turner, three carrots well cleaned and split into quarters, a stock of ice lettuce, the top crust of a penny loaf, a little pepper and salt, half a peck of green peas, two to three large onions. When it comes to the boil scum well. Then put in three pound of the back ribs of mutton, cut into handsom stakes, and let it boil an hour on a moderate fire. Then take out the lettuce and bread, and serve up the soup in a tureen.

To make pottage of chopped herbs
Mince, very fine, spinage, chives, Parsley, Marigold flowers, succory, Strawberry and Violet leaves, stamp them with oatmeal in a bowl, put chopped greens in with it: you may either put Broth or Water to them: if Water, boil a good piece of butter in it; put Sippets in the Dish, and pour it over them.

A Mussel Soup
Get a pint of mussels, scald them and wash them clean, put them in a pan with three mutchkins of strong broth and a Mutchkin of their own liquor, a Bunch of Sweet herbs, an onion stuffed with cloves, Pepper, mace, and salt; put on the Crumbs of Bread to thicken it; you may put a Gill of White Wine in it; boil till it is smooth; you may squeeze in it a little lemon juice, so serve it up hot.

A Turnip Soup
Pare and cut in Dice Twelve Turnips which will make a dish full, fry them in clarified Butter a light brown, put them in two chopins of good Gravy and Crusts of fine bread, let them drain from the fat, boil them till tender: You may put a Fowl in the middle.

To make Spring Soup
Take twelve letices, cut them in Slices and put them in strong broth; get six green cucumbers, pare them, and cut out the Cores, cut them into little bits, and scald them in boiling Water, and put them into your Broth; let them boil very tender, with a mutchkin of young Pease and some Crumbs of Bread.

A very good Pease Soup
Boil three pounds of lean beef in eight Chopins of Water, and three pounds of pease, till the meat is all in rags, then put in two or three Anchovies, a Faggot of Thyme, Spearmint, Parsley, and Ginger, Pepper, Salt and Cloves, with some Onions; then boil it for a while and strain it off in a clean pan; then give it another boil, stirring in it a good piece of Butter. Fry some Forc'd-meat Balls, Bacon cut in thin slices, and Bread cut in Dice, with Spinage boil'd green and chopped small, with a bit of butter and salt, and roll'd in Balls: Put all in the Dish, and pour the soup boiling hot over them.

To roast or bake a Salmon
Score it on the Back, season with Salt, Pepper, Mace and Nutmeg; put grated bread, the Grate of a Lemon, Parsley, Thyme, Salt, and Butter in every Score, and in the Belly: put it in a close covered pan in the Oven, with some Butter on the top and Bottom. You may give it either Oyster or Lobster Sauce or Plain Butter.

To make Oyster, Lobster or Shrimp Sauce
Pick your oysters, clean, and scald them, strain their own liquor and put it on them then put Gravy, if you have it, or a little water in it, put in it a good

piece of Butter worked into Flour, a whole Onion, the Rind of a lemon; you may put in Ketchup if you have it. The lobsters must be cut in Pieces, and white wine in it.

To pot Herrings
Cut off the Heads and Fins, put them in a Pan: season them with Pepper, Salt and Vinegar: If you put in a little Sherry in them put the Juice of Lemon instead of Vinegar: cover them close, and bake them in a slow Oven. They are to be eaten when cold.

To boil Mackerel
Boil them in Salt and Water, with a little Fennel: The sauce is the Fennel chopped small, with beat Butter or Scalded Gooseberries, with butter and sugar.

Beef Steaks with Oyster Sauce
Cut your Steaks off any under Part of the Beef, flat them with your chopping knife, and put them on to hot clean Brander on a clear quick fire, turning them often that the Gravy does not run out; have your sauce ready, make it up thus: Scald your Oysters, and wash them clean in their own liquor, then strain the liquor into a saucepan, put to it a piece of butter worked in flour, two or three shallots, pounded pepper, Cloves, and Nutmegs, salt it to your taste; put a Glass of white wine and the rind and Juice of a Lemon in it: So pour it on your ashet of Steaks boiling hot. Garnish them with pickles.

A Carrot Pudding
Boil as many good carrots as will be half a pound, cut them and pound them fine with half a pound of fine sugar; then beat ten eggs and three whites and mix them with the carrots; grate an orange in it, and just as you are going to put it in the oven put into it half a pound of clarified butter.

Anonymous Manuscript, undated. Catalogue of library books at one end of the note book, recipes at the other. Given to me by the late Ted Renolds (Senior Lecturer in Catering at The Scottish Hotel School, also joint author of the *Chef's Compendium*) who found it among some second-hand books at the Glasgow 'Barras'. The library catalogue suggests it dates from the early eighteenth century.

To make Punch*
Take a Gallon of good Brandy, six Sevile Oranges, six Lemons, pare them so thin that there may be none of the white seen, put your Peels to steep in the Brandy twenty four hours, then take six quarts of Water, three pound of double refined sugar, three whites of Eggs beaten, when it begins to boil scum it, let boil a quarter of an hour when your syrup is gold then put your fruit and squeeze them, and when your Brandy has stood the time, strain the

Brandy from the peels, and mix all together, so turn it up in your vessell and stop it close, let it stand six days, and then bottle it, and when you come to drink it, mix it with watter to your taste.

* This method of making Punch was typical of the early tavern method of bottling the mixture for use as required. Some tavern punch bowls could hold several gallons. One in the People's Palace in Glasgow, which was used in the Saracen Head, holds 14 pints (25 l).

Lemon Bisketts Mrs Smiths way
Take four ounces of dry'd flower, half a pound of fine sugar, and the yolks of five eggs, and the whites of two beat the whites by themselves a quarter of an hour, then put in the yolks by degrees, and beat it half an hour more, then put in the sugar by degrees and beat that half an hour more, then stir in the flower with a spoon, and have ready the juice of a Lemon and the yellow rind of a Lemon grated, and put into it, your oven must be ready, and your tins – Buttered, sift some fine sugar over them just as you set them into the oven.

THE NINETEENTH CENTURY

1826

Mistress Margaret (Meg) Dods of the Cleikum Inn, St Ronan's, *The Cook and Housewife's Manual*
Published in Edinburgh and written, not by the fictious Meg Dods, but by Christian Isobel Johnstone, a minor novelist and editor, who chose to publish the book anonymously. (4th edition, 1929)

To Boil a Round of Beef (Beef and Greens)
A round or buttock of salted beef may either be boiled whole, divided into two, or cut into three pieces, according to the size of the meat, and the number of the guests or family. It is a common error of vanity to boil too much of a ham or round at once. If boiled whole, the bone may be cut out; if divided, it is desirable to give each piece an equal proportion of the fat. Wash the meat, and, if over salt, soak it in one or more waters till it be sufficiently softened or freshened. Skewer it up tightly, and of a good shape, wrapping the flap or tongue-piece very firmly round. Bind it with broad strong tape, or fillets of linen. The pot should be roomy, and the water must fully cover the meat. A fish drainer is convenient to boil this and other large pieces of meat on. Heat very gradually; take off the scum, of which a great deal will be thrown up, till no more rises, and throw in some cold water to refine the liquor if needful; cover the pot close, and boil slowly, but at an equal temperature, allowing about three hours to from 12 to 16 pounds, and from that to four or five hours for a weightier piece. Turn the meat once or twice in the pot during the process. Put in the carrot and turnip about two hours after the meat. If the liquor is to be afterwards used for soup, these roots instead of

hurting will improve the flavour. Greens may be either boiled in the same pot, or better separately in some of the pot-liquor. . . ; garnish with large sliced carrots, (or with greens or cabbage instead) and serve mashed turnip and greens in separate dishes.

To Boil Poultry

Be careful in picking, not to break the skin. Let the fowls stand from two to five days; for the most delicate fowl will be tough and thready if too soon dressed. When to be used, draw, singe without blackening, and wash thoroughly, passing a stream of water again and again through the inside. Boiled fowls must be very neatly trussed, as they have small aid from skewers; and nothing can be more indecorous than to see unfortunates on the table –

'Whose dying limbs no decent hands composed!'
Put them on with plenty of water, a little warmed. Having, as usual skimmed very carefully, simmer by the side of the fire from twenty-five minutes to an hour, according to the age and size of the fowl. A small tureen of very good barley or rice broth, seasoned with shred parsley and young onions, may be made at the same time, if a shank, or small chops of neck or ribs of mutton be added; which last may be frugally served in the broth. Some good cooks put fresh suet and slices of peeled lemon to boil with fowls; white-legged fowls are most worthy of attention, whether for eating or appearance.

To serve Oysters in the Shell

Let the opener stand behind the eater's chair, who should make a quick and clean conveyance. If not so placed, wash, brush and open and beard the oysters, and arrange them on rows on a tray; or if pinched for room, heap the shells in piles; the fresher from the sea, and the more recently opened the better. The French serve lemon-juice with raw oysters; we serve this or vinegar, pepper and toasted crusts.

An apple-pudding

Pare and grate three quarters of a pound of juicy apples. Put to them six ounces of butter beat cold to a cream, four beat eggs, two pudding-biscuits pounded, the rind of a lemon grated, sugar to taste, a spoonful of brandy, and another of orange-flower-water. Bake in a puff-paste marked in leaves round the border, and, when done, strew candied lemon or orange peel sliced over the top.

Oatmeal Cakes

The proper making of these cakes requires both skill and care, Have for the best kind, finely ground double-sifted oatmeal, such as is only seen to the north of the Spey. Add a little salt; make, one by one, cakes about five inches diameter, with barely enough scalding water to moisten the oaten flour. Knead with hands, but as little as possible, and toast very slowly at a distance from the fire, first on one side and then the other, on a toaster of open bars that lets the moisture escape.

Girdle Cakes

The meal used for oat-cakes is usually ground finer than that for porridge. Make the cakes, one by one, with hot water and salt enough. Roll out from five to seven inches in diameter, keeping round. Bake on one side on the girdle and the other toast before the fire. Keep dry meal below and above the cake on the baking-board to prevent sticking. Butter, or even dripping is used by good housewives for these cakes; and milk or sweet whey instead of water. Soda also begins to be employed. They keep long, but if above a week, should be re-toasted when wanted, like most other cakes. They look best rolled very thin, but do not eat better, as more water must be used to make the dough hold together. They take no injury by lying over for some hours before being baked.

Auld man's milk

Beat the yolks and whites of six eggs separately. Put to the beat yolks, sugar and a quart of new milk, or thin sweet cream. Add to this rum, whisky, or brandy to taste (about a half-pint). Slip in the whipped whites, and give the whole a gentle stir up in the china punch-bowl, in which it should be mixed. It may be flavoured with nutmeg or lemon-zest. This Highland morning-cup is nearly the egg-nog of America.

Oatmeal Dumpling or a fitless cock –

This antique Scotch dish, which is now seldom seen at any table, is made of suet and oatmeal, with a seasoning of pepper, salt and onions, as for white puddings, the mixture bound together with an egg, and moulded somewhat in the form of a fowl. It must be boiled in a cloth, like a dumpling.

1829

Mrs Dalgairns, *Practice of Cookery*, published in Edinburgh

Bunch of Sweet Herbs

Is made up of parsley, sweet marjoram, winter savour, orange and lemon thyme, the greatest proportion is parsley.

Oatmeal Porridge

Boil some water in a sauce pan with a little salt, and stir oatmeal into it with a thevil [porridge spurtle]; when of proper thickness let it boil for four or five minutes, stirring all the time; then pour it into a dish, and serve it with cream or milk. It is sometimes eaten with porter and sugar, or ale and sugar, if made with milk instead of water, less meal is requisite, and it is eaten with cold milk.

Welsh Rabbit

Pare the crust off a slice of bread, toast it nicely, divide it in two, butter it, and lay upon each half a thin slice of cheese with has been toasted in a Dutch

oven; if when put upon the toast, it is not sufficiently browned hold a sala-
mander, or hot shovel over the top serve very hot.

Caledonian Cream
Mince a tablespoon Orange Marmalade add it, with a glass of brandy some
pounded loaf sugar, and the juice of a lemon, to a quart of cream; whisk it
for half an hour and pour into a shape with holes in it, or put into a small hair
sieve, with a bit of thin muslin laid into it.

Raspberry Cream
Gather the fruit upon a dry day, mash and drip it through a jelly-bag; to
every pint of juice add a pound of pounded loaf sugar, and when it is completely dissolved, bottle it in a pint and half pint bottles, filling them only to
the neck. When to be used, mix it with rich cream, add more sugar, and
whisk till thick. It may be made the day before it is required.

1846–59

Janie Ellice, *Recipes*
A manuscript collection, delightfully illustrated by the author whose
family were the Balfours of Balbirnie in Fife. (Facsimile published by
Macdonald, 1974)

Toasted Cheese which is not toasted at all but boil'd . . .
Take 4 ounces of Cheese, Single Gloucester or Dunlop do well. 2 ounces of
fresh Butter; 1 tablespoonful of cream. Cut the cheese into thin slices. Put
them all in a small pan. Set it on a very slow fire and keep stirring it till it boils
and is quite smooth. Take off the Pan and break an egg into it, white and
yolk. Stir it quickly, put it into a dish and brown it before the fire in a tin
oven. From Lord Lauderdale, Thirlestane Castle.

How to make Friar's Chicken
Having caught your fowl, deprived it of life and feathers, boil it in its own
broth. Cut it up as for a fircasse. (The Broth must be made good, trimmings
of fowl or knuckles of Veal might be added). When the soup is finished about
three eggs for this quantity of soup must be broken into it. Season with salt,
pepper and a little shred parsley.
Rabbits make this very well, or rather it is very good when made of Rabbits.
Friars are supposed to be particularly fond of this dish. From my mother.

1886

Charles Elme Francatelli, *The Modern Cook*; *A Practical Guide to the
Culinary Art*
Published in London. He was a pupil of Carême and Chief Cook of Her
Majesty the Queen. (28th edition, 1886)

In the soup and stock recipes there are similarities with the old Scottish methods of 'strong broth' making.

Nutritive Soup

Into a three-gallon stockpot, put a knuckle of veal, six pounds of the shoulder part of beef (commonly called the gravy-piece), and a bone of roast beef or mutton. Fill the stockpot with cold water to within two inches of the brim, and set it upon a stove-fire to boil, taking care not to hurry its ebullition, but allow it to take place gently, so that it may have time to throw up its skum this should be removed, as it rises to the surface, and a little cold water should be thrown in occasionally to effect that purpose.

When the stock has thrown off all its skum, which will easily be perceived by the water becoming clear again, lift it off the stove, and put it by the side. Then proceed to garnish it with four leeks and two heads of celery, trimmed and tied together, two good-sized carrots, two turnips, and two onions, into each of which two cloves have been inserted; add one good tablespoonful of salt, and let the whole boil gently for about three-quarters of an hour. During this time, an old hen and a partridge should be partially roasted, and then put into the stock; this should continue to boil during five hours unremittingly: care being taken that the stockpot be kept full.

Previously to the soup being served, take off every particle of fat that appears on the surface, with a ladle; take out the vegetables – carefully placing them on a napkin, then remove the fowl and the partidge from the stock: these operations should be so managed as not to disturb the brightness of the broth. Cut the fillets of the fowl and the partridge into slices, and place them in the soup tureen and upon these put some of the vegetables (which have been drained on the napkin) neatly cut with a vegetable cutter a quarter of an inch in diameter; then pour in the broth, to which add a little brown *consommé* of veal to give it colour. Let it be sufficiently seasoned with salt, and a few grains of minionette pepper, then serve.

Empotage, or Consommé for Soups in General

When preparing for company, take about thirty pounds of gravy beef, and a similar quantity of knuckles of veal, together with four wild rabbits, and put the whole into a large stockpot which has been previously spread with butter, add common broth in sufficient quantity so as nearly to cover the meat. Put the stockpot on the stove-fire to boil until the broth is reduced to a light coloured glaze; then fill it up with the remainder of the grand stock, and after it has boiled and been skimmed, garnish it with carrots, turnips, leeks, onions, and celery; add also two blades of mace and six cloves. In all cases be sparing of salt, especially in the first stages of preparation. Allow the broth to boil gently on the side of the stove for six hours, and then pass it into kitchen-pans for further use.

In connections with this subject, I may here point out that, if it be contemplated to have as one of the removes a piece of beef braized, a saving of provision may be effected, by using in the first instance, instead of about thirty pounds of stock beef, only ten pounds of that quality in preparing the grand stock, the deficiency being made up by twenty pounds of sirloin. This latter must be boned, and the fillet taken out, whither to be used to ornament the remove or for an *entrée*, as occasion may require; the meat must then be rolled up tightly and strung round in the manner of Hambro'beef. This will thus answer the double purpose of giving strength to the *consommé*, and of serving afterwards as a remove.

When the beef thus prepared has boiled gently in the stockpot for about five hours, take it out and put it in press between two dishes till wanted; it must be then trimmed and placed in a long braizing-pan with a little good stock to warm it in; glaze it nicely, and having dished it up, garnish the remove with such vegetables as have been prepared for the purpose.

Brown Consommé of Pheasants or Partridges
Roast off two pheasants, after having taken out the fillets for the purpose of making them into an *entrée*, or four partridges may be used (removing the fillets in the same way); put them into a stockpot with a small knuckle of veal, and about one pound of lean of ham; fill up with water, then set it to boil on the stove-fire. Meanwhile slice up a carrot, an onion, two turnips, a head of celery, and a leek; fry these roots in a stewpan, with a small piece of butter, till they become slightly browned, then throw them into the *consommé* after having previously well skimmed it. Add three cloves, a piece of mace, and a little salt; let it boil gently about three hours, and then strain it off for use.

Quenelle of Fowl
Take of panada and prepared udder, or fresh butter, half a pound of each, to these add ten ounces of prepared fillets of chicken, as directed above, and pound all three together in a mortar; when they are well mixed, add salt, and as much grated nutmeg as will cover a sixpence, a little pepper, and one egg; pound the whole together till thoroughly mixed, then add another whole egg and two yolks, and a tablespoonful of *Béchamel* or *Suprême* Sauce. Pound the whole thoroughly and quickly, and after having taken the force-meat out of the mortar and put it into a kitchen basin, keep it in a cool place until wanted for use.

Previously to taking the quenelle up out of the mortar, its consistency should be thus ascertained. Take a piece of the force-meat the size of a large nut. Roll it with a little flour into the form of a round ball, put it into a small stewpan half full of boiling water; place it by the side of the fire to simmer for three minutes, after which take it out and cut it in halves; taste it in order to ascertain if it be correctly seasoned, and see that when cut asunder, the inner part presents a smooth, light, compact surface.

Grand Sauces

Espagnole, or Brown Sauce
Let the stock *Espagnole* (No 2) be turned out into a large stewpan, adding

thereto some essence of mushrooms and sufficient *blond* of veal to enable the sauce to clarify itself, stir it over the fire till it boils, and then set it down by the side to continue boiling gently. When the sauce has thoroughly cleared itself, by gentle ebullition, and assumes a bright velvety smoothness, reduce it over a brisk fire to the desired consistency, and then pass it through a tammy for use.

White Velouté Sauce
To finish this sauce, proceed in every respect the same as for the Espagnole, substituting white consommé of veal or fowls, for the blond of veal in order to clarify it; and the essence of mushrooms must be white in order to prevent the sauce from taking a dark hue, contrary to its special character.

Béchamel Sauce
Divide the Velouté sauce (according to the quantity required) into three parts; put one-third into a stewpan, and having reduced it, add thereto a quart (more or less) of boiling cream:-after allowing the sauce to boil a few minutes longer, stirring it the whole time, pass it through the tammy into a basin, or *bain-marie**, for use.
* This is a French term for a distinct set of copper saucepans, tinned both inside and outside, and used only for the Special Sauces, when finished.

Butter Sauce
Butter sauce, or as it is more often absurdly called, melted butter, is the foundation of the following sauce, and requires very great care in its preparation. Though simple, it is nevertheless a very useful and agreeable sauce when properly made; so far from this being usually the case, it is too generally left to assistants to prepare as an insignificant matter; the result is therefore seldom satisfactory.

When a large quantity of butter sauce is required put four ounces of fresh butter into a middle-sized stewpan, with some grated nutmeg and minionette pepper; to these add four ounces of sifted flour; knead the whole well together, and moisten with a pint of cold spring water; stir the sauce on the fire till it boils, and after having kept it gently boiling for twenty minutes (observing that it be not thicker than the consistence of common white sauce), proceed to mix in one pound and a half of sweet fresh butter, taking care to stir the sauce quickly the whole time of the operation. Should it appear to turn oily, add now and then a spoonful of cold spring water; finishing with the juice of half a lemon, and salt to palate; then pass the sauce through a tammy into a large *bain-marie* for use.

Red Currant-Jelly Sauce for Venison
Bruise one stick of cinnamon and twelve cloves, and put them into a small stewpan with two ounces of sugar, and the peel of one lemon pared off very thin, and perfectly free from any portion of white pulp; moisten with three glasses of port wine and set the whole to simmer gently on the fire for a quarter of an hour; then strain through a sieve into a small stewpan contain-

ing a pot of red currant-jelly. Just before sending the sauce to table, set it on the fire to boil, in order to melt the currant-jelly, so that it may mix with the essence of spice etc.

Black Currant-Jelly Sauce for Venison
This sauce is made exactly in the same manner as the foregoing – substituting black currant-jelly for red; it is preferred by many to the other, as it posesses more flavour.

1891

Lady Clark of Tillypronie, *The Cookery Book of Lady Clark of Tillypronie.*
Lady Clark of Tillypronie in Aberdeenshire died in 1891 leaving sixteen notebooks containing nearly three thousand pages of manuscript recipes. Her collection was edited by Catherine Frere and published in 1909.

Salmon Pudding*
From pieces of cooked fish. Use a plain mould buttered and breadcrumbed inside. If your fish has been cooked before it should be freed of skin and bone, and chopped fine, Half a pound of fish – this quantity will require a quarter of a lb of nicely boiled and mashed potatoes passed thro a sieve when hot and then mixed with two ounces of fresh butter and two tablespoonfulls of cream – also two raw eggs and a little pepper and salt – Into this mix your fish with a teaspoonful of Essence of Anchovy – Cover your mould with a paper lid and steam for 2 hours – Put the lid on the pan in which it steams. Turn out onto a very hot dish (you can bake it for a change).

* This recipe is not in the published collection but is one of many which she scribbled onto the back of envelopes, bills, scraps of available paper. This one, on a sheet of Tillypronie-headed writing paper, was found inside a copy of the book but with no date or details of where she got the recipe.

"Dripping Potatoes." (Mrs Husthwaite.)
Wash the potatoes and peel them very thin; boil them 10 minutes with a little salt, and then put them in a Yorkshire pudding tin under the joint which is roasting before an open fire, to catch the gravy; when enough moistened, put them into the oven, still in the tin, turn the potatoes often, and baste them with a little dripping, till crisp and brown.
Serve very hot, but NOT round the joint, or they will become sodden.
Potatoes done this way are mealy inside and crisp on the outside.

Feather Fowlie No. 1(Isa. Emslie. 1893)
A luncheon soup. The name is a corruption of "Oeufs Files."
Take 1 fresh fowl; joint it, and lay the pieces to soak for ½hr, well covered by cold water in which is a dessertspoonful of salt; next wash it well under the tap, and put it into a stewpan with a slice of ham, fat and lean, a stick of

celery cut up, an onion cut up, thyme, parsley, and a bit of mace. Cover all with 1 qt. of cold water; put the lid on and let it boil up; then draw to the side to cook more gently for 1½ hours; strain off, and at once clear off all the grease with paper. Put it into another stewpan, and add a dessertspoonful of chopped parsley and a ladleful of first stock – all to heat up 15 minutes; add minced white meat of chicken. When taken off the fire, stir in 3 strained yolks of egg and a dessertspoonful of warmed cream. Have soup tureen ready very hot.

Feather Fowlie. No. 2 (1888)

If you have 2 chickens, boil one of them in 2 oz cold water, with 1 onion, 1 carrot, and celery, and keep the liquor it was boiled in; when this fowl comes down from the dining-room keep also any white bits that may be left on it.

Joint the second chicken, carcass and all, and use the livers and gizzards of both; cover all with the chicken stock of the first fowl, just as it is, adding 1 raw whole onion, 1 raw whole carrot, and a little celery, 6 white peppercorns; add some raw ham also, and if the chicken stock is not enough, add a ladleful of fresh water, or of pork liquor, drawn from uncooked bones and trimmings, or veal stock, mutton stock, or failing that, enough to cover all; put the lid on, and let it just come to the boil; then simmer uncovered 1 hour at the side of the stove, strain off and pick out all nice white meat for use.

Return liquor and white meat to the pan, add a little pepper and salt, and a tablespoonful of finely chopped parsley-leaf , blanched and well squeezed in a cloth, all to simmer, still uncovered, ½ hour, then take off and stir in quickly 2 whole raw eggs. Stir, one way only, quickly, and serve in a very hot tureen.

Green Ginger Cake

(sent by Mrs Abel to Mrs Proctor, N. Berwick. 1879)

½ lb pounded sugar, ½ lb fresh butter, 4 eggs, ¼ lb Oswego [?] flour, ¼ lb fine flour, ¼ lb ginger taken out of syrup, chopped fine, ½ teaspoonful powdered ginger, ½ teaspoonful baking powder, a pinch of salt.

Beat sugar and butter together till very light; add the eggs, one by one, beating each thoroughly well in as you add it. Mix all well together, the Oswego flour, fine flour, salt, etc., and then add them to the mixed butter, sugar, and eggs; mix in lightly, and bake in a moderate oven.

(This makes an excellent pudding, if you add more ginger, and serve with a custard sauce flavoured with the syrup of the ginger.)

Lemon Pound Cake

(Mrs Thomas)

Beat ½ lb butter to a cream. Work in well ½ lb crushed sugar flavoured with the rind of 1 large or 2 small lemons (rub lump sugar on the best parts of the rinds, then grate the sugar fine), next add 5 eggs one after another, beating each well in as you add it. Then add, very gradually, as for a sponge cake, ½ lb of well dried flour. Mix in with the hand in cold weather but with a spoon in summer. Add a few carraway seeds if desired.

Bun Loaf Auchentorlie
(Mrs Buchanan)
3 lbs of dough, 1 lb butter melted, 1 lb sugar, 3 lbs sultana raisins, 3 ozs candied peel, 8 eggs, a little spice, add a little more flour, and mix all with the dough. Let this cake stand 2 hours before baking.

"Castle Cake"
(Mrs Innes of Learney. 1874)
(Rather strongly lemon flavourd. Sometimes called "Lemon Cake")
3 eggs, their weight in sugar, in flour, and in butter, the butter to be beaten to a cream. Beat the yolks and whites of egg together; next, add the sugar to the eggs; then, alternately, put in first a little of the butter, next a little of the flour, then butter again, and so on. Before putting the mixture into a buttered cake mould, add the grated rind of 3 lemons. Mix. Bake a nice brown.

Chocolate Cake
½ lb butter beaten to a cream, 7 eggs – yolks and white beaten separately, the whites stirred in at the last; ½ lb best vanilla-flavoured chocolate scraped down and heated in the oven, then beaten into the butter with 3 ozs flour, ½ lb sifted sugar, 4 ozs pounded almonds, and a teaspoonful sal volatile. Bake in a slow oven; frost over with sugar.
This cake is best when not quite newly baked.

Fresh Fruit Syrups for Pudding Sauces
(Mrs Wellington)
Raspberry: pick ripe raspberries and look them all over care-fully, rejecting any that are bruised or mouldy. Draw them down with a little cold water to simmer gently till all the juice is drawn out, then strain through a cloth. Add clarified syrup, and boil again for 10 minutes.
For this syrup, for every quart of raspberries use a pint of cold water and 1 lb of sugar; all to come to the boil, and to be well skimmed before you add it to the fruit juice.
Strain into a bottle, or for immediate use, into a crock.
For Raspberry juice, Mrs Sherwood prefers to draw down the fruit in a jar, without water, after carefully picking off stalks, etc. She puts the jar in the oven to draw out the juices, then strains the juice through a sieve and sweetens to taste, putting it on the fire to come to the boil, and bottles it when cold.
Strawberry juice requires less sugar than other fruit juice, but if bottled for winter use it must be more of a syrup, or it will not keep. It is best in summer made fresh every two or three days. It can then be served warm in a sauce boat with puddings.
Blackcurrant juice is also good for pudding, or the juice of redcurrants and raspberries mixed, made as above.

Orange Marmalade "Excellent"
(A Scotch Recipe from Miss Forsyth, View Park, Elgin)
Put 12 lbs sugar (large lumps) in 4 pts of water, and allow it to remain all night.
Next morning take 6 lbs of oranges and boil them whole until the <u>head</u> of a pin can pierce them; cut them in quarters, taking out the pulp; put back the skins, and boil them until they are transparent; then cut into very thin chips, carefully avoiding any bitter white part.

Boil the sugar and water until it becomes a syrup, carefully skimming it all the time; then put every part of the oranges, except the white part and the pips, into this syrup, and boil from 5-10 minutes.
Lemons may be added if you wish.

THE TWENTIETH CENTURY

1916

Robert Gordon's Technical College, Aberdeen School of Domestic Science, 352 King Street, *Plain Cookery Recipes* (Fourth Issue) Price sixpence, To be had at the School.

Colcannon
½ lb boiled cabbage. ½ lb boiled potatoes, a piece of boiled onion, 1 desertspoonful melted dripping, Salt and Pepper.
1. Mash altogether and season highly.
2. Pack tightly into a greased pie-dish.
3. Brush over with milk, if liked.
4. Mark neatly on top.
5. Bake in a hot oven till quite heated through.
6. Serve at once.

Oatmeal Biscuits
2½ oz flour, ½ oz sugar, ½ egg, Pinch of Salt, 3½ oz oatmeal, 2 ozs dripping or butter, Milk (if necessary), Pinch of carbonate of soda.
1. Grease a baking sheet.
2. Mix the flour, oatmeal, salt and carbonate of soda.
3. Rub in the dripping, add the sugar.
4. Mix to a stiff paste with beaten egg and milk if necessary.
5. Knead the mixture, roll to ⅛ of an inch in thickness.
6. Cut into rounds or squares.
7. Bake in a moderate oven for twenty to thirty minutes.

1929

F Marian (Flossie) McNeill, *The Scots Kitchen, Its lore and recipes*, published in Glasgow by Blackie.

Nettle Kail (Highlands and Hebrides)

'This simple but delicious soup is associated specially with the month of March, when nettles are young and fresh and the black March cockerel is exactly a year old, with young and tender flesh. The nettles were picked commonly on the old drystone dykes or the walls of the drystone-built 'black' houses, now rapidly vanishing. In the old days, March time was tonic time, and it was believed that nettle kail, taken three times during the month – sometimes on three consecutive days – purified the blood, cleared the complexion, and in general, ensured good health during the ensuing year. Shrove Tuesday was a very special night for a nettle kail supper. All the members of the family were expected to be present, and a blessing was invoked on the spring work.' – Rachel Macleod, Barra, in a letter to the author, accompanying the recipe.

A year-old cockerel, young nettles, oat or barley meal, butter, salt, pepper, wild garlic or onion or mint, water.

Gather a sufficient quantity of young nettles from the higher part of the wall, where they are clean. (It is advisable to wear gloves). Strip off the young, tender leaves at the top (discarding the coarser ones), and wash in several changes of salted water. Dry in a clean cloth and chop finely, unless the leaves are very small. Put the dressed and stuffed bird into the kail-pot with two quarts of cold water. Bring slowly to the boil, and add the nettles – about three-quarters of a pint – and a handful of oat or barley meal, stirring well. Add salt to taste, a good pat of butter, and a little wild garlic, onion or mint, as preferred. Simmer until the bird is tender then season the kail to taste.

For the stuffing, rub a piece of butter into twice its weight in oatmeal or barley meal, or substitute finely chopped suet for the butter. Season with salt, pepper and a little wild garlic or mint (fresh or powdered). Mix the ingredients well and stuff the bird. Insert a skewer in the opening.

In some districts whole barley is substituted for meal, but it should then be put on in cold water. Nettles make an excellent substitute for spinach in early spring.

'In Scotland I have eaten nettles, I have slept in nettle sheets and I have dined off a nettle tablecloth . . . The stalks of the old nettles are as good as flax for making cloth. I have heard my mother say that she thought nettle cloth more durable than any other species of linen.'

Thomas Campbell (the poet), quoted by Mrs Grieve in *A Modern Herbal*.

To Dress and Keep Dry Salted Tusk, Ling, or Cod Fish *Mrs Dalgairns recipe*

Cut in square bits, or put one large piece in water overnight; wash it clean in fresh water, and put it on to boil in cold for one hour and a half; then cool the water, so that the fish may be easily handled; take it out of the saucepan and pick out the loose bones and scrape it clean without taking off the skin. Put it on in boiling water, and if the fish is too fresh add a little salt with it and let it boil gently from one hour to one and a half. The very thick part will take this time, the thin bits less, to dress. When dished, garnish with hard-boiled eggs and parsley.

Plain boiled parsnips and a butter tureen of egg sauce are served with it. (In Morayshire, dried fish were served with home-made mustard, the seeds, freshly gathered in the cottage garden, being pounded in a mortar.)

When the fish is put on the second time some people prefer boiling it in milk and water. To keep any of this sort of fish for winter use it ought to be cut or sawed in pieces, and when perfectly dry, laid in a small cask or wooden box with oatmeal, oatmeal seeds, or malt dust between each layer.

Blawn (Wind-Blown) Fish
(Traditional Method)
Obtain the fish – whiting, haddock or other white fish – as fresh as possible, clean and skin them, take out the eyes, cover the fish over with salt, immediately after which take them out and shake off the superfluous salt, pass a string through the eye-holes, and hang them up to dry in a passage, or some place where there is a current of air; the next morning take them off, just roll them lightly in a little flour, broil them gently over a slow fire, and serve very hot, with a small piece of fresh butter rubbed over each, or serve quite dry, if preferable.

Note: When I (F.M.McN) was a child in Orkney, this was my favourite breakfast dish. Many years later I was much gratified to find the following passage in a cookery book by the great Soyer:

'Of all the modes of preparing and dressing whitings for breakfast I cannot but admire and prize the system pursued by the Scotch, which renders them the most light, wholesome, and delicious food that could possibly be served for breakfast.'

The small whiting, hung up with its skin on, and broiled without being rubbed in flour, is excellent. A wooden frame, called a *hake*, is used for drying fish. In Orkney cuiths (which in Shetland they call piltocks and in the Hebrides cuddies) are prepared in this way, care being taken that the fish are perfectly fresh, newly gutted, and thoroughly cleaned, and that the salt is rubbed well in along the bones from which the guts have been removed. They may be either boiled or brandered [grilled] – if boiled, they are eaten with butter, melted. They are particularly good with buttered bere bannocks or wheaten-meal scones and tea. – F.M.McN.

Arbroath Smokie
Smokies, pepper, butter
Heat the fish on both sides (it has already been cooked in the long smoking process) open it out, remove the backbone, mill black pepper over the fish, spread with butter, close up and heat for a few minutes in the oven or under

the grill. (In the old days it was brandered.) Serve piping hot. The Smokie, like the finnan-haddie, makes an excellent savoury.

To Fry Venison Collops
(Supplied to the Cleikum Club by P. Winterblossom, Esq)
Venison, gravy, lemon or orange, claret, pepper, salt, cayenne, nutmeg.
Cut oblong slices from the haunch, or slices neatly trimmed from the neck or loin. Have a gravy, drawn from the bones and trimmings, ready thickened with butter rolled in lightly browned flour. Strain into a small stew-pan, boil and add a squeeze of lemon or orange and a small glass of claret, pepper to taste, a saltspoonful of salt, the size of a pin's head of cayenne, and a scrape of nutmeg. Fry and dish the collops hot, and pour the sauce over them.

Caledonian Ice (Iced Stapag)
Cream, vanilla, sugar, oatmeal
Whip some cream stiffly; sweeten it and flavour with vanilla; set it to freeze. When nearly frozen stir in coarse toasted oatmeal, well dried in the oven without being browned. Serve in a glass dish or in individual glasses.

Cranachan or Cream-Crowdie
(A special dish at the Kirn, or Harvest Home)
Oatmeal, cream, sugar, and flavouring to taste
Toast some coarse oatmeal lightly before the fire or in the oven. Beat some cream to a stiff froth and stir in the oatmeal. Do not make it too substantial. It may be sweetened and flavoured to taste. The toasted oatmeal gives an agreeable somewhat nutty, flavour to the dish.
Note: This is a very old dish, commonly served in farmhouses on festive occasions. In the Scottish National Museum of Antiquities [now the National Museums of Scotland], there is to be seen, in the section of domestic articles, one of the old fro'ing sticks, having a wooden cross surrounded with a ring of cow's hair at one end, formerly used for beating cream and whey.
Raspberries in Cream-Crowdie: A few handfuls of raspberries buried in a bowl of cream-crowdie make an excellent sweet. F.M.McN.

1929

Aberdeen Education Authority, *Cookery Book*, for use in School and Home. Published in Aberdeen.

Perkins
8 oz flour; 8 oz oatmeal; 4 oz lard; 4 oz sugar; 4 oz syrup; 1 small egg; 1½ teaspoonfuls bi-carbonate of soda; 1½ teaspoonfuls ginger; ½ tea-

spoonful cinnamon, ½ teaspoonful mixed spices (makes 32 perkins) Mix all the dry ingredients and rub in the lard. Melt the syrup and add to the dry ingredients along with beaten egg. Mix to a stiff paste. Roll out like a sausage and cut in small pieces. Roll in balls, place on slightly greased tins, and flatten a little. Bake in a sharp oven for 10 to 15 minutes.

This copy belonged to Dora Cable, a pupil at Forfar Academy in 1929. She has written in many additional recipes at the back of the book, among them the following:

"I made a lovely new cake this weekend – 4 oz Gr Almonds, 4 oz Castor Sugar, 3 eggs – a few drops Almond Ess – Beat the sugar and egg yolks, add the Gr Almonds and Ess and fold in the whites beaten stiffly. Put into a lined tin and bake ½ hour in a moderate oven. (I used the tin in which I bake shortbread). It is extravagant and doesn't look very special but it tastes delicious, especially if after it is kept for a day or two for the almonds to give out their richness. It comes out about one inch thick and is very light in texture."

1920s or 30s

The Dundee Homecraft Book, Cookery, Laundry, Housewifery for use in School and Home.
Printed in Dundee for Dundee Education Committee. Undated, but certainly in existence in the 1930s. It was my first school cookery book (late 1940s, early 1950s).

Fish Custard
4 fillets White Fish, Salt and Pepper, 1 Egg, 1 gill Milk.
1. Wash, season, and roll up fillets skin side inside.
2. Arrange in greased pie-dish.
3. Add milk to beaten egg and pour over fish.
4. Bake in a moderate oven until custard is set (about ½ hour).

Coburg Sandwich
½ lb Flour, 3 oz Brown Sugar, 4 oz Margarine, 2 Eggs, ¾ teasp. Gr. Cinnamon. ¾ teasp. Mixed Spice, 1 tablesp. Syrup, 3 tablesp. Hot Water, ½ teasp. Baking Soda, ½ teacup Sour or Buttermilk.
1. Cream margarine and sugar, then add flour and eggs alternately.
2. Add spices then syrup melted in water.
3. Dissolve soda in milk and add.
4. Bake in greased sandwich tins in hot then moderate oven 20–30 minutes.
5. Cool on a wire tray.
6. Fill with butter icing.
   If liked the mixture may be baked in greased cake tin or patty tins.

Buns
Foundation Mixture
½ lb Flour, 3 oz Margarine, 3 oz Sugar, 1 teasp. Baking Powder, 1 egg, Milk.
Distinctive Ingredients:
ROCK – 3 oz currants
CHOC. – 2 tablesp. Chocolate powder
COCONUT – 1½ ozs coconut
LEMON – Grated rind of ½ lemon, 2 teasp. lemon juice.
Method:
1. Rub margarine into flour.
2. Add other ingredients.
3. Mix to elastic dough.
4. Place in rough small heaps on greased tray.
5. Bake in hot oven about 15 minutes.
6. Cool on wire tray and serve on plate with a d'oyley.

RASPBERRY BUNS [the favourite]
Make mixture into small balls, form a hollow in centre of each and put in a little raspberry jam. Bake in the same way as others.

1954

Gabriel Tschumi, *Royal Chef*
Recollections of life in royal households from Queen Victoria to Queen Mary.

Balmoral Shortbread
Queen Victoria had a little of this almost every day.
Ingredients: ¾ lb flour, ½ lb butter, ¼ lb sugar
Method: Rub in butter and sugar on a board, then work in flour lightly with fingertips. Roll out about an eighth of an inch thick, cut into circles, prick with a fork and bake on a greased tray in a moderate oven for about 15 minutes.
These were always pricked in the same way at Buckingham Palace, in a domino pattern with three rows of three dots.

Queen Alexandra's Birthday Cake
This makes a 36 lb. cake and was made regularly at Buckingham Palace from 1902–10.
Ingredients: 3½ lb butter, 4 lb Lisbon sugar, 5 lb flour, 6 lb currants, 2 lb sultanas well washed and dried, 1 lb filleted almonds, 1½ lb orange peel, 1½ lb lemon peel. 3 lb Cedrat peel all cut small, 40 eggs well beaten, grated rind of 8 lemons, ½ bottle brandy, ½ bottle rum; and the following spices mixed well together: 1½ tablespoonfuls allspice, 2 tablespoonfuls cinna-

mon, 1 tablespoonful mace, 1 tablespoonful cloves, 1 tablespoonful nutmeg.
Method: Mix together dry ingredients, then stir in eggs, brandy and rum.
Bake for 11 hours in medium oven. Top with almond paste and sugar icing
with orange-flower water flavouring.

Grouse à la Balmoral
(sufficient for sixteen people)
Take eight grouse which are too old for roasting and boil until tender in good
strong game stock for about 3 hours.
When cold slice meat from breast, clean, and arrange the pieces on a silver
dish. Make a thick jelly with the stock, flavouring it with sherry and brandy,
and when almost set pour it over the grouse. Serve garnished with a plain
green salad.

1960s

Scottish Council of the British Deer Society, *Venison Recipes*, compiled
by Mr A M McArthur of the Highland Branch.
A small booklet containing, several old 'handed down' recipes using up
the bits and pieces. When I first came across it while cooking in the Highlands these recipes were not to be found in any other cookery book.

Venison Ham
Cut venison, as thinly as possible from the top of the haunch. Sprinkle each
slice with freshly grated nutmeg and freshly ground black pepper. Place one
slice on top of the other and leave for not less than an hour. Fry in a little fat
and serve with fried eggs.

Venison Roll
Mince together about 1 lb roe venison, the heart, liver, 1 onion and two
tomatoes. Mix well together with half-lb diced streaky bacon, grated rind of
lemon, two tablespoonfuls fresh breadcrumbs, 1 well-beaten egg, salt and
pepper. Grease a bread size baking tin and fill with the mixture. Cover with
aluminium foil and cook in oven for 1½ to 2 hours – Regulo Mk 5. Serve
cold with salad.

Venisonburgers
If the weather is very cold, and a hot venison is required the above recipe
[Venison Roll] may be used, the diced bacon should be omitted and ½ lb
pork sausage meat substituted. The mixture should be put through the
mincer twice, formed into flat round cakes, dipped in beaten raw egg and
breadcrumbs and fried in hot fat until well browned on each side. Thicken
the gravy with a little flour, a tablespoonful of redcurrant jelly and add a
squeeze of lemon juice. Season to taste.

For Dressing the Velvet on Deer's Horns
Strip the fur off the horns with the fingers, cut in small pieces, put some good dripping or lard into a frying pan and let it boil, put in the fur, fry till quite tender, put into a hot dish with a little cayenne pepper and salt. Add no gravy but what comes from the fry after it has been put in on the hot water dish.

Stag's-Head Soup
Take two heads, also the necks: soak the heads in water for one night; keep them on in a stock pot with water. When the scum rises to the top skim it all off nicely; then put in carrots, turnips and onions, celery, thyme, and bay leaves (three). Boil all the goodness out of the heads; take a piece of the cheek and press it; strain off the soup and put it away to get cold; then take off the fat, clarify the soup, and reduce it to the quantity you require. Cut up the pressed cheek in nice small pieces, and place them in the tureen with some cut-up French beans just before you take the soup. Pour a glass of port wine in it; let it boil up, put the consommé in the tureen, and serve.

Fried Stag's-Feet for breakfast
Boil the feet six hours strain the stock from them; put the stock away to make jelly, take all the bones out of the feet while they are hot; mix them with chopped parsley, pepper, and salt and lemon juice to taste; let stand until cold; then cut them out in nice small pieces; egg-and-breadcrumb them, and fry in hot fat. Stag's-feet make a nice jelly, using them as calves'-feet are used.

1960s

Janet Murray, *Traditional Scottish Recipes*
Published by the BBC as a selection of her recipes broadcast on 'Morning Call'. She later wrote 'With a Fine Feeling for Food' (Impulse 1972).

Butteries
Making butteries is rather like making a flaky pastry, only you use yeast; and while baking utensils are as cold as possible for pastry, they must be warm for a yeast mixture.
Here are the quantities for a batch of about 15.
12 oz plain flour; 1 large teaspoonful salt; 2 large teaspoonfuls sugar; ½ oz yeast; ¼ pint tepid water; 3 oz butter; 4 oz lard.
Sift the flour with the salt into a warm roomy bowl. Cream the yeast with the sugar and add some of the tepid water to it. Pour it into the flour and mix to a smooth firm dough, adding more of the water if necessary. Knead the dough well on a well-floured baking board. (Kneading is not just pounding. You lift the edge of dough with the right hand and fold it into the centre of the dough with the knuckles of the left hand and keep on turning the dough round and

round as you work.) Put the dough back into the bowl, cover it with a cloth wrung out of warm water, and set it in a warm corner for an hour. After an hour it should have risen to twice its size. Knead it again. It will fall back almost to its original size or pretty near it, so do not be disappointed. Roll it out on a floured board.

There are two methods of adding the fat. You can do it in tiny pieces over the dough, or you can mix the butter and lard to a cream and spread it on. I prefer the latter method.

Having creamed the butter and lard, spread a third of it evenly over the dough and dust with flour. Fold the dough in three and roll it out. Repeat the operation twice. The final rolling should leave the dough thin and flattish. Cut it in squares. Take up each square, tuck the four corners underneath, flatten with the hand and put on a floured, warm baking sheet. Leave them for half an hour, then bake in a hot oven for 15 minutes until they are a golden brown and crusty, above and below.

For those who like to know the temperature – for an electric oven, 450 degrees F; for a gas oven, mark 6.

Pitcaithly Bannock

Pitcaithly in Perthshire was at one time noted for its mineral wells and it is said that one of the landladies, who catered for the visitors who flocked to the health resort, made a rich cake of a biscuit nature. This is the traditional recipe:

4 oz almonds; 4 oz mixed peel; 8 oz butter; 4 oz castor sugar; 12 oz plain white flour.

Skin the almonds and chop them. A few minutes in a pan of boiling water will slacken the skin, and it will come away easily.

Shred the peel finely. Beat the butter and the sugar until it is creamy, then add the nuts, the peel, and the flour slowly, mixing well all the time. Use a wooden spoon for mixing, but finish by kneading firmly with the hand to get a smooth, firm dough.

Turn it out on to a floured board and knead into a round shape. It should be fully half an inch thick. Pinch round the edge of the bannock, then stab over the surface with a fork. Put the bannock on a floured baking sheet and leave it for at least a couple of hours to become firm.

Pin a strip of greaseproof paper round the bannock and bake in a moderate, even a slow oven. Bake for 1 hour.

It should be a pale golden colour. A few minutes before removing it from the oven, dredge it liberally with castor sugar. The bannock, if stored in an airtight tin will keep for a long time.

1961

Robert McDonald, *Highland Recipes*
Published in Inverness by Charles Keith. A collection of recipes from the people of his parish and around Dornie.

Father's Favourite Friday Soup

A few potatoes, an onion, ½ pt milk, piece of margarine, pepper and salt.
Cut up the potatoes and onion into small pieces and cover with water in a
pan. Add salt and boil. When boiled, mash up potatoes and onion and pour
in almost ½ pt of milk, add a slice of margarine and some pepper, bring to
the boil and let simmer. Serve hot.

Fish Cakes

(from Mrs Campbell, Shiel House, Glenshiel)
½ lb cooked fish, 1 egg, ½ lb mashed potatoes, 2 teaspoons chopped
parsley, pepper and salt.
Bone and flake fish and mix well with other ingredients and bind with
beaten egg. Shape into round cakes and fry in shallow fat till brown on
both sides.

Cheese Potatoes

(from Helen Fisher, Aberdeen)
Large sound potatoes, nut of butter, hot milk, grated cheese.
Scrub the potatoes, prick with a fork and bake in a moderate oven till soft.
Cut in halves lengthwise, scoop out the insides. Mix them with butter, a little
hot milk and grated cheese – about two-thirds with potato to one-third of
cheese. Season well. Pile the mixture back into the potato cases, sprinkle
with grated cheese and put back in the oven or under the grill to brown.

Junket and Cream

(from Mrs Campbell, Shiel House, Glenshiel)
To 2 pints warm milk add ½ teaspoon rennet and 1 teaspoon sugar. Stir and
leave to set in a glass dish. Grate nutmeg on top and serve with double cream,
plain or whipped.

Highland Shortbread

(from Mrs Campbell, Shiel House, Glenshiel)
8 oz plain flour, 4 oz cornflour, 4 oz icing sugar, 8 oz butter.
Sift flours and sugar into a bowl. Rub butter into this, knead and blend till a
stiff consistency. Form into four rounds about ¼ inch thick, prick over top
and flute edges with finger and thumb. Bake in slow oven for about 40
minutes till pale biscuit colour. Sprinkle with castor sugar and store in
airtight tin.

Scotch Shortbread

(from Mrs Kennedy, Inverinate)
5 oz plain flour, 2 oz castor sugar, 1 oz rice flour, 4 oz butter.
Sieve together flours, sugar and pinch of salt. Put butter into dry mixture
until crumbly, knead until it binds together. Mould into tin, turn on to lined
baking sheet. Prick surface, crimp edges. Bake ¾ – 1 hour.

Walnut Tablet
(from Mrs McLeod, Tigh-na-Bruaich, Dornie)
2 lbs granulated sugar, 2 ozs chopped walnuts, 1 tin condensed milk, 1 cupful sweet milk.
Put the sugar, condensed milk and sweet milk into a saucepan and stir until the mixture boils. Boil for 20 minutes, then remove from heat, add walnuts and stir until the mixtures thickens. Turn into a greased tin and cut when cold.

Toddy

"Sit roun' the table well content
An steer aboot the toddy."

(from Mrs Forbes, Fernaig)
Whisky, hot water, sugar, lemon (if liked)
Pour boiling water slowly into a tumbler till half full. Let it remain until the crystal is thoroughly heated then pour out. Put in loaf sugar to taste with a glassful of boiling water. When melted pour in ½ glass of whisky and stir well, add more hot water and another ½ glass whisky. Stir – serve hot! Can be flavoured with lemon if wished.

The Tonic
(from Mrs MacDonald, Plockton)
6 eggs, 4 lemons (juice of lemons), 1 pint cream, 1 lb demerara sugar, 1 gill brandy or rum.
Break eggs, including shells, and soak in sugar and juice of lemons for three days, stirring frequently. Mixture having been strained well mix in brandy, or rum if preferred, with cream and add to egg mixture. Beat well and bottle. Take wine glassful twice a day.

Late 1960s

Anonymous, undated, manuscript recipes from Lewis
These were given to me by a schoolteacher in Garve with Lewis connections. They had been written by a cookery teacher at the Nicolson Institute in Stornoway who had collected them from local people.

Salt Herring and Potatoes
Salt herring; potatoes of an equal size; cold water
Put herring in cold water, bring to the boil and pour off that water. Cover with boiling water and place on top potatoes in their jackets which have been cleaned. Cook until the potatoes are ready.

Fried Herring
Oatmeal; pepper and salt; dripping
Clean and dry the herring. Sprinkle with pepper and salt and toss on coarse

oatmeal. Put the dripping in a frying pan and when smoking hot put in the herring and brown them nicely on both sides. Drain them on paper and serve very hot.

Cooking of Lobsters and Crab
Have a large pan ready with boiling water. Plunge crabs and lobsters into boiling water when living. Cook for 20 minutes. Remove from boiling water break shell and flake flesh. Mix flesh with a tablespoon of cream and serve in washed shell.

Stags Liver
Stags liver; milk; pepper and salt
Soak stags liver in milk to improve the flavour. Dip in flour and fry in the usual way.

Carrageen (Sea Moss Jelly)
Gather the weed on the rocks. Wash the salt and sand well out of it and spread it on the rocks or on a white cloth on the grass and leave it there for several days to bleach and dry. When thoroughly dry put it into bags and hang these up in a dry place preferably in the kitchen. When required, allow a heaped tablespoon to each quart of milk and put both into pan. Let it simmer till milk begins to thicken, strain and pour it into a bowl and allow it to cool and set. Serve with cream.

Barley Meal Porridge
1 handful of barley meal; 1 pint boiling water; salt
Boil water and add barley meal allowing the meal to sift through the fingers of the left hand, stirring frequently. Cook for two hours and serve with cream.

Crowdie
Set pan with freshly sour or thick milk on a slow heat and watch till it curdles, not letting it simmer or boil or it will harden. When set, let it cool before drawing off the whey. Use a muslin cloth. When whey is completely squeezed out mix crowdie with a little salt until you find it very soft in your hands, mix with cream or top of milk and set out in dishes. The mixture can also be pressed in a colander to remove whey and a weight placed on top. The crowdie can then be sliced like cheese.

1968

Margaret B Stout, *Shetland Cookery Book*
Compiled for Home and School and published by T & J Manson, Lerwick. A comprehensive collection of Shetland fish recipes, particularly old ways of dealing with the livers, stomachs, etc.

Pickled Mackerel
Three large Mackerel
One ounce of Pepper
Three Nutmegs grated
Mace or Mixed Herbs
One handful of Salt
METHOD
Mix the seasonings together. Wash, clean and dry mackerel, cut into five or six pieces. Make two or three holes in each piece and fill these with seasoning, pushing it in with the finger; rub each piece all over with seasoning; fry in oil or dripping and set aside till cold. Lay the pieces in a tight fitting vessel, cover with vinegar (will keep longer, if cold, boiled) cover tightly. This will keep for some time and is very tasty.

Salt Fish Pie
One teaspoonful chopped Parsley
One pound of Salt Cod
One pint of Bread Sauce
One tablespoon of Butter
METHOD
Soak, boil, and flake fish. Make the bread sauce, add fish, butter and parsley; season with pepper and mustard. Turn into pie-dish, brown in oven or cover with paste and bake 20–30 minutes.

Pickled Mutton*
Three and a half pounds Salt
Four quarts of water
Six ounces of Sugar
Two to three ounces of Saltpetre
About sixteen pounds of Mutton
METHOD
Wipe meat and lay in salted water over night. Pour off liquid. Bring salt and other ingredients to boil in the water, allow to cool, pour into a stone crock, lay in the meat and leave for 14–21 days; hang up and use as required.

* This is the mutton which they describe as *reested*, a Shetland name from the Scandinavian *riste* meaning to broil or grill. It makes a very fine tasting broth and is available in Lerwick butchers (see Traditional Scottish Food Suppliers, p. 243).

Shetland Seasoning for Saucermeat
The poorer cuts of meat, generally beef, minced and seasoned with the following may be made into bronies and fried, or into meat loaf and baked. A Mixture of spices in the following proportion is first made.
Quarter of an ounce of Allspice
Quarter of an ounce of Cloves
Quarter of an ounce of Ginger
Quarter of an ounce of White Pepper
Quarter of an ounce of Black Pepper

Eighth of an ounce of Mace
Eighth of an ounce of Jamaica Pepper
Eighth of an ounce of Cinnamon
This along with 6 oz salt, will season 12 lb minced meat.

SAUCERMEAT BRONIES
One pound of Saucermeat
One pound of minced Steak
One teacupful of Breadcrumbs
One tablespoonful of Chopped Onion
Pepper and Salt
One Egg or Milk to moisten
METHOD
Mix all thoroughly together with the hand in a basin, form into cakes about
¾ inch thick; fry on both sides in smoking hot fat; reduce heat and allow to
cook through more slowly for 10–15 minutes; drain and serve hot.

Stovies
One and a half pounds of Mutton
One pound of Potatoes
Pepper and Salt
One Onion
Half a small Turnip
One tablespoonful of Suet
METHOD
Cut mutton up finely; chop suet; put these into pan and pour on enough
boiling water to cover; simmer gently for one hour. Chop onion finely, cut
potato and turnip up roughly, add these and stew gently for another hour;
season and serve hot.

Whipkull*
One dozen Yolks of Eggs (fresh)
One pound of Castor Sugar
One pint of Rum or Mead
One quart of sweet Cream
METHOD
Beat the yolks and sugar together till thick and creamy, add cream and rum
or any spirit. Allow to stand for some time until ingredients are thoroughly
blended; pour into glasses and serve.

* A Yule-time celebration drink (hence the quantities). It had Scandinavian origins,
compare with Norwegian *Eggedosis*.

1977

A Mull Companion, edited by Janet M Nelson
A collection of recipes from the people of Mull, some handed down

through generations, all reflecting the environment of the island. Published to raise funds for the Queen's Silver Jubilee Fund. Printed by Mackenzie and Storrie, Edinburgh.

Broth Achaban
About 3 pints of mutton stock, 1 large onion or leek, 4 large carrots, 2 medium turnips, Half a small cabbage, 2 tablespoons of parsley, 1 breakfast cup barley.
Simmer a gigot bone, to which some meat adheres, for at least an hour. Strain, cool, and skim off the fat. Finely chop the onion or leek, two carrots, cabbage, turnips and parsley. Finely grate the other two carrots. This gives the broth a nice orange colour. Add all the vegetables to the stock with the barley and seasoning. Cover the pan and cook for 2 hours. The essentials are the mutton stock, the barley, and the grated carrot. Otherwise any vegetables in season can be used.

Whelk Soup
Wash whelks very thoroughly, preferably in sea water. Place in pan with fresh water and bring to the boil. Boil for 4–5 minutes. Then pour through colander and reserve water. Shell the whelks and return to the water with a well chopped onion and a good sprinkling of oatmeal. Boil slowly for ½ hour. Season to taste.

Duileasg Bree
(Dulse Soup)
Dulse is a dark red seaweed with wedge shaped fronds. It can be eaten fresh in salads or washed and dried for later use. Wash the seaweed well in running water. Soak for two hours in cold water and strain. Put in a large pan, cover with cold water and simmer gently for 3–4 hours with the lid on. Drain well. Then beat in pepper, salt, butter, and a little lemon or orange juice. Take 1 cup of this cooked seaweed, add 3 pints milk and ½ lb cooked mashed potato and simmer together for 20 minutes. Then beat well or liquidise. Season to taste. Add melted butter and lemon juice. Beat up again, heat and serve piping hot. Serves 6.

Cockles
Wash the cockles thoroughly in several changes of water. Boil until they open. Separate meat from shells. Roll the cockles in oatmeal and fry in butter until golden. The water used in boiling can be saved to make a delicious cockle soup, using some of the cockles. Sprinkle the soup with chopped chives.

Razor Fish or Spout Fish
Wash the shells thoroughly and boil until they open. Remove meat and cut off each end. Roll in oatmeal and fry until golden in butter.

Poached Scallops
Wash and beard the scallops, removing black part. Place in a pan and cover with milk. Add about 1 oz butter and seasoning. Poach gently for 8–10 minutes. Remove the scallops from pan and replace them in their shells. Make white sauce using liquid in which scallops were cooked and pour over scallops in shells. Sprinkle with chopped parsley.

To Dry Fish
Take some freshly caught Saithe (or Cuddies*). Cut and wash. Put in a large basin with plenty of coarse salt for 36 hours. Then bone by running one's thumb down bone. Lay out flat on slate roof to dry. They are lovely half-dried (after one day in the sun and wind). The hard dried fish will keep in a dry place all winter and just need to be soaked for 2–3 hours before cooking.

* In this part of the world a young coal fish is first called a cuddie and then, as it grows, a saythe. The Gaelic word *ceiteanach* was used to describe the young fish caught in May in the first year of its life.

Ham and Haddie
Simmer 1 large smoked haddock in water for 4 minutes. Remove, skin and fillet. Heat 2 tablespoons of butter in frying pan and cook 2 large slices of smoked ham, turning once. Put fish on top, season with pepper, cover and simmer gently for 3 minutes. Pour ½ cup of thick cream on top, and brown under the grill. Top with poached egg and serve at once.

Boiled Beef and Hodgils*
For each person allow 1 cupful of medium oatmeal. Place in a bowl, season with salt and black pepper. Add 1 dessertspoon chopped chives. Mix with fat skimmed from top of beef broth. Shape into balls and stand for 10–20 minutes. Then pop into pan of boiling beef broth. Cover and cook for 20 minutes. Serve with second course of boiled beef after first supping of broth.

* I have spoken to many people in the Highlands who remember when these oatmeal dumplings were very common in broth.

Bramble Cake
Cake: 4 oz butter, 4 oz sugar, 1 egg, 8 oz plain flour, 2 teaspoons baking powder, pinch salt, ¼ pint milk.
Make sponge in the usual way, beating to smooth batter with the milk. Pour into a buttered tin about 7″ × 11″.
Topping: 8 oz firm ripe brambles, 2 oz butter, 4 oz sugar, 2 oz flour, ½ teaspoon cinnamon.
Wash and drain brambles well. Cream butter and sugar and then work in flour and cinnamon to make crumb mixture. Sprinkle cake with berries, then crumbs. Bake at 350F for 1 hour.

RECIPES

Oatmeal Drink
Pour 1 pint of cold water on to 2 heaped tablespoons of oatmeal. Leave for 15 minutes, then pour the liquid through a sieve and put in a cool place. This makes a very refreshing drink. Bottles of it were taken to the moors during peat-cutting and were kept ice-cold by being submerged in a bog or burn until needed.

1978

Willie Fulton, *Hebridean Kitchen*
A light-hearted look at aspects of cooking (and other habits) in the Western Isles of Scotland. Published by Buidheann-foillseachaidh nan Eilean an Iar, Steornabhagh.

Cuddies
The young of the saithe or coalfish (member of the cod family) . . .
These small, but voracious fish are plentiful among the rocks and by jetties etc, during the winter months. They will devour almost any small bait, but now small feathers or sheep's wool tied onto 2 or 3 hooks and suspended from a long bamboo pole is the usual method. Around four or five fish, 4 to 6 ins. long, per person. Cut, clean, but retain the little livers.
Simmer fish and livers for a few minutes, till ready.
Serve with spuds and veg.
More often than not the juice is kept, milk, salt and pepper added, and a nutritious drink it is too, taken hot.
I prefer them fried in butter after rolling in oatmeal. Remove from pan, after a few minutes then the crisp little fish eaten using the fingers . . .

Mackerel (Rionach)
(Must be fresh and head removed and fish cleaned when caught).
Mackerel, Brown Sugar, Salt, Vinegar.
A fish much underrated – has a unique strong taste, when eaten fresh – plentiful in the autumn months, when they will take any bait, anything that shines on a hook.
Fillet fish by removing generous slices from each side (a little wasteage is fine they are very meaty).
Place mackerel fillets, brown sugar, salt in alternate layers in a dish and leave overnight.
Next day, wash in cold water (the fish also) and boil in equal parts of vinegar and water till cooked (10 minutes approx). Leave to cool and serve with salad. Can also be treated as herring and fried in oatmeal.

Cormorant (Sgaibh)
A large sea-bird, existing throughout the islands. Feeds on fish and can be seen, in groups, sometimes with open wings, drying in the wind.
To catch your bird, take one rowing boat, oars and shotgun. Row quietly to

230

the corner before where you know the birds to be, then quickly row into view. Shoot, while they are surprised, collect when they fall.
Pluck, singe with hot iron (or moderate blow lamp) boil for 1 ½ to 2 hours till tender.
Eat hot with potatoes and vegetables.
Soup can be made with the stock, plus:-
½ cup oatmeal
handful of barely
chopped onion
salt and pepper to taste.

Cup of tea
(Strupag or cupa tea)
The hospitable and open nature is demonstrated in the island home when visiting, either as a friend or complete stranger. Having been given a seat, (usually the best beside the fire) a tray is prepared for one's sole use. Hot tea, fresh scone and cheese, biscuits or such like. With the tea and food, a dram for a man, sweet sherry for the lady. ''Just a little drop to warm the mouth.''

1978

Jenni Simmons, *A Shetland Cookbook*. Published by Thuleprint, Shetland

Sassermaet*
(Sausagemeat)
For 6 lbs minced beef:
1 tsp allspice
1 tsp black pepper
1 tsp white pepper
1 tsp ground cloves
½ tsp Jamaica pepper
½ tsp cinnamon
3 oz salt
Mix all the spices with the salt first, then stir through the minced meat very well.

* Almost the same recipe as Margaret Stout's but I include this one since the quantity of salt is reduced by half, a modification it seems as modern tastes change but yet cling to old methods.

Reested Mutton (see also p. 102)
The mutton is first salted, then hung and dried in the roof by the fire; the peat reek gives a unique smokey flavour to the mutton tee. The veggil [a wood or rope framework] is where the meat is hung to reest.

Vivda
Vivda is mutton dried by the wind, not salt. Its flavour is greatly to be esteemed, the meat being cut in very thin slices. The meat was hung in a skjeo (a stone larder built so that air could blow freely through the walls).

Boiled Salt Mutton
2 lb salt meat, 1 carrot, sliced, pinch pepper, 1 lb potatoes, cut small, 1 large onion, sliced.
Wash meat and cook in 1 breakfastcupful water for 1 hour. Then remove, and cut in small pieces and return to the pot. Add vegetables and seasoning and simmer 1 hour. This can be done in a casserole (or lidded dish) in a slow oven. Cook for two hours.

Cabbage
Shetland cabbage have good solid hearts. Peel off the outer leaves and quarter (make the first cut lengthways.) Put in boiling water, salted, and boil rapidly till tender. Drain well and butter. Eat with Fatty Brunnies (see p. 172).

Bibliography

COOKERY

Aberdeen Education Authority, *Cookery Book*, Aberdeen, 1929

Annlan is Eile, compiled by Catriona Dunn and a group of girls from the Nicolson Institute in Stornoway for Comhairle Mod na Eillean, Alba, Inverness, 1978

British Women's Cookery Book, compiled by Mrs A S Wilkinson (Perth) and Miss Flora Patterson (Edinburgh), 1950

Brown, Martha, unpublished manuscript of recipes in Cunningham District Library, 1712

Carter, Charles, *The Complete Practical Cook*, first published 1730, facsimile published by Prospect Books, 1984

Ceserani, Victor and Kinton, Ronald, *Practical Cookery*, Arnold, 1962

Clark, Lady of Tillypronie, *The Cookery Book of Lady Clark of Tillypronie*, edited by Catherine Frere, published 1909

Clayton, Bernard Jr, *The Complete Book of Soups and Stews*, Simon and Schuster, New York, 1984

Cleland, Elizabeth, *A New and easy method of Cookery . . .*, printed in Edinburgh, 1755

Cookery and Domestic Economy for Young Housewives, A work of plain and practical utility, William and Robert Chambers, Edinburgh, n.d.

Dalgairns, Mrs, *Practice of Cookery*, Edinburgh, 1829

Davidson, Alan, *North Atlantic Seafood*, Macmillan, 1979

Dods, Mistress Margaret (Meg) of the Cleikum Inn, St Ronan's, *The Cook and House vife's Manual*, Edinburgh, 1826 (written anonymously by Christian Isobel Johnstone)

Drysdale, Julia, *The Game Cookery Book*, Collins, 1975

Dundee Homecraft Book, The, Dundee Education Committee, n.d.

Ellice, Janie, Manuscript collection of 'Recipes' with illustrations by the author, 1846–59, facsimile published by Macdonald, 1974

Fitzgibbon, Theodora, *A Taste of Scotland: Scottish Traditional Food*, Dent, 1970

Francatelli, Charles Elme, *The Modern Cook, A Practical Guide to the Culinary Art*, London, 1886

Fraser, Mrs, *The Practice of cookery and pastry . . .*, Edinburgh, 1791

Fuller, John and Renold, Edward, *The Chef's Compendium of Professional Recipes*, Heinemann, 1963

Fulton, Willie, *Hebridean Kitchen*, Buidheann-foillseachaidh nan Eilean an Iar, Stornoway, 1978

Glasgow Cookery Book, The, published for the Glasgow and West of Scotland College of Domestic Science by John Smith, revised edition, 1962

Glasse, H, *The Art of Cookery Made Plain and Easy*, Edinburgh, 1738

Greene, Bert, *Greene on Greens: over 450 incomparable vegetable recipes*, Equation, British edition, 1987

Grigson, Jane, *Observer Guide to British Cookery*, Joseph, 1984

Heptinstall, William, *Gourmet Recipes from a Highland Hotel*, Faber, 1967

Hope, Annette, *A Caledonian Feast*, Mainstream, Edinburgh, 1987

Johnston, Mrs, *Receipts for all sorts of pastry, creams, puddings, custards, preserves, marmalets . . .*, Edinburgh 1740 (first 92 pages identical to Mrs McLintock's *Receipts*)

Lappe, Frances Moore, *Diet for a Small Planet*, Ballantine Books, New York, 1971

Lockhart, Martha (Lady Castlehill), Manuscript recipes, 1712 (a quarter of the manuscript recipes published by Molindinar (1976) as *Lady Castlehill's Receipt Book*, ed. Hamish Whyte)

McArthur, A M, *Venison Recipes*, Scottish Council of the British Deer Society, n.d.

Macdonald, Robert, *Highland Recipes*, Inverness, 1961

MacIver, Suzanna, *Cookery and pastry. As taught and practised by Mrs MacIver, teacher of those arts in Edinburgh*, Edinburgh, 1773

McLintock, Mrs, *Receipts for Cookery and Pastry-Work*, 1736 (the first published cookery book in Scotland), facsimile published by Aberdeen University Press (1986) with introduction by Iseabail Macleod)

McNeill, F Marian, *The Scots Kitchen, Its lore and recipes*, Blackie, Glasgow, 1929

Madison, Deborah, *The Greens Cook Book*, Bantam, 1987

Murray, Janet, *Traditional Scottish Recipes*, published by the BBC as a selection of recipes broadcast on 'Morning Call', n.d.

National Trust for Scotland, *A Taste of Apples, Recipes from Priorwood Orchard*, n.d.

Nelson, Janet M, *A Mull Companion*, Edinburgh, 1977

Old Highland Cookery Book, The Feill Cookery Book, published by An Comuan Gaidhealach, Glasgow, 1907

Phillips, R, *Mushrooms*, Pan, 1981

——, *Wild Food*, Pan, 1983

——, *Seaweeds and Seashells*, Hamilton, 1987

Rance, P, *The Great British Cheese Book*, Macmillan, 1983 (revised edition, 1988)

Reid, Nancy (ed.), *Highland Housewives' Cook Book*, Highland Printers, 1971

Robert Gordon's Technical College, Aberdeen School of Domestic Science, *Plain Cookery Recipes*, 1916 (to be had at the school price sixpence)

Robertson, Una A, *Let's Dine at Hopetoun*, Hopetoun House, 1981 (details from a volume in the Hopetoun House archives dealing with domestic food supplies, drink and menus from 1745–55)

Scottish Women's Rural Institutes, *Traditional Scottish Recipes Cookery Book*, 6th edition, 1946

Shapinsay SWRI Cookery Book, A Collection of Members' tried and tested recipes, n.d.

Simmons, Jenni, *A Shetland Cook Book*, Shetland, 1978

Stout, Margaret B, *Shetland Cookery Book*, T & J Manson, Lerwick, 1968

Strawberry Leaves and Syllabubs, Recipes collected by the Duchess of Buccleuch from old family cookery books, Buccleuch Recreational Enterprises Ltd., 1979

Traditional Scottish Recipes: Over 150 recipes still used by members of the Scottish Women's Rural Institutes, some of which have been handed down over many generations, SWRI, Edinburgh, n.d.

Tschumi, Gabriel, *Royal Chef, recollections of life in royal households from Queen Victoria to Queen Mary*, William Kimber, 1954

Ward, Ruth, *A Harvest of Apples*, Penguin, 1988

Wilson, C Anne, *The Book of Marmalade: its antecedents, its history and its role in the world today*, Constable, 1985

Wolfe, Eileen, *Recipes from the Orkney Islands*, Gordon Wright, 1978

Women's Institute and Smith, M, *A Cook's Tour of Britain*, Willow, 1984

GENERAL

Anson, Peter, *Fisher Boats and Fisher Folk*, Dent, 1930

Berry, R J and Firth, H N, *The People of Orkney*, The Orkney Press, 1986

Binney, Marcus, *Lost Houses of Scotland*, London, 1970

Black, Maggie, *Food and Cooking in 19th Century Britain: History and Recipes*, Historic Buildings and Monuments, 1985

Blair, Anna, *Tea at Miss Cranston's: A Century of Glasgow Memories, Recorded conversations with the Glasgow people of their memories of past times*, Shepheard-Walwyn, London, 1987

——, *Croft and Creel: a Century of Coastal Memories, Recorded conversations round the coast of past lifestyles*, Shepheard-Walwyn, London, 1987

Brears, Peter, *Food and Cooking in 17th Century Britain: History and Recipes*, Historic Buildings and Monuments, 1985

Brown, George Mackay, *An Orkney Tapestry*, Gollancz, 1969

——, *Fishermen with Ploughs*, The Hogarth Press, 1971

——, *Under Brinkie's Brae*, Gordon Wright, 1979

Brown, Hume, *Early Travellers in Scotland, 1295–1689*, first published 1891, facsimile by James Thin, 1978

Burnett, J B, *Plenty and Want*, Nelson, 1966

Burt, Edward, *Letters from the North of Scotland*, 5th edition, London, 1822

Cameron, David Kerr, *The Ballad and the Plough: A Portrait of the Life of the Old Scottish Farmtouns*, Futura, 1978

Carter, Ian, *Farm Life in North East Scotland: 1840–1914*, Donald, 1979

Chambers, Robert, *Domestic Annals of Scotland: From the Reformation to the Revolution*, 2 vols, Edinburgh, 1858; 3rd vol: *From the Revolution to the Rebellion of 1745*, 1861

——, *Traditions of Edinburgh*, Edinburgh, 1868

Cheape, Hugh and Sprott, Gavin, *Angus Country Life: A Companion to the Angus Folk Museum, Glamis*, The National Trust for Scotland, Edinburgh, 1980

Cheke, Val, *The Story of Cheesemaking in Britain*, Routledge and Kegan Paul, 1959

Cockburn, Henry Thomas: Lord Cockburn, *Circuit Journeys*, Edinburgh, 1842

——, *Memorials of His Time*, Edinburgh, 1874

Colville, James (ed.), *The Ochtertyre House Book: 1737–1739*, Scottish History Society, Edinburgh, 1907

Cooper, Derek, *The Road to the Isles: Travellers in the Hebrides 1770–1914*, Routledge and Kegan Paul, London, 1979

Cutting, C L, *Fish Saving: A History of Fish Processing from Ancient to Modern Times*, Hill, 1955

Davidson, Alan, *A Kipper with my Tea, A blend of curious and amusing information and reflections for everyone in the kitchen*, Macmillan, London, 1988

Davidson, Caroline, *A Woman's Work is Never Done*, Chatto and Windus, London, 1982

Driver, C, *The British at table: 1940–1980*, Chatto and Windus-Hogarth, 1983

Duff, David (ed.), *Queen Victoria's Highland Journals*, Webb and Bower, 1980

Durant, David, *Living in the Past: An insider's social history of Historic Houses*, Aurum, 1988 (chapter on provisioning and eating)

Faujas de Saint-Fond, B, *Travels in England, Scotland and the Hebrides, etc.*, London, 1799

Fenton, A, 'Sowens in Scotland', *Folk Life*, Vol. 12, 1974

——, *Scottish Country Life*, Edinburgh, 1976

——, *The Northern Isles, Orkney and Shetland*, Edinburgh, 1978

——, *The Hearth in Scotland*, National Museum of Antiquities, 1981

——, *The Scottish Ethnological Archive, Edinburgh*, National Museums of Scotland, 1988

Fergusson, Thomas, *Scottish Social Welfare 1864–1914*, Edinburgh, 1958

Field, Rachel, *Irons in the Fire*, Crowood, 1984

Firth, John, *Reminiscences of an Orkney Parish, together with old Orkney words, riddles, and proverbs*, Orkney Natural History Society, Stromness, 1974

Foulis, Sir John, *Foulis of Ravelston's Account book: 1671–1707*, Scottish History Society, 1894

Fullarton, Allan and Baird, Charles R, *Remarks on the Evils at Present Affecting the Highlands and Islands of Scotland*, 1838

Fyfe, J G, *Scottish Diaries and Memoirs*: Vol. 1, 1550–1746; Vol. 2, 1746–1843, Maclean, Stirling, 1928

Galt, John, *Annals of the Parish and The Ayrshire legatees*, Macmillan, London, 1895

Gauldie, Enid, *The Scottish Country Miller, 1700–1900*, John Donald, Edinburgh, 1981

Glasgow Herald, The, 'Housekeeping sixty years ago', Tuesday 29 June 1897

Graham, Henry G, *The Social Life of Scotland in the 18th Century*, 2 vols, London, 1899

Grant, Ann of Laggan, *Letters from the Mountains: concerning Highland Affairs*, 2nd edn., Scottish History Society, 1807

Grant, David 'Castlegreen', *Tatties an' Herreen*, Thurso, 1961

Grant, Elizabeth of Rothiemurchus, *Memoirs of a Highland Lady: 1797–1827* (edited by her neice, Lady Strachey, and first published in 1898). A vivid picture of domestic and public life in Edinburgh, the Highlands and London, new edition published by John Murray, 1972

Grant, I F, *Everyday Life on an Old Highland Farm*, Longmans Green, 1924

——, *Highland Folk Ways*, Routledge, 1961

Grant, J, *Old and New Edinburgh*, Edinburgh, 1779

Gray, Malcolm, *The Highland Economy 1750–1850*, Edinburgh, 1957

——, *The Fishing Industries of Scotland 1790–1914*, Oxford University Press for Aberdeen University, 1978

Griggs, Barbara, *The Food Factor: An Account of the Nutrition Revolution, and the history of the ploneering researchers and writers who suffered derision and hostility for their views on healthy eating*, Penguin, 1988

Haldane, A R B, *The Drove Roads of Scotland*, Edinburgh, 1952

——, *New Ways through the Glens*, Edinburgh, 1962

Hamilton, Elizabeth *The Cottages of Glenburnie*, 7th edn., Edinburgh, 1822

Harrison, Molly, *The Kitchen in History*, Osprey, 1972

Hartcup, Adeline, *Below Stairs in the Great Country Houses*, Sidgwick and Jackson, 1980

Hoey, Brian, *Invitation to the Palace: How Royalty Entertains*, Grafton, 1989

Hunter, James, *The Making of a Crofting Community*, Edinburgh, 1976

Jamieson, J H, 'The Edinburgh Street Traders and their Cries', *The Book of the Old Edinburgh Club*, Vol. II, Constable, 1909

Kay, Billy and Maclean, Cailean, *Knee Deep in Claret: A Celebration of Wine in Scotland*, Mainstream, Edinburgh, 1983

Kitchen, A H, *The Scotsman's Food*, Livingston, 1949

Leith Lives: a look at unemployment and making ends meet between the Wars - the history of Leith through oral reminiscences of people who lived and worked in Leith since the turn of the century, published by the Leith Local History Project, n.d.

Lochhead, Marion, *The Scots Household in the 18th Century*, Moray Press, 1948

Lockhart, G W, *The Scot and His Oats*, Luath Press, 1983

Lockhart, J G, *The life of Sir Walter Scott, Bart*, Edinburgh, 1871

Low Life in Victorian Times by a Medical Gentleman, Edinburgh, 1815 (reprinted by Paul Harris, n.d.)

McCance and Widdowson's The Composition of Foods, eds, Paul, A A and Southgate, D A T, HMSO revised edition, 1978

McCarrison, Sir Robert, *Nutrition and Health*, The McCarrison Society, London, 1982

MacClure, Victor, *Scotland's Inner Man*, Routledge, 1935

——, *Good Appetite, My Companion*, Odhams Press, 1955

Macculloch, John, *A Description of the Western Islands*, 1819

——, *The Highlands and Western Isles of Scotland*, 1824

Macdonald, Jessie, and Gordon, Anne, *Down to the Sea, An account of life in the fishing villages of Hilton, Balintore and Shandwick*, Northern Publishers, Aberdeen, n.d.

MacDougall, Hope, *Island of Kerrera: Mirror of History*, Oban, 1979

MacDougall, Jean, *Highland Postbag, the Correspondence of Four MacDougall Chiefs 1715-1865*, Shepheard-Walwyn, London, 1984

MacGibbon, David and Ross, Thomas, *Castellated and Domestic Architecture of Scotland, From 12th to 18th Century*, 5 vols, Edinburgh, 1887-92

Mackay, John, *A History of the Burgh of Cannongate*, Edinburgh, 1891

Mackenzie, Osgood Hanbury, *A Hundred Years in the Highlands*, Bles, 1972

Mackenzie, William, *A History of the Highland Clearances*, Inverness, 1883

Maclean, V, *A short-title catalogue of household and cookery books published in the English tongue 1710-1800*, Prospect, 1981

McNeill, F Marian, *The Scots Cellar: its Traditions and Lore*, Reprographia, Edinburgh, 1973

Marshall, Rosalind, *The Days of Duchess Anne: Life in the Household of the Duchess of Hamilton - 1656 to 1716*, Collins, Glasgow, 1973

Martin, Martin, *A Description of the Western Islands of Scotland etc. 1703*, Stirling, 1934

——, *A Voyage to St Kilda*, reprinted by James Thin, 1970

Marwick, H, *The Orkney Norm*, Oxford, 1929

——, *Orkney*, London, 1951

Mitchell, J O, *Burns - and His Times*, Glasgow, 1897 (chapter on Food and Drink)

Muir, Edwin, *Scottish Journey*, London, 1929

Oakley, Charles, *The Second City*, Blackie, 1967 (revised edn)

Ochtertyre, The Ochtertyre House Book, Scottish History Society, ed. James Colville, 1907

Orphir, James Omond, *Orkney Eighty Years Ago: with special reference to Evie*, Kirkwall Press, 1980

Orr, Sir John Boyd, *Food and the People*, The Pilot Press, London, 1943

Oxford Symposia on Food and Cookery:
   National and Regional Styles of Cookery, 1981
   Cookery: Science, Lore and Books, 1984, 1985
   Taste, 1987
Published by Prospect Books, 45 Lamont Road, London, SW10 OHU

Page, E B and Kingsford, P W, *The Master Chefs: A History of Haute Cuisine*, Arnold, London, 1971

Patten, M, *We'll eat again: a collection of recipes from the war years selected by M. Patten in association with the Imperial War Museum*, Hamlyn, 1985

Pennant, Thomas, *A Tour in Scotland, 1769*, Chester, 1771

Petits Propos Culinaires: Essays and Notes on Food, Cookery and Cookery Books, Prospect Books, back nos: 45 Lamont Road, London, SW10 OHU

Plant, Marjorie, *The Domestic Life of Scotland in the 18th Century*, Edinburgh University Press, 1952

Pococke, Richard, *Tours in Scotland, 1747, 1750, 1760*, Scottish History Society, Edinburgh, 1887

Ramsay, John, of Ochtertyre, *Scotland and Scotsmen of the 18th Century*, 2 vols, Edinburgh, 1888

Reid, John, *The Scots Gardener: the Gard'ners Kalander . . . for the Climate of Scotland*, Edinburgh, 1721

Robertson, George, *Rural Recollections*, Irvine, 1829

Rodgers, Murdoch, *Italiani in Scozia: the Story of the Scots Italians*, Odesey, 2nd collection, ed. Billy Kay, Edinburgh, 1982

Rogers, Charles, *Social Life in Scotland from Early to Recent Times*, Edinburgh, 1884–86

——, *Scotland, Social and Domestic*, London, 1869

Salaman, Redcliffe N, *The History and Social Influence of the Potato*, Cambridge University Press, revised edn, 1970

Scotland's Magazine:
   'A Hole in the Wa': the story of the Box Bed', February 1960;
   'A Gude pat o' Kail', December 1960;
   'The Mussel Gatherers' (good pictures), November 1961;
   'Seaweed', May 1962

Scots Magazine:
   'The Work of the Bakers', October 1971, March 1972;
   'Ice Cream Men', by Dorothy K Haynes, July 1970

Scott, M A, *Island Saga: The Story of North Ronaldsay*, Aberdeen, 1968

Scott-Moncrieff, W S Robert (ed.), *The Household Book of Lady Griselle Baillie (1692–1733)*, Scottish History Society, 1911

Scottish Field:
  'Friendship is a Clootie Dumpling', by Jennifer Green, July 1966
  'Sweetie Shops', December 1970
Smith, W J (ed.), *A History of Dundee* (first published, 1873), David Winter, Dundee, 1980
Smout, T C, *A history of the Scottish People 1560–1830*, Collins, Glasgow, 1972
——, *A century of The Scottish People 1830–1950*, Collins, Glasgow, 1986
  Both are classic works of social history
Sommerville, Thomas, *My Own Life and Times 1741–1814*, Edinburgh, 1861
Stead, Jennifer, *Food and Cooking in 18th Century Britain: History and Recipes*, Historic Buildings and Monuments, 1985
Steuart, John, *The Letter-Book of Baillie John Steuart of Inverness, 1715–1752*, Scottish History Society, Edinburgh, 1915
Steven, Maisie, *The Good Scots Diet*, Aberdeen University Press, 1985
Stevenson, R L, *Men and Books*, Chatto, 1900
Stromness: Late 19th Century Photographs, Stromness Museum, Orkney Natural History Society, 3rd impression, 1986
Stuart, Marie W, *Old Edinburgh Taverns*, Hale, 1952
Swann, Elsie, *Christopher North (John Wilson)*, London, 1934
Tannahill, Reay, *Food in History*, Paladin, St Albans, 1975
Thompson, Francis, *Harris and Lewis: a factual study which explores the topography, the people, the economy, the history and the problems*, Newton Abbot, 1968
——, *The Crofting Years*, Luath Press, Barr, 1984
Thomson, Gordon, *The Other Orkney Book*, Edinburgh, 1980
Topham, Edward (ed.), *Letters from Edinburgh, written in the years 1774 and 1775*, London, 1776
Tulloch, Peter A, *A Window on North Ronaldsay*, Kirkwall Press, 1974
Warrack, J, *Domestic Life in Scotland 1488–1688 (furniture and plenishings)*, London, 1920
Wilson, C Anne, *Food and Drink in Britain*, Constable, 1973
Wilson, John, *Noctes Ambrosianae*, 4 vols, Blackwood 1855
Wilson, Professor Daniel, *Memorials of Edinburgh in Olden Times*, Edinburgh, 1886
Wordsworth, Dorothy, *A Tour in Scotland in 1803*, Edinburgh, 1874
Wright, Lawrence, *Home Fires Burning: The History of Domestic Heating and Cooking*, Routledge and Kegan Paul, 1964
Yarwood, Dorren, *The British Kitchen*, Batsford, 1981
Young, Douglas, *Edinburgh in the Age of Walter Scott*, Oklahoma, 1965
Youngson, A J, *Beyond the Highland Line, Three Journals of Travel in 18th Century Scotland*, Collins, 1974

Traditional Scottish Food Suppliers

The aim of this list is to provide information about some producers and distributors whom I have found striving for high standards of Scottish products – it is not definitive.

In any such list of producers and suppliers, given the variables involved in terms of companies being taken over or going bankrupt, etc., there is always the constant need to update. While the list was as accurate as possible at time of going to press, you may find some errors. It would be extremely useful to hear of good suppliers which I have missed and you think ought to be included; also suppliers which I have listed, and who, in your opinion, are not satisfactory for whatever reason. I would be pleased to hear from you c/o John Murray, 50 Albemarle Street, London WlX 4BD.

Those in the list show the rich variety to be found in Scottish produce. A distinctly Scottish variety which, looking to the future, will come under increasing commercial challenge as more and more continental foods appear on supermarket shelves in the movement towards harmonization in Europe in the 1990s. Another threat is competition from multinational food companies, of whatever nationality, who find it cheapest and simplest to standardize food throughout the country.

If the regional diversity in traditional foods is to be maintained, small local producers, bakers, butchers and specialist food shops who preserve the differences in our food supplies must have consumer loyalty. Only with this commitment will standards be maintained and improved. This raises the question of quality, which many maintain has greatly deteriorated since the food industry in Britain adopted the 1960s super-market philosophy of 'make it cheap and pile it high'. In the last twenty years, Britain has lost more small independent food shops than any other country in Europe where there has been less enthusiasm for the giant stores and greater local loyalty.

While some argue that our food supplies are better now than they ever were, there are just as many others who claim the opposite. Whatever the truth, there can be no doubt that the British consumer's demand for cheap food since the end of the Second World War has had a number of significant effects on quality.

Bread is probably as good an example as any. Two-thirds of the production was taken out of traditional bakeries as the large milling companies bought out the family high street bakeries in the sixties and seventies. The result is that most bread in Britain is now no longer produced by traditional slow-fermented methods to give a matured flavour, but by fast modern bread plants using cheap flour and such a speedy process, to keep the cost down, that bread has lost both its good flavour and keeping quality. And the effect on sales? Consumption has fallen in Britain from 55 ounces (1.5 kg) a week per person in 1955 to 29 ounces (800 g) in 1989 [National Food Survey (MAFF)].

There are many other basic items which have suffered the same fate. As with regional variation, the question of quality should not be left to the producers to decide. The point of sale is where the power lies: either we compacently accept the mediocre, the poor quality, the boringly standardized, or we use that power to take a stand for better quality.

CONTENTS

1 Meat, game and poultry

Alexander, Robert
8 Cromdale Road, Port Glasgow PA14 6LT
(0475) 705833
Traditional butcher.
Catering and wholesale.
Contact: Drew McKenzie

Ardgay Game
South Bonar Industrial Estate, Bonar
Bridge, Sutherland
(086) 32 247
Highlands
Wild venison, saddles, haunches and
goulash in Cyrovac packs for catering.
Oven-ready game products include rabbit,
hare, pheasant, grouse, wild duck and a
special game pie mix.
Retail and export; refrigerated distribution
throughout the UK. Mail order.
Contact: Leslie Waugh

Argyll Quail
Eilean Beag, South Ledaig, Connel, by
Oban, Argyll PA37 1RT
(0631 71) 597
Highlands
Fresh oven-ready quail, fresh and smoked
eggs, smoked quail in vacuum packs, quail
liver pâté.
Mail order.
Contact: Margo McIntyre

Bain, John
Duthie Road, Tarves, Ellon, Aberdeenshire
(065) 15 675
Northeast
Beef, lamb and pork. Wild venison, roe and
red deer, and game of all kinds.
Wholesale, retail and export.
Mail order in Scotland.
Contact: John Bain

Band's of Perth
135 Glover Street, Perth, Perthshire PH2
OJB
(0738) 24222
Central
Pheasant, partridge, grouse, venison, rabbit
and wild duck. Also fish.
Salmon by mail order.
Contact: R H Critchell

Bell, John A Ltd
Butchers, Ballygrant, Isle of Islay, Argyll
PA45 7QL
(049 684) 656
Inner Hebrides
Islay beef and lamb (all animals naturally
reared and butchered on the island).
Retail, wholesale and catering.
Contact: Donald Bell

Braehead Foods
Craufurdland Castle, Kilmarnock, Ayrshire
KA3 6BS
(05606) 402
Southwest
Gressingham duck and guinea fowl,
venison, smoked duck, guinea fowl, quail,
pigeon, pheasant.

Cockburn, James
26 Market Street, Galashiels
(0896) 2120
Borders
Traditional butcher.

Craigrossie Smoke House
Hall Farm, Auchterarder, Perthshire PH3
1HD
(0764) 62596
Central
Smoked duck, smoked wild vension
haunch.
Smoked eel, smoked wild Tay salmon,
smoked Orkney and Shetland farmed
salmon.
Mail order, wholesale.
Contact: Mr Lockett

Crawford Farm Enterprises Ltd
Cluanie, By Beauly, Inverness IV4 7AE
(0463) 782534
Highlands
Farmed venison, lamb and beef, sausages
and puddings. Sometimes free range eggs,
pork, local beef and lamb. Restaurant
adjoining produce shop.
Contact: Archie Crawford

Crombie's Quality Meats
97–101 Broughton Street, Edinburgh EH1
3RZ
(031) 556 7643
Traditional butcher. Beef, lamb, pork, pies,
puddings and haggis (own recipe).
Delicatessen foods in adjacent shop,
Scottish cheeses.
Haggis by mail order.
Contact: Sandy Crombie

Ewing's
83 Main Street, Baillieston, Glasgow G69
6AD
(041) 773 0724
Traditional butcher. Beef, lamb, pork,
Scottish pies, sausages and cooked meats.
Contact: J Ewing

Fassock Game Farm
Dalry House, Fassock, Kiltarlity, Inverness-
shire 1V4 7HT
(0463) 74559
Highlands
Quail (fresh, frozen and smoked), eggs
(fresh pickled or in brine).
Contact: Terry Hall

Fleming, W
27 West Port, Arbroath
(0241) 73252
East
Traditional butcher. Home-made beefsteak
pies.
Contact: Bill Fleming

Forsyth, W T S & Sons
21–25 Eastgate, Peebles EH45 8AD
(0721) 20833
Borders
Traditional butcher. Beef (hung for three
weeks), pies and bridies, haggis.
Contact: Malcolm Forsyth

Fraser, Duncan Ltd
17 Queensgate, Inverness IVI IDF
(0463) 232744
Highlands
Game Dealer. Wild venison deer, roe and
sika. Fresh and smoked fish, wild smoked
salmon.
Retail, wholesale and mail order.
Contact: Duncan Fraser

Fyne Game of Inveraray
Unit 3 Upper Riochan, Inveraray, Argyll
PA32 8UR
(0499) 2443/2055
Highlands
Venison, red, roe and sika deer, pheasant,
grouse, duck, partridge, hare and rabbit.
Contact: Gordon Slaughter

Gillespie, Andrew
1623/1634 Great Western Road, Glasgow
(041) 959 2015
Traditional butcher. Aberdeen Angus beef,
own steak pies, haggis, black pudding,
potted hough, cooked meats.
Contact: Charles Hopes

Grants of Dornoch Ltd
Shore Road, Dornoch, Sutherland IV25
3LS
(0862) 810327, mail order tel. (0862) 810000
Highlands
Scotch beef, lamb and pork. Haggis and
black pudding.
Wholesale, catering and mail order.
Contact: D F Grant

Greenway Organic Farms
Freepost, Edinburgh EHI OAQ
(031) 557 8111
Organic Scotch beef and lamb, French
black leg chicken, guinea fowl, duck.
Mail order and home deliveries.
Contact: Stewart McKenna

Highland Glen Producers
1 Crieff Road, Aberfeldy, Perthshire PH15
2BJ
(0887) 20666
Central
Lamb and mutton.
Contact: Mark Lumsden

Highland Venison Marketing Ltd
Woodlands Industrial Estate, Grantown on
Spey, Morayshire
(0479) 2255
Highlands
Wild venison, red and roe deer.
Home and export.
Contact: Kerry Keysell

J Kerr Little, Master Butcher
58–60 High Street, Dumfries DG1 2BS
(0387) 53818
Southwest
Beef (hung for min. 10 days), lamb, pork,
bacon, hams, sausages and puddings.
Contact: J Kerr Little

James McIntyre
74 Montague Street, Rothsay, Isle of Bute
PA20 OHL
(0700) 3672
Strathclyde
Beef, pork, lamb, bacon, and ham. Game.
Contact: James McIntyre

John M Munro Ltd
12 High Street, Conon Bridge, Dingwall,
Ross and Cromarty
(0349) 61398
Highland
Beef, lamb and pork. Fresh and smoked
salmon.

Kennedy of Scone
31 Perth Road, Scone, PH2 6JJ
(0738) 51752
East
Prime Scotch beef, haggis, puddings,
smoked venison pâté.
Contact: Dorothy Kennedy

MacBeth's
20 High Street, Forres, Moray 1V36 ODB
(0309) 72254
Highlands
Native beef breeds only, including West
Highland beef. Game in season.
Retail, wholesale and catering.
Contact: Michael and Susan Gibson

McIntosh, J
The Square, Stonehaven, Grampian
(0569) 62835
Northeast
Traditional butcher.

Macleans of Aultbea
Birchburn, Aultbea, Ross-shire IV22 2HZ
(044 582) 357
Highlands
Traditional butcher. Black and white
puddings, haggis and fruit puddings from
traditional Highland recipes.
Contact: John Rippin

Macsweens of Edinburgh
130 Bruntsfield Place, Edinburgh, EH10
4ES
(031) 229 1216

Traditional butcher. Pies, puddings, haggis, vegetarian haggis, Shetland lamb. Yellow turnip and potatoes.
Mail order.
Contact: John Macsween

Meikle Knox Farm Shop
Meikle Knox, Castle Douglas, Dumfriesshire DG7Y INS
(0556) 2736
Southwest
Sausages and meat products, haslet.
Contact: C Irving

Mitchell Game Ltd
338 Clepinton Road, Dundee; 2 Woodside Rd, Letham, Forfar
(0382) 827088; (030) 781 220
East
Game from Angus Glens and Highlands: venison, grouse, pheasant, rabbit.
Contact: Gordon Mitchell

Moor of Rannoch Game Butchery
Rannoch Station, Perthshire PH17 2QA
(08823) 238
Highlands
Wild venison from local estates, butchering and processing. Suppliers of smoked and fresh salmon, prawns, Loch Fyne kippers, smoked pheasant, grouse and venison. Rabbits and hares.
Mail order.
Contact: Phillip Turner

Organic Meat and Products (Scotland)
Endrigg, Jamesfield, Newburgh, Fife KY14 6EW
(073) 88598
East
Organic beef, lamb and pork. Organic vegetables (experimental organic farming research funded by SDA, EC and Safeway Foods).
Contact: Ian Miller

Orkney Foods
Waird, Marwick, Orkney KW17 2HY
(085672) 223
Orkney
Islands pâtés: farmhouse, country, smoked mackerel, crab.
Contact: Mrs A E Morrison

Orkney Meat Ltd
Haston Industrial Estate, Kirkwall, Orkney
(0856) 4326
Northern Isles beef and lamb, boned-out, vacuum-packed and carcasses.
Contact: E Balfour

Palmer, David
3 High Street, Jedburgh TD8 6AQ
(0835) 63276
Borders
Traditional butcher. Award-winning haggis, puddings, pies and bridies.
Contact: David Palmer

Pitlochry Game Service Ltd
Ferry Road, Pitlochry, Perthshire PH16 5DD
(0796) 3254
Central
Venison, pheasant, grouse and other game. Duck. Salmon, trout and lobster.
'No customer order too big or too small, be it one pigeon for the housewife or 20 tons of venison for export.'
Contact: Martin Shore

Proudfoot, Ian
6 Learmonth Avenue, Edinburgh; 136 Comiston Road, Edinburgh; IA/3 Drumbrae Avenue, Edinburgh
(031) 315 2056; (031) 447 1307; (031) 339 1962
Traditional butcher. All beef hung in traditional Scottish manner for 14 days. Pies, puddings, haggis, Ramsay's bacon. Game in season. Home deliveries.
Contact: Alistair Proudfoot

Ramsay of Carluke
Wellrigs Factory, 22 Mount Stewart, Lanarkshire ML8 5ED
(0555) 72277
Glasgow
Pork (fresh, butchered on premises), lamb and beef. Ayrshire Bacon (traditional cure), hams.
Contact: John Ramsay

Rannoch Smokery
Kinloch Rannoch, by Pitlochry, Perthshire PH16 5QD
(08822) 344
Central
Traditional smoked venison, game pâtés and pastes.
Mail order.
Contact: Leo Barclay

Reawick (Shetland) Lamb Marketing Co Ltd
Skeld, Reawick, Shetland ZE2 9NJ
(059586) 261
Shetland lamb.
Contact: W H Barcas

Reid, James Ltd
Rowanbank, 140 Coupar Angus Road, Birkhill, Dundee DD2 5PG
(0382) 580251
East
Traditional butcher. Puddings and pies, haggis.
Contact: James Reid

Robertson, Allan
234 Brook Street, Broughty Ferry; 34 Union Street, Dundee
(0382) 73927; (0382) 21362
East
Traditional butcher.

Rothiemurchus Estate
Dell of Rothiemurchus, by Aviemore,
Inverness-shire
(0479) 810703
Highlands
Red deer, farmed venison. Beef. Smoked
salmon, fresh and smoked trout. Herb
plants available at shop.
Contact: Sibyl Ballantine

Rutherford Guinea-Fowl
Rutherford Lodge, Kelso TD5 8NW
(0835) 23757
Borders
Guinea fowl, Gressingham ducks. Belted
Galloway beef.
Contact: Johnny Rutherford

Scone Palace Produce Shop
Perth, Perthshire, Tayside PH2 6BD
(0738) 52300
Central
Estate game. Smoked Tay salmon. Home-
made bread, fruit loaves, shortbread,
chutney and marmalade.

Shearer
1 Sir John's Square, Thurso
(0847) 62781
Highlands
Traditional butcher. Black and white
puddings and haggis.

Sheridan, Michael
11 Bridge Street, Ballater, Aberdeenshire
AB3 5QP
(03397) 55218
Northeast
Traditional butcher.
Catering and wholesale.
Contact: Michael Sheridan

Smith & Co
61 Commercial Street, Lerwick, Shetland
(0595) 3306
Traditional butcher, cures reestit (salted and
smoked) mutton, available all year.
Contact: Jim Grunberg

Strachan, Archibald
16 Keptie Street, Arbroath DD11 1RG
(0241) 73345
East
Haggis, potted hough, jellied tripe,
additive-free sausages, pies and bridies.
Mail order.
Contact: David Strachan

Strathardle Natural Farm Produce
Crowhill, Bridge of Cally, Blairgowrie,
Perthshire PH10 7PX
025 086 316
Central
Organic lamb and goat. Free-range corn-fed
chicken, free-range eggs. Dairy products.

Strathmore Larder
Memmus, Angus
(03566) 238
East
Free-range poultry and pigs, eggs.
Contact: Graham Malcolm

Strathmore Meat, Ltd
Carseview Road, Forfar, Angus DD8 3NG
(0307) 62333
East
Pies and puddings, Scotch pies, black
puddings.
Contact: Colin Muir

Summer Isles Foods
The Smokehouse, Achiltibuie, Ullapool,
Ross-shire
(085482) 353
Highlands
Smoked meats and poultry, lamb, venison
and sausages. Oak smoked fish, salmon,
trout and eel.
All available in shop and by mail order.
Contact: Keith Dunbar

Taygame Limited
Units 5/6 Whitefriars Street, Perth PH1
1PP
(0738) 36357
Central
Hare, pheasant, pigeon, rabbit, venison,
snipe, woodcock and partridge. Duck,
turkey and geese. Salmon.
Contact: Ian Thomson

Teviot Game Fare Smokery
Kirkbank House, Kelso TD5 8LE
(08355) 253
Borders
Traditionally smoked Borders game. Tweed
and Teviot eels lightly brined with fresh
herbs.
Mail order.
Contact: Denis Wilson

Urquhart & Son
Main Street, Lairg, Sutherland
(0549) 2475
Highlands
Traditional butcher. Pies and black
puddings, haggis.
Contact: I E MacDonald

Watson
39 High Street, Paisley
(041) 889 2691
Glasgow
Traditional butcher.
Contact: Mr Watson

Wilson, Charles – Totally Organic Meat
416 Morningside Road, Edinburgh
(031) 452 9110
Organic meat.

2 Fish

Abrahams, A
  The Strand, Colonsay, Argyll PA61
  7TR
  (09512) 365
  Inner Hebrides
  Farmed oysters and mussels, smoked
  oysters and mussels. Heather honey (40
  hives). Wholesale.
  Contact: A Abrahams
Achnamara Shellfish
  Knapdale Sea Farm, by Lochgilphead
  (054 685) 288
  Highlands
  Oyster hatchery. Farmed oysters.
  Contact: Allan Berry
Allan and Dey Ltd
  8 Raik Road, Aberdeen AB9 8AG
  (0224) 581000
  Northeast
  Fresh and smoked salmon (wild and
  farmed), smoked mackerel, Finnan
  haddock, kippers. Wholesale, export and
  mail order.
  Contact: C Copping
Armstrong, George
  80 Raeburn Place, Stockbridge, Edinburgh
  EH4 1HH
  (031) 315 2033
  Wide range of fresh fish including
  sometimes turbot, brill, Dover sole, tuna,
  grey mullet, John Dory. Own-smoked
  salmon, undyed haddock, and mackerel
  and cod's roe in season. Shellfish. Free-
  range eggs.
  Contact: Ian Breslin
Benesther Shellfish
  Old Schoolhouse, Deerness, Orkney KW17
  2QH
  (0856) 74267
  Smoked fish, farmed shellfish.
  Contact: Dennis Gowland
Beveridge, Alan
  306 Byres Road, Glasgow G12
  (041) 357 2766
  Arbroath smokies, Orkney marinated
  herring, Loch Fyne kippers, Finnan
  haddock, Shetland salt herring, West Coast
  shellfish. Wide range of fresh fish including
  sometimes shark and turbot. Other
  branches in Glasgow.
  Contact: Tom Bell
Burgon (Eyemouth) Ltd
  Harbour Road, Eyemouth, Berwickshire
  (08907) 50272
  Borders
  Fish, shellfish, winkles, lobster, crab.
  Wholesale and export.
  Contact: Graham Sinclair

Colfin Smokehouse
  Lochan, Portpatrick, Wigtownshire
  (0776) 82622
  Southwest
  Smoked products, wild Atlantic salmon,
  smoked Galloway mussels and smoked
  salmon, kipper, and trout pâté.
  Mail order.
  Contact: Allan Logan
Crannog Ltd
  5B1 Blar Mhor, Fort William, Inverness-
  shire PH33 7NG
  (0397) 3919
  Highlands
  Fresh fish, frozen and cooked Norway
  lobster, crab and lobster, smoked salmon,
  trout and mussels.
  Contact: Finlay D Finlayson
Cromack Ltd
  Bath Street, Fraserburgh, Aberdeenshire
  AB4 4DX
  (0346) 27850
  Northeast
  Smoked mackerel, marinated herring,
  undyed kippers, undyed smoked Aberdeen
  fillet.
  Contact: Peter Duthie
Cromarty Mussels
  George Street, Cromarty, Ross-shire
  (03817) 314
  Highlands
  Farmed mussels.
  Wholesale.
  Contact: Robert Davie
Daniels Sweet Herring Ltd
  Dell of Inches, Inverness, IVI 2BG
  (0463) 225349
  Highlands
  Marinated herring.
  Contact: Rosemary Griffin
Fascadale Fisheries
  Fascadale, Achateny, Acharacle, Argyll
  PH36 4LG
  (097) 23243
  Highlands
  Fresh and smoked wild Atlantic salmon.
  Mail order.
  Contact: Mark James
Fastnetfish (Highlands) Ltd
  Unit 2, Blar Mhor Industrial Estate, Fort
  William, Inverness-shire
  (0397) 5940
  Highlands
  Fresh Norway lobster dispatched daily for
  UK and export, wild and farmed salmon,
  prime Scottish fish.
  Contact: N Tudor
Fish Shop, The
  Victoria Street, Stromness, Orkney
  (0856) 850840

Fresh and smoked fish, scallops, crabs, salted ling and cod. Smoked Orkney farmhouse cheese.
Mail order.
Contact: Raymie Manson

Framgord Ltd
O I L Base, Gremista, Lerwick, Shetland ZE1 ORY
(0595) 4262
Fresh salmon, salmon trout, scallops, whitefish, shark, Norway lobster.
Home and export.
Contact: Frank Odie

Fynecraft Seafoods
Wood Cottage, Otter Ferry, Argyll, PA21 2DH
(070) 082 237
Highlands
Traditionally cured (with no artificial colouring or preservatives) smoked fish, salmon, kippers, mackerel and eels.
Suppliers of salmon, turbot, Dover sole, lobsters, prawns, scallops, crabs, also gravadlax.
Contact: M Buchanan

Fynefish Products
Churchill, Tarbert, Argyll PA29 6ST
(08802) 439
Highlands
Quality Scottish smoked salmon and Loch Fyne kippers, undyed.
Contact: Duncan Blair

Gairloch Sea Foods Ltd
The Pier, Gairloch, Ross-shire 1V1 2BQ
(0445) 2244
Highlands
Langoustines, scallops, crabs, white fish.
Export.
Contact: William Brown

Ghillie and Glen Ltd
Unit 26, Kirkhill Industrial Estate, Dyce, Aberdeen AB9 7AS
(0224) 771701
Northeast
Smoked salmon and other smoked products.
Mail order.
Contact: Richard Berry

Great Bernera Ltd
The Pier, Kirkbost, Great Bernera, Isle of Lewis PA86 9LX
(0752) 847114
Outer Hebrides
Crab and crab products, prawns and mussels.
Home and export.
Contact: M K Alway

Hebridean Shellfish Growers (Lewis and Harris) Ltd
42 Balallan, Isle of Lewis PA86 9PT
(0851) 83 271
Outer Hebrides
Rope-cultured mussels grown in the sea lochs of the Outer Hebrides.
Contact: Jerry Luty

Hebrides Harvest Ltd
Scott Road, Tarbert, Isle of Harris PA85 3BG
(0859) 2323
Outer Hebrides
Salmon, farmed and wild, fresh and smoked.
Contact: Jerry Luty

Highland Aquaculture Ltd
Scalpay House, Broadford, Isle of Skye IV49 9AB
(04712) 539
Inner Hebrides
Fresh farmed scallops from the Isle of Scalpay.
Contact: B T Fullerton

Inverawe Smokehouses
Taynuilt, Argyll
(08662) 446
Highlands
Smoked Scottish eels, cod roe, kippers, and Loch Etive trout. Smoked venison, Argyll ham, mutton and beef. Pâtés.
Mail order.
Contact: R G Campbell-Preston

Inverness Salmon Co Ltd
8 Riverside Field, Dingwall, Inverness IV15 9TN
(0349) 61565
Highlands
Oak and peat smoked salmon, gravadlax. Mustard and dill sauce.
Mail order.
Contact: Roy Stevens

Islay Seafoods Ltd
Glenegedale, Port Ellen, Isle of Islay, Argyll PA42 7AS
(0496) 2300
Inner Hebrides
King scallops.
Contact: B Fullerton

Isle of Skye Oysters
9 Harport Cottages, Carbost, Isle of Skye IV47 8SS
(047 842) 313
Inner Hebrides
Farmed oysters and Manila clams.
Contact: Kenny Bain

John Steer
The Lobster Pond, Ferry Road, Stromness, Orkney SW16 3AE
(0856) 850 465
Live lobsters, crabs, oysters and scallops.
Contact: John Steer

Johnston, Joseph & Sons
3 America Street, Montrose DD10 8DR
(0674) 72666
East
Salmon fishers. Wild salmon and sea trout
from Highlands and Islands. Full range of
traditionally smoked products. Game, fresh
and oven ready.
Mail order.
Contact: Jonathon Stansfeld

Jolly, William
Haston Industrial Estate, Scott's Road,
Kirkwall, Orkney
(0856) 2417
Scallops, crabs, fresh and smoked haddock
fillets, smoked salmon, salt herring.
Retail, wholesale and mail order.
Contact: Billy Jolly

Keracher, Andrew
106 Market Street, St Andrews, Fife; 168
South Street, Perth; 20 Lady Wynd, Cupar,
Fife
(0334) 72541; (0738) 38454; (0334) 52668
Extensive range of fresh fish, own smoked
wild and farmed salmon, dyed and undyed
kippers, West Coast shellfish. Game in
season.
Smoked fish by mail order.

Knapdale Sea Farms
PO Box 1 Lochgilphead, Argyll
(054685) 288
Highlands
Pacific oysters, native oysters, hard shell
clams (Palourdes), abalone. Specialists in
high quality tray-grown shellfish.
Contact: A W Berry, D Chirnside

Lang-Geo Oysters
Lang-Geo, Finstown, Orkney KW17 2EL
(0856) 76544
Fresh oysters, princess scallops, king
scallops, mussels and velvet and brown
crabs.
Wholesale.
Contact: Dave Bichan

Lawrie & Sons (Mallaig) Ltd
8 Industrial Estate, Mallaig, Inverness-shire
PH41 4QD
(0687) 2102
Highlands
Mallaig kippers (undyed), smoked mackerel
(undyed), traditionally cured salmon, wild
and farmed, salt herring, salt mackerel
fillets, Finnan haddock.
Mail order.
Contact: G E Lawrie

Loch Fyne Oysters Ltd
Ardkinglas, Cairndow, Argyll PA36 8BH
(04996) 264
Highlands
Wild Atlantic and farmed salmon, fresh
and smoked, gravadlax, smoked mussels,
oysters, Norway lobster, lobster, smoked
trout, marinated herring, kippers, scallops.
Mail order.
Contact: Andrew Lane, Mark Sands

Loch Hourn Mussel Growers
Arnisdale, Kyle, Ross-shire IV40 8JJ
(059982) 358
Highlands
Rope-grown mussels. Wholesale throughout
the UK.
Contact: Rick Rohde

Lochetive Mussels
Tigh Na Speir, Connel, Argyll PA37 1PH
(063171) 505
Highlands
Fresh mussels in one-stone bags.
Contact: Janet Church

Macdonalds Smoked Produce
Glenuig, Lochailort, Inverness-shire PH38
4NG
(06877) 266
Highlands
Smoked salmon, trout, mussels, queen
scallops and oysters. Smoked cream cheese,
quail eggs and exotic fish.
Contact: Simon R Macdonald

MacKechnie, James
350 Scotland Street, Glasgow G5
(041) 429 1609
Fresh fish, Arbroath smokies, Finnan
haddock, kippers, own-smoked salmon and
mackerel (any fish smoked to order).
Speciality: whole filleted lemon sole stuffed
with fresh salmon steak, squat lobster tails
and prawns. Game.
Contact: Peter MacKechnie

Mermaid Fish Supplies
Clachan, Locheport, North Uist, Outer
Hebrides
(08764) 209
Outer Hebrides
Peat smoked salmon from the Outer
Hebrides (whole sides ready sliced, unsliced
or in packs), undyed peat smoked cod,
haddock and whiting.
Small orders welcome, and mail order.
Contact: George Jackson

Mill Smoke House
Cessintully Mill, Thornhill, Stirling FK8
3QE
(0786) 85 348
Central
Smoked trout, salmon, Loch Fyne kippers.
Smoked chicken.
Mail order.
Contact: Mr Routledge

Monach Seafoods Ltd
Gramisdale, Benbecula, Western Isles PA88
5LZ
(0870) 2304
Outer Hebrides

Norway lobster, scallops, crabs, lobster, winkles, mussels and salmon.
Contact: W Macdonald

Morayfish (Portree) Ltd
The Pier, Portree, Isle of Skye IV51 9DE
(0478) 2414
Highlands
Fresh and frozen king scallops, queen scallops, shell-on Norway lobster tails, peeled Norway lobster, whole Norway lobster, squid.
Contact: Catriona Matheson

Muckairn Mussels
West Cottage, Achnacloich, Connel, Argyll PA37 1PR
(0631) 71653
Highlands
Rope-cultured mussels.
Contact: Walter Speirs

Mull Shellfish Ltd
Dunan, Ardtun, Bunessan, Isle of Mull, Argyll PA67 6DH
(06817) 295
Innner Hebrides
Mussels, live and smoked. Mail order, wholesale and retail.
Contact: Alice McKay

Murray McBay
Lobster Merchants, Johnshaven, Montrose DD10 0EZ
(0561) 62207
Northeast
Lobsters, local shellfish, scallops and prawns.

Neil, S L
80/128 Strathmore Road, Glasgow G22 7TH
(041) 336 6411
Smoked salmon, wild and farmed, smoked mackerel, Finnan haddock, Arbroath smokies, kippers. Wholesale, export and mail order.
Contact: Hamish Neil

Old House Smoked Salmon
Old House, Kilpheder, South Uist, Outer Hebrides PA81 5TB
(0878) 272
Outer Hebrides
Peat smoked salmon.
Mail order.
Contact: Ian Forrester

Orkney Fish Farms (Herring) Ltd
Cairston Road, Stromness, Orkney KW16 3JS
(0856) 850514
Herring marinated to traditional Danish recipes in five flavours: sour, plain, dill, Madeira and sherry.
Contact: Kenneth Sutherland

Orkney Fishermen's Society Ltd
26 Alfred Street, Stromness, Orkney KW16 3DF
(0856) 850 375
Live lobster, processed crab.
Contact: J Malloch

Paterson, William & Son
Salmon Fisheries, The Anchorage, Hilton, Fearn, Ross-shire
(086 283) 2277
Highlands
Fresh salmon from Moray and Dornoch Firths.
Contact: P W J Paterson

R & M George
Sunart Sea Farm, Salen, Acharacle, Argyll PH36 4JN
(096785) 332
Highlands
All Scottish species of crustacea and molluscs (except prawns), live, fresh and frozen.
Contact: Rodney George

Race, Andy (Fish Merchants)
15 Industrial Estate, Mallaig, Inverness-shire PH41 4PX
(0687) 2626
Highlands
Salmon, trout, fresh fillets of white fish, whole fish, smoked cod and haddock, shellfish.
Contact: A Race

Ritchie's of Rothsay
37 Watergate, Rothsay, Isle of Bute
(0700) 3012
Strathclyde
Loch Fyne kippers, smoked wild salmon.
Mail order.
Contact: Neil Ritchie

Rousay Processors Ltd
Trumland Pier, Rousay, Orkney KW17 2PU
(085682) 216
Own-smoked salmon and mackerel, fresh and frozen crab (white and brown meat, hand picked), scallops and lobster, live oysters.
Contact: Pier Lees

Scotimpex Ltd
The Industrial Estate, Strathpeffer Road, Dingwall, Ross-shire
(0349) 64198
Highlands
Lobsters, king and queen scallops, prawns and crabs, wild and farmed salmon.
Chanterelle mushrooms in season.
Contact: G M Leslie

Scotts Fish Shop
3 Bridge Street, Kirkwall, Orkney
(0856) 3170

Traditional fishmonger. Farmed and wild salmon, fresh and smoked, salted ling, haddock. Orkney cheese and butter (in season).
Mail order.
Contact: Helen Watson

Seacroft Oysters (Shellfish Farms)
Baravalla, Tarbert, Argyll PA29 6YD
(08802) 583/342
Highlands
Pacific and native oysters, other shellfish. Stonefield Blackface lamb and venison (in season).
Contact: Neil Duncan

Seafish Industry Authority
Marine Farming Unit, Ardtoe, Acharacle, Argyll PH36 4LD
(096) 785666
Highlands
Shellfish, princess scallops.
Contact: Jeremy Paul

Shetland Norse Preserving Company
Mid Yell, Shetland ZE2 9BN
(0957) 2112
Shetland
Crabs, scallops, queens, and crab claws.
Contact: A Alfredsson

Shetland Seafoods Ltd
North Road, Lerwick, Shetland ZE1 0PQ
(0595) 3292
Fresh shellfish and white fish processors.
Contact: Campbell Williamson

Shetland Smokehouse
Skeld, Shetland ZE2 9NS
(059586) 251
Range of smoked and marinated produce including kippers, smoked mackerel, smoked haddock (no artificial additives).
Contact: David Hammond

Shin Game Dealers
3 Terryside, Shinness, Lairg, Sutherland 1V27 4DL
(0549) 2300/2275
Highlands
Live lobsters and brown crab, prawns, wild and farmed salmon, fresh and smoked. Wild venison (whole carcasses, haunches, saddles, diced).
Fresh and frozen to home market, catering and retail trade, mail order.
Contact: Douglas Macleay

Smoked Salmon of Perth
Springwells, Dunkeld, Perthshire PH8 OBA
(035 02) 639
Central
Smoked wild salmon.
Mail order.

Spey Valley Smokehouse
Cromdale, Grantown-on-Spey, Morayshire PH26 3LN
(0479) 3078
Highlands
Smoked wild and farmed salmon. Smoked game.
Mail order.
Contact: Mr Coulson

Spink, R R & Sons
35 Seagate, Arbroath, Angus
(0241) 72023
East
Arbroath smokies.
Mail order.
Contact: R Spink, Jr

Strom Dearg Fish Ltd
Suilisgeir, Lochmaddy, North Uist PA82 5AE
(08763) 253
Outer Hebrides
Raft-grown mussels, farmed salmon.
Contact: Donald MacLeod

Teacuis Mariculture
Claggan, by Lochaline, Morvern, Argyll PA34 5XB
(096784) 281
Highlands
Mussels, scallops and oysters.
Contact: Matthew Wilson

Watmaugh, Ken
Thistle Street, Aberdeen
(0224) 640321
Northeast
Traditional fishmonger.
Contact: Ken Watmaugh

Westend Shellfish Ltd
Glenborrodale, Acharacle, Argyll PH36 4JP
(097) 24 235
Highlands
Princess scallops, fresh, frozen and smoked.
Contact: A C Bowker

3 Fruit and vegetables

Acheson, C A and D B M
Easter Ballindean Farm, Inchture, Perthshire PH14 9QS
(0828) 86256
East
Raspberries, tayberries, strawberries, brambles, blackcurrants.
Retail and wholesale.
Contact: C A Acheson

Ballingall Farm
Leslie, Fife KY6 3HD
(0592) 742963
East

Strawberries (Cambridge Favourite, Hapil, Saladin, Silver Jubilee), raspberries (Malling Jewel, Glen Clova, Glen Moy). Pick-your-own farm. Farm shop selling ready-picked sprouts, broccoli, cauliflower, potatoes, swedes, lettuce.
Contact: Robert Watson

Balmachie Farm
Carnoustie, Angus
(0241) 53260
East
Raspberries, strawberries, blackcurrants and tayberries.
Pick-your-own and ready-picked.
Farm shop selling farm produce, sugar and lemons.
Tearoom selling home-baked pancakes, scones and strawberry tarts.

Blackshaw Park Farm
West Kilbride, Ayrshire, Strathclyde
(0563) 34257
Strathclyde
Vegetables. Farm shop selling home-made jams, jellies and chutneys.
Only open March – September.

Border Berries
Rutherford Farm, Kelso TD5 8ND
(0835) 23763
Borders
Raspberries, strawberries and blackcurrants.
Retail and wholesale.
Contact: Martin Johnson

Coldstream Mains Farm
Coldstream, Berwickshire TD12 4ES
(0890) 2613
Borders
Strawberries (Cambridge Favourite, Cambridge Vigor, Bogota), raspberries (Malling Jewel, Glen Clova, Glen Moy), red and blackcurrants, gooseberries. 200 acres of pick-your-own.
Contact: Margo MacGregor

Cranston, David & Sons
Netherraw Farm, Lilliesleaf, Melrose TD6 9EP
(08357) 214
Borders
Raspberries and strawberries .
Retail and wholesale.
Contact: Alastair Cranston

Darnaway Farm Visitor Centre
Tearie Brodie, By Forres, Moray, Grampian
(0309) 469
Northeast
Farm shop selling potatoes and milk.
Victorian farm, 240 milking cows.

E C L Organic Ltd
Ednam, Kelso TD5 7QH
(0573) 24988
Borders
Organic mushrooms.
Contact: D Peddie

E P O Growers
Duntochter
(0389) 75337
Strathclyde
Organic baby vegetables (25 varieties).
For specialist catering market, and wholesale. Organic golden and red gooseberries and strawberries.
Supplies families in the area with weekly delivery of box of mixed organic vegetables.
Contact: Echo Mackenzie

Erskine Home Farm
Bishopton, Renfrewshire, Strathclyde PA7 5PN
(0505) 862305
Strathclyde
Pick-your-own farm. Ready-picked strawberries (Cambridge favourite, Hapil, Temella, Cambridge Vigor), raspberries.
Contact: Peter Kerr

Eshiels Market Garden
9 Eshiels, Peebles EH45 8NQ
(0721) 21479
Borders
Organic raspberries (Glen Prosen, Glen Moy, Malling Jewel), strawberries (Cambridge Favourite).
Pick-your-own. Organic vegetables in season. Retail.
Contact: C Hall

Fieldfare Organic Growers
Bograxie, Inverurie, Aberdeenshire
(0467) 42518
Northeast
Organic vegetables, curly kale.
Contact: David Benson

Gagie House Farm
Gagie House, by Dundee DD4 0PR
(082621) 303
East
Strawberries, raspberries (newest varieties), tayberries, gooseberries, red and blackcurrants, brambles and blueberries. Specializing in late varieties cropping from late June to early October.
Contact: France Smoor

Gowrie Growers
Waterbutts Farm, Grange, Errol, Perthshire
(082) 12228
East
Lettuce (oak leaf, lolla rosa, lolla blonda, quattro stagioni), curly endive.
Contact: R O Wilson

Gray, J and F
House of Auchrennie, Carnoustie, Tayside
(0241) 52800
East
Lochlair swedes. Home and export.
Strawberries and raspberries.
Contact: Jim Gray

Knowes Farm Shop
Knowes Farm, Dunbar, East Lothian EH42
1XJ
(0620) 860221
Edinburgh
Potatoes (Maris Piper, Pentland Hawk,
Romano, Golden Wonder), leeks, sprouts,
cauliflowers, cabbage, parsley and chives
(all grown without artificial fertilizer).

Lowes Fruit Farm
Camp End, Dalkeith, Lothian EH22 2HJ
(031) 660 2128
Edinburgh
Brambles, tayberries, raspberries and
strawberries.
Local cheese.

Monktonhill Farm, C W S
Prestwick
(0292) 74118
Southwest
Blackcurrants, raspberries, strawberries and
redcurrants. Pick-your-own and ready-
picked. Radishes, peas, broccoli, runner
beans and asparagus (pick your own). Farm
shop selling vegetables, fruits and freshly
picked herbs.

Morris, P and C
1 Houston Place, Kinning Park Industrial
Estate, Glasgow G5 8SG
(041) 429 6068
Vegetables.
Contact: Robert Morris

Muir, T & W
Torquham Stow, Galashiels TD1 2RX
(05786) 230
Borders
Strawberries (mainly), also raspberries,
gooseberries and blackcurrants.
Contact: T Muir

Perth and Angus Fruit Growers Ltd
Lochside Road, Forfar, Angus DD8 3JD
(0307) 62181
East
Co-operative processing frozen soft fruit.
Contact: David Leighton

Polytun Growers Ltd
Pitkeathly Wells, Bridge of Earn, Perth
PH2 9HA
(0738) 39560
Central
Organic vegetables including fresh
butterhead and iceberg lettuce, cabbage,
broccoli, turnips, celery, leeks and potatoes

Priorwood Garden
Melrose, Borders TD6 9PX
(089682) 2965
Borders
Herbs from herb garden. Apple products
(juice, jams, jellies, chutneys) from abbey
orchard.
Apples (Permain and Oslin), originally
grown by monks from eleventh to
eighteenth century.

Rendall, David & Son
Stiellsmuir Farm, Rosemount, Blairgowrie,
Perthshire
(0250) 2237
East
Strawberries, raspberries, blackcurrants,
brambles and gooseberries.
Contact: Mrs Rendall

Roots and Fruits
457 Great Western Road, Glasgow
(041) 334 3530
Range of organic vegetables, fresh herbs,
wild mushrooms (in season), curly kale,
fresh spinach.
Contact: Garth Gulland

Sandy Braid Farms Ltd
Channel Farm, Kinross KY13 7HD
(059284) 236
East
Strawberries, blackcurrants, raspberries and
brambles. Pick-your-own and ready-picked.
Farm shop selling fresh farm vegetables and
ready-picked fruit.
Contact: Sandy Braid

Scottish Crop Research Institute
Invergowrie, Perthshire
(0382) 562731
East
Vegetables, especially potatoes, fruit.
Experimental development of varieties of
fruits and vegetables suitable for Scottish
soil and climate.
Contact: Murray Cormack

Sea Vegetable Co Ltd
Pitkerrie, Balmuchy, Fearn, Easter Ross
1V20 ITN
(086287) 272
Highland
Dried sugar ware, finger ware, dabberlocks,
grockle, summer and autumn dulse, purple
nori.
Gathered from unpolluted shores around
the north coast.
Mail order.
Contact: Julian Clokie

Simply Organic
Holding No 3, Walnut Grove, Kinfauns, Nr
Perth, Perthshire
(0738) 20390
Central

Extensive range of organic vegetables.
Contact: Ken Paterson
South West Fullarton Farm
  Meigle, Perthshire
  (082 82) 391
  Central
  Organic raspberries, strawberries, tayberries
  and blackcurrants.
  Pick-your-own and ready-picked.
Valvona and Crolla
  19 Elm Row (top of Leith Walk),
  Edinburgh
  (031) 556 6066
  Wild mushrooms, picked locally in season.
  Wide range of Italian delicatessen foods,
  and ice creams.
  Mail order.
  Contact: Philip Contini

4 Grains

Boardhouse Mill
  Birsay, Orkney
  (085672) 363/223
  Orkney
  Stoneground oatmeal, beremeal (Northern
  form of barley) organically grown on
  Orkney, peasemeal.
  Last surviving water-powered meal mill in
  northern isles.
  Mail order.
  Contact: Fergus Morrison
Border Oats Ltd
  Edington Mill, Chirnside, Duns TD11 3LE
  (089081) 252
  Borders
  Oatmeal, oatflakes, oat flour (stoneground,
  kiln-dried).
  Mail order.
  Contact: R A Black
Grassroots
  498 Great Western Road, Glasgow
  (041) 334 1844
  Oatmeal (all grades, organic and ordinary),
  Orkney beremeal, peasemeal, pearl barley.
  Sour dough bread from Glasgow
  Wholefood Bakery.
Green City Wholefoods
  23 Fleming Street, Glasgow G31 1PH
  (041) 554 7633
  Organic oatmeal and pearl barley,
  Boardhouse beremeal.
  Heather honeys. Wholesale only, workers'
  co-operative.
  Contact: Giles Boddington
Hamlyn Milling Ltd
  44 Glengate, Kirriemuir, Angus DD8 4HG
  (0575) 72121
  East

Scottish grown oats (pinhead, coarse,
medium, fine and oat bran), oatflakes and
jumbo oats.
Wholesale, and retail and mail order.
Contact: David Valentine
Hogarth, John Ltd
  Kelso Mills, Kelso TD5 7HR
  (0573) 24224
  Borders
  Oatmeal, oatflakes, pearl barley
  (stoneground).
  Contact: I G A Miller
John Ridley Products Ltd
  The Mill, Blair Atholl, Perthshire PH18
  5SH
  (079) 681321
  Central
  Stoneground oatmeal. Cakes, scones,
  oatcakes, home-made jams, marmalades
  and pickles.
  Teas, snack lunches.
  Contact: John Ridley
Mill of Towie
  Drummuir, by Keith, Banffshire AB5
  3JE
  (054281) 307
  Northeast
  Oatmeal (all grades, stoneground,
  kiln-dried). Honey from mill's bees,
  jams and ice creams. Shop and
  restaurant.
  Contact: Priscilla Gordon-Duff
Montgarrie Mills
  Alford, Aberdeenshire AB3 8AP
  (09755) 62209
  Northeast
  Oatmeal (six grades from superfine flour to
  pinhead, stoneground, kiln-dried). Alford
  oatcakes.
  Tour of the mill, by appointment, Tuesdays
  and Thursdays.
  Contact: Donald MacDonald
North Eastern Farmers Ltd
  Bannermill Beach Boulevard, Aberdeen
  (0224) 641255
  Northeast
  Oatflakes.
  Contact: Uel Morton
Real Foods
  37 Broughton Street, Edinburgh; 8
  Brougham Street Edinburgh
  (031) 557 1911 (mail order, retail); (031) 228
  1651 (retail only)
  Organic oatmeal (fine, medium, pinhead,
  flour and jumbo oats), Orkney beremeal.
  Range of organic produce. Heather
  honey.
  Mail order.
  Contact: Janet Lockwood

5 Herbs

Mordon Herbs
    Mill Farm, Kemnay, Inverurie, Grampian
    AB5 9NY
    (0467) 43167
    Northeast
    Herbs (64 varieties, free from artificial
    chemicals and sprays).
    Wholesale and retail.
    Contact: Morag Milne
Old Semell Herb Garden
    Strathdon, Aberdeenshire, Grampian AB3
    8XJ
    (09756) 513
    Northeast
    Herb plants, seeds and pots (100 varieties of
    culinary herbs, free from chemical
    fertilizers and sprays).
    Retails and wholesale. Tea-room and shop.
    Contact: Gillian Cook
Poyntzfield Herb Nursery
    Black Isle, by Dingwall, Ross and Cromarty
    1V7 8LX
    (03818) 352
    Highlands
    Herbs (800 varieties). Specialists in
    cultivation of herb plants and seeds using
    organic and biodynamic methods. Mail
    order.
    Contact: Duncan Ross
Scotherbs
    Waterybutts, Grange by Errol, Perth PH2
    7SZ
    (08212) 228
    East
    Herbs (extensive selection in pots and fresh
    cut in packs), herb oils, vinegars and
    mustards. Courses in herb cooking and
    preserving by Sue Turner (08212) 680.
    Contact: Stanley Turner, Rob Wilson
West of Scotland College of Agriculture
    Auchincruive, Nr Cumnock, Ayrshire KA6
    5HW
    (0292) 520331
    Southwest
    Herb advisory service: proof of suitability
    to Scottish environment of over 150
    different herb species has been determined.
    Other farming research.
    Contact: Dr K Svoboda

6 Cheese

Biss, K and D
    Achmore, Plockton, Wester Ross
    (059987) 203
    Highlands
    Cow's milk crowdie, Coulommiers-type soft
    cheese, curd cheese with chives and mixed
    herbs (all pasteurized). Courses on
    cheesemaking, yogurt manufacture, sheep
    milking.
    Contact: Kathy Biss
Brecks Farm
    Shapinsay, Orkney
    (085 671) 272
    Orkney farmhouse cheese (3–4 lb cheeses,
    made by traditional methods, semi-soft).
    Friesian cows, unpasteurized milk.
    Contact: Mrs Minnie Russell
Campbeltown Creamery Ltd
    Campbeltown, Argyll PA28 6JU
    (0586) 52244
    Highlands
    Scottish mature cheddar: Mull of Kintyre
    1 lb 4 oz truckle, extra mature; Highland,
    2½ kilo block.
    Contact: Ian Ireland
D'Arcy's Comestibles and Bespoke
Sandwiches
    The Courtyard, Princes Square, Glasgow
    (041) 226 4309
    Full range of Scottish farmhouse cheeses.
    Contact: Alan Laing
Easter Weens Enterprises
    Easter Weens, Bonchester Bridge,
    Roxburgh TD9 8JQ
    045086 635
    Borders
    Bonchester (Camembert-style cheese from
    pedigree Jersey milk, unpasteurized,
    available May to December, 4 oz and
    10 oz), Teviotdale (full fat hard, slightly
    crumbly cheese from Jersey milk,
    unpasteurized, 2½ lb), Belle d'Ecosse
    (medium hard, slightly pressed cheese from
    Jersey milk, unpasteurized).
    Mail order (minimum order required).
    Contact: John Curtis
Errington, H J & Co
    Ogscastle, Carnwath, Lanarkshire ML11
    8NE
    (089) 981 257
    Borders
    Lanark Blue (mould ripened cheese from
    unpasteurized ewes' milk, made to the same
    traditions as a cheese produced on the farm
    in the nineteenth century and ripened in the
    original ripening rooms), Dunsyre Blue
    (mould ripened soft blue cheese from
    unpasteurized Ayrshire cows' mllk).
    Mail order.
    Contact: Humphry Errington
Farmhouse, The
    Chapel Street, Aberdeen, Grampian
    (0224) 640681
    Northeast

Wide range of hand-made Scottish cheeses.
Fresh fruit, vegetables and herbs. Cold
meats, smoked fish, vegetarian haggis.
Honeys, mustards and Scottish preserves.
Contact: Alistair Massey

Flockhart, M
Bunloit, Loch Ness, Inverness-shire
(06678) 268
Highlands
Soft goats' milk cheese.
Contact: Ruth and Michael Flockhart

Grinigoe Farm
Shapinsay, Orkney
(085 671) 256
Orkney farmhouse cheese (semi-hard, from
unpasteurized cows' milk, 1 lb to 3 lb).
Contact: Jean Wallace

Hennyston Farm
Sorn, Mauchline, Ayrshire KA5 6NF
(0290) 51422
Southwest
Cheese, milk, ewes' milk.
Contact: Laura Blythe

Highland Fine Cheese Ltd
Knockbreck, Tain, Ross and Cromarty
(0862) 2034
Highlands
Caboc (rich double cream, old Highland
recipe), also traditional Highland crowdie,
garlic crowdie, gru dhu, crowdie and cream
cheese mixture rolled in crushed
peppercorns.
Contact: Jamie Stone

Highland Goat Products
Corglass Farm, Ballindalloch, Banffshire
AB3 9BS
(08072) 269
Northeast
Ballindalloch (from unpasteurized goats'
milk, hard, wax-covered), Strathspey (full
fat, semi-hard, from goats' milk).
Contact: Jane Heape

Howgate Dairy Products
Walltower, Howgate, Penicuik, Midlothian
(0968) 72263
Edinburgh
Crowdie, Camembert-type cheese, Brie-type
cheese, peat smoked soft cheese, cream,
milk and yogurt.
Contact: M T R Marwick

Ingle Smokehouse Ltd
Unit 8, Shore Road, Perth PH2 8BD
(0738) 30121
Central
Gowrie (full fat hard pressed cheese from
unpasteurized cows' milk, also available
with fresh herbs, 6 lb), Craigrossie (hard
cheese, from unpasteurized ewes' milk,
5 lb), Madoch (hard cheese from
unpasteurized goats' milk, coated in ash

from smokehouse), Inglesmoked cheddar
(smoked pasteurized cheddar).
Mail order.
Contact: Ann Brow

Islay Creamery Co Ltd
Port Charlotte, Isle of Islay, Argyll PA48
7TY
(049685) 229
Inner Hebrides
Islay Dunlop (hard cheddar-type cheese).
Contact: John J Kissock

Kirkton Farm
Lockerbie
05762 2591
Southwest
Dryfesdale full fat soft cheese.
Contact: Mrs Wilson

McLelland, A & Sons
Cheese Market, Albion Street, Glasgow
(041) 552 2962
Scottish cheddar.
Wholesale.
Contact: Mr McLelland

Meason, Kenny
Fruistigarth, Shapinsay, Orkney
(08571) 261
Orkney farmhouse cheese.
Contact: Kenny Meason

Meiklejohns Croft Organic Cheese
Meiklejohns Croft, Lamington,
Invergordon, Easter Ross, IV18 OPE (086)
284 2358
Highlands
Strathrusdale goats' milk cheese, Strathorie
ewes' milk cheese, Caise na bo, Ayrshire
herd milk. Soft cheeses from unpasteurized
cows', goats', and sheeps' milk, flavoured
with garlic, rolled in oatmeal, sesame,
thyme and seaweed.
Unpasteurized.
Contact: Alasdair Hutchison

Minty, Mr
4 Dockhart Place, Comrie, Perthshire
(0764) 70110
Central
Supplier of speciality cheeses to the catering
trade throughout Scotland.
Contact: Mr Minty

Nairnside Farm
Cawdor, Nairn, Moray IV12 5XS
(06677) 621
Northeast
Clava (full fat hard sheep's milk cheese),
Clava Croft (semi-soft, Coulommiers-type
sheeps' milk cheese), Clava Cottage
(Scottish crowdie-type sheeps' milk cheese,
also with added chives or spring onion).
Sheeps' milk yogurt and sheeps' milk ice
cream.
Contact: David Rose

North of Scotland Milk Marketing Board
Kirkwall, Orkney
(0856) 2824
Orkney cheese (plain, coloured and
smoked), hard, modified Dunlop cheese,
from pasteurized milk (1 lb round Cryovac
wrapped), Claymore crowdie.
Contact: David Watt

Peckhams
100 Byres Road, Glasgow
(041) 357 2909
Range of Scottish cheese. Oatcakes and
shortbread. Other Scottish foods.
Other Branches in Glasgow include Central
Station and Clarence Drive.
Contact: Tony Johnston

Perratt Dairymen
Ashton Road, Rutherglen, Glasgow G73
1UB
(041) 647 9801
Crème fraîche, cream cheese.
Wholesale.
Contact: G Perratt

Porter's Speciality Food Suppliers
Unit 7, Young's Road, East Mains
Industrial Estate, Brocksburn EH52 5AU
(0506) 852015
Edinburgh
Full range of Scottish farmhouse cheeses.
Foie gras, truffles, wild mushrooms,
saffron, oils, vinegars, hams, couverture.
Wholesale.
Contact: Alistair Clark

Read, J & C I
Sgriob-ruadh Farm Dairy, Tobermory,
Mull
(0688) 2235
Inner Hebrides
Isle of Mull (hand-made cheddar from
unpasteurized milk, with vegetable rennet,
matured 6 to 9 months). Sold in whole 50 lb
cheeses only, most sold on the island.
Contact: Christine Read

Real Cheese Company, The
9–11 Braeview Place, Nerston East
Industrial Estate, East Kilbride, Glasgow
G73 3XH
(03552) 66071
Full range of farmhouse and traditional
cheeses.
Wholesale.
Contact: David Taylor

Robrock Dairy Goat Products
Drum Farm, Lumsden, Near Huntly
(04646) 732
Robrock: wide range of unpasteurized
goats' milk cheese (natural, Red n' White,
vine leaf wrapped, with chives, with sage,
wine dipped (roset), in approximately 5 lb
wax-dipped cheeses and 2 oz or 6 oz cheeses
with various coatings)
Contact: Rosie Brocklehurst

Rowlands
42 Howe Street, Edinburgh
(031) 225 3711
Lanark and Dunsyre Blue, Clava (from
unpasteurized ewes' milk), Robrock (from
unpasteurized goats' milk), Sgriob-ruadh
(Cheddar-type cheese from unpasteurized
cows' milk), and other Scottish cheeses
subjects to availability.
Contact: Rowland Robinson

St Michael's, Boreland Road,
Lockerbie, Dumfries and Galloway DG11
2RH
(05762) 3386
Southwest
Unpasteurized goats' milk cheese, *petit
fromage blanc*, Coulommiers-type
cheese, hard cheese. Also retail from
farm, and sold at Alternative in
Dumfries.
Contact: Kay Wakefield-Richmond,
Secretary, The Dumfries and Galloway
Goat Keepers' Association

Scottish Goat Products Ltd
Co-operative Society, Station Road,
Newtonmore PH20 IAR
(05403) 592
Highlands
Soft goats' milk cheese, goats' milk and
yogurt.
Contact: Tim Dearman

Scottish Milk Marketing Board Creamery
Kilmory, Arran
(077 087) 240
Strathclyde
Arran (Softer modified Dunlop, coloured,
2¼ lb small drums, and blocks), Dunlop
(waxed), Scottish cheddar (60 lb cylinders);
all from pasteurized cows' milk.
Contact: Neil McLean

Seater, Hilda
Grimister, Finstown, Orkney
(085 676) 318
Orkney
Orkney farmhouse cheese.
Contact: Hilda Seater

Stichill Jerseys
Garden Cottage Farm, Stichill, Kelso TD5
7TJ
(05737) 263
Borders
Stichill cheese (hard Wensleydale-type
crumbly cheese from unpasteurized Jersey
milk, 1 lb mini or larger 3–5 lb), Kelsie
(similar to Stichill but made using
a yogurt starter. Jersey double cream and
yogurt.
Contact: Brenda Leddy

Swannay Farm
Birsay, Orkney
(085672) 365
Orkney
Scottish cheddar (9 lb wheels, Cryovac wrapped), 1 lb farmhouse cheddars dipped in black wax; all from pasteurized cows' milk.

7 Baking

Argo Bakery
Stromness, Orkney
(0856) 850245
Orkney
Baker, making traditional slow-fermented breads, local specialities.
Contact: Ian Argo

Asher, James
46 Church Street, Inverness IVI IEH
(0463) 234388
Highlands
Baker, making traditional slow-fermented breads, using one of the few remaining Scotch ovens. Shortbreads, oatcakes, Scottish teabread, Scotch perkins, Aberdeen butteries, softies, black bun. Other branches in Forres and Nairn.

Bradfords
245 Sauchiehall Street, Glasgow
(041) 332 5071
Baker, making traditional slow-fermented breads. Scotch pies and Forfar bridies made with 100 per cent beef, Scottish teabread, shortbread, oatcakes. Caramel walnuts. Traditional tearoom above shop with afternoon teas including tiered cake stand of Bradfords teabread and cakes.
Contact: Hugh Bradford

Chalmers Bakery
13-15 Auchmill Road,
Bucksburn, Aberdeen
(0224) 712631
Northeast
Baker, making traditional slow-fermented breads. Aberdeen butteries.

Clifton Coffee House and Craft Centre
Tyndrum, Perthshire FK20 8RY
(08384) 271
Highlands
Range of traditional shortbreads. Preserves, jams and chutneys, Moniack Castle preserves. Scottish cheeses, undyed kippers, smoked game and poultry.
Mail order.
Contact: Derek Wilkie

Cumming and Spence
Albert Street, Kirkwall, Orkney KW15 1HP
(0856) 2034

Baker, making traditional slow-fermented breads. Oatcakes, black bun, beremeal bannocks, biscuits (carvey, rice, cabin, butterflake and perkins); all handmade to traditional Orkney recipes.
Mail order.
Contact: T R Laird

Dalgetty, Alexander & Sons
21 Island Street, Galashiels TD1 1NZ
(0896) 2508
Borders
Baker, making traditional slow-fermented breads. Selkirk bannock, shortbreads.
Contact: Bill Murray

Dean's of Huntly
52 Deveron Street, Huntly AB5 5BZ
(0466) 2086
Northeast
Dean's Home Recipe shortbread.
Wholesale, home and export, mail order.
Contact: Helen Dean

Diggens
135 Byres Road, Glasgow
(041) 334 0430
Baker, making traditional slow-fermented breads. Scottish teabread, shortbread, black bun, Scotch pies (large and small, with and without potatoes). Other branches throughout Glasgow.

Duncan's Bakery
King Street, Aberdeen
(0224) 645616
Northeast
Baker, making traditional slow-fermented breads, butteries.

Fisher Donaldson
13 Church Street, St Andrews
0334 7220
East
Baker, making traditional slow-fermented breads, speciality Scottish baking and chocolates.

Forbes Bakeries
Muir of Ord
(0463) 870240
Highlands
Traditional baker. Oatcakes and shortbread.
Contact: John or Martin Forbes

Glasgow Wholefood Bakery
30 Laverockhall Street, Glasgow
(041) 554 9294
Baker, making traditional slow-fermented breads, sour dough breads, other wholemeal breads. Wholesale only.

Goodfellow and Steven
83 Gray Street, Broughty Ferry, Dundee, Angus
(0382) 77214
East

Baker, making traditional slow-fermented breads. Shortbread, thick rough oatcakes, chocolate violets, black bun, Scottish teabreads. Other branches at Arbroath, Monifieth, Barnhill, Dundee, Carnoustie and Perth (head office [0382] 730181).

Hossack, R T
50 Horsemarket, Kelso TD5 7AE
(0573) 24139
Borders
Baker, making traditional slow-fermented breads, Selkirk bannock, pies, bridies.
Contact: Robert Jack

Houstons (Bakers) Ltd
16 Bourtree Place, Hawick TD9 9HW
(0450) 72218
Borders
Baker, making traditional slow-fermented breads, Selkirk bannock, shortbread.
Mail order.
Contact: Paul Martin

Jenners
Princes Street, Edinburgh
(031) 225 2442
Baker, making traditional slow-fermented breads. Shortbread, teabreads, Selkirk bannock, Aberdeen butteries, oatcakes. Heather honey and blossom honey. Scottish chocolates. Macsween's Haggis, Glentarkie free-range pork and bacon.
Mail order.

Kennedy
Merkland Street East, Aberdeen
(0224) 633612
Northeast
Baker, making traditional slow-fermented breads.

Leiper, A & K
South Crown Street, Aberdeen
(0224) 582427
Northeast
Baker, making traditional slow-fermented breads, butteries.

Low's Bakeries
Victoria Road, Torry, Aberdeen
(0224) 876572
Northeast
Baker, making traditional slow-fermented breads.

Lunn, Jackie
Chanell Street, Galashiels
(0896) 3877
Borders
Baker, making traditional slow-fermented breads. Borders teabread.

McKenzie's Biscuits
41 Main Street, Turrif, Grampian AB5 5GB
0888 62425
Northeast

Traditional Scottish biscuits and oatcakes.
Contact: Gerry McKenzie

Muirs of Orkney
2–4 Graham Place, Stromness, Orkney KW16 3BY
(0856) 850213
Handmade biscuits.
Mail order.
Contact: R Muir

Orkney Islands Oatcake Company
18 Bridge Street, Kirkwall, Orkney KW15 1HT
(0856) 3165
Orkney
Orkney oatcakes, biscuits (ten varieties).
Mail order.

Robertson, G A
Allardyce Street, Stonehaven
(0569) 62734
Northeast
Baker, making traditional slow-fermented breads. Aberdeen butteries.
Contact: G Robertson

Scott, John
10 Roxburgh Street, Kelso TD5 7DH
(0573) 24819
Borders
Baker, making traditional slow-fermented breads. Shortbread, Selkirk bannock.
Contact: Neile McArthur

Scotts Kitchen, The
Block 8, Unit 4, Motherwell Foodpark, Bellshill, Lanarkshire
(0698) 844933
Glasgow
Specialist bakers, using traditional recipes. Cakes and teabreads, sugar-free teabread, rich chocolate cakes, gingerbreads, Glasgow cake, carrot cake and banana cake; all free from artificial flavourings and colourings. Lanark Blue quiche, frozen Rumbledethumps, Apple Frushie.
Wholesale.
Contact: Ian Scott

Short's Pies
Skirving Street, Glasgow; Barscube Terrace, Paisley
(041) 632 2100; (0630) 887
Glasgow
Short's pies (plain, onion and steak), full range of bakery goods.
Retail and wholesale.
Contact: Mr Strannigan

Shortbread House of Edinburgh
14 New Broompark, Edinburgh EH5 1RS
(031) 552 0381
Butter shortbread (presentation packs and tins), Dundee cake.
Contact: Anthony Laing

Stag Bakery
   60 Bayhead, Stornoway, Isle of Lewis PA87
   2DZ
   (0851) 2733
   Outer Hebrides
   Baker, making traditional slow-fermented
   breads. Scottish batch loaves, speciality
   baking.
   Contact: Malcolm Maclean
Thain's Bakery
   341 George Street, Aberdeen
   (0224) 638698
   Northeast
   Baker, making traditional slow-fermented
   breads, butteries.
Walkers' Shortbread Shop
   Aberlour, Grampian AB3 9PB
   (03405) 555
   Northeast
   Walkers' shortbread, traditional fruit cakes,
   Dundee cake, black bun, traditional
   oatcakes, bran oatcakes.
   Mail order.
   Contact: James Walker
Waterside Bakery
   Strathaven
   (0357) 12160
   Glasgow
   Baker, making traditional slow-
   fermented breads. Traditional Scottish
   teabread, treacle crumpets, currant
   crumpets.
   Contact: Alexander Taylor
Wilson, George
   33 Tower Street, Selkirk TD7 4LR
   (0750) 20766
   Borders
   Baker, making traditional slow-fermented
   breads. Selkirk bannock, home recipe
   shortbread.
   Contact: Fiona Lees
Wooley's of Arran Ltd
   Invercloy, Brodick, Isle of Arran KA27
   8AJ
   (0770) 2280
   Strathclyde
   Baker, making traditional slow-fermented
   breads. Scottish cakes, oatcakes,
   bannocks, shortbread, coffee buns, water
   biscuits.
   Contact: A G Lindsay Keir

Fazzi Bros Ltd
   64 Cambridge Street, Glasgow; 232 Clyde
   Street, Glasgow
   (041) 332 0941; (041) 221 9411
   Italian Colpi ice cream, hand-made aniseed
   ice cream wafers (cialde).
   Contact: Julie Ferarri, Mario Gizzi
Iannetta & Sons
   9 Faraday Street, Dryburgh Industrial
   Estate, Dundee DD2 3QQ
   (0382) 811622
   East
   Dairy ice cream, fresh fruit sorbets, goats'
   milk ice cream.
   Contact: Graeme Webster
Ice of Skye Ltd
   The Diary, Castle View, Kyleakin, Isle of
   Skye, Inverness-shire
   (0599) 4713
   Inner Hebrides
   Dairy ice cream (full cream).
   Retail and wholesale.
   Contact: Alexander McDiarmid
Lucas
   34 High Street, Musselburgh
   (031) 665 2237
   Edinburgh
   Ice cream
Luvians
   Bonnygate, Cupar
   (0334) 54820
   East
   Italian dairy ice cream, fresh fruit sorbets,
   Sicilian ice cream bombes, mele stragata
   (black apples), chocolate-coated ice creams.
   Window at back of shop for viewing
   manufacture of ice cream.
   Contact: V Fusaro
Nardini
   8 Greenock Road, Largs, Ayrshire KA30
   8NF
   (0475) 674555
   Strathclyde
   Traditional Italian ices.
   Contact: Robbie Nardini
Rizza's
   16 Gordon Street, Huntly, Aberdeenshire
   (0466) 3907/2847
   Highlands
   Italian ice creams made with full cream
   milk and butter.
   Retail and wholesale.

8 Ice cream

Colpi, R & Son
   38 Main Street, Milngavie, Glasgow
   (041) 956 2040
   Italian dairy ice cream.
   Contact: R Colpi

9 Drinks

Braithwaite, J A
   Castle Street, Dundee, Angus
   (0382) 22693
   East

Speciality teas and coffees. Heather, clover and blossom honey.
Mail order.
Contact: George or Allan Braithwaite

Broughton Brewery Ltd
The Brewery, Broughton, Biggar ML12 6HQ
(08994) 345
Borders
Greenmantle, Merlin's and Old Jock ales, Broughton Special Bitter, Broughton Ale.
Contact: J Younger

Caithness Spring Water
Berridale, Caithness KW7 6HD
(05935) 253
Highlands
Caithness Spring, still and carbonated, low mineral spring water.
Contact: Bill Paterson

Chip Wine Shop
Ashton Lane, Glasgow
(041) 334 7109

Drysdale & Co Ltd
107 Grove Street, Edinburgh EH3 8AE
(031) 229 1313/4
Speciality teas and coffees.
Mail order.
Contact: David Ogg

Gordon & MacPhail
58–60 South Street, Elgin, Morayshire 1V30 1JY
(0343) 45111
Northeast
Specialist malt whiskies. Retail, wholesale and export.
Mail order.
Contact: Mr Grant

Highland Spring Ltd
35 Headford Place, London SW1X 7DE
(071) 235 0954
Highland Spring mineral water, still and sparkling.
Contact: John Biggs

Hogg, J E
61 Cumberland Street, Edinburgh
(031) 556 4025
Extensive range of malt whiskies.

Pearce, W M & Sons
St Ronan's Works, Miller Street, Innerleithen EH44 6QS
(0896) 830324
Borders
St Ronan's Natural Spring Water.
Contact: George Clapperton

Scotch Malt Whisky Society Ltd
The Vaults, 87 Giles Street, Edinburgh EH6 6BZ
(031) 554 3451

Association of connoisseurs of single malt whisky. Membership includes opportunity to sample single malts taken straight from the cask at 100 per cent proof and over, undiluted and retaining the original character.
Retail and wholesale. Quarterly newsletter.
Mail order.
Contact: Philip Hill

Strathmore Mineral Water Company
126 West High Street, Forfar, Angus DD8 1BP
(0307) 66147
East
Strathmore Spring, still and sparkling mineral water, also flavoured with lime, lemon or orange.
Contact: D Critchley–Salmonson

Thomsons
Burnfield Ave, Thornliebank, Glasgow G46 7TL
(041) 637 3808
Speciality teas and coffees.
Shop: Renfield Street, Glasgow.
Mail order.
Contact: R Addison

Traquair House Brewery
Traquair House, Innerleithen EH44 6PW
(0896) 830323
Borders
Traquair Ale, Bear Ale (named after the Bear Gates).
Contact: Flora Maxwell Stewart

10 Preserves

Arran Provisions Ltd
The Old Mill, Lamlash, Isle of Arran KA27 8JU
(07706) 606
Strathclyde
Mustards, chutneys, jams and marmalades.
Mail order.
Contact: Iain Russell

Baxters of Speyside Ltd
Fochabers, Morayshire IV32 7LD
(0343) 820393
Northeast
Jams, marmalades, preserves, chutneys and pickles.
Mail order.
Contact: Miss M E Foster

Black Isle Apiaries
Dungriannach, Millbank Road, Munlochy, Ross-shire IV8 8ND
(046381) 309
Highlands
Heather and Scottish blossom honey (80 hives).
Contact: Alastair Taylor

Galloway Lodge Preserves
24–28 High Street, Gatehouse of Fleet
(05574) 357
Southwest
Chutneys, marmalades, mustards.
Contact: Nigel Hesketh

Heather Hills Honey Farm
Bridge of Cally, Perthshire PH10 7JG
(025086) 252
Central
Heather and blossom honey (750 hives),
Strathardle brand.
Contact: Athole Kirkwood

Mackays of Carnoustie
21 Thistle Street, Carnoustie, Angus, DD7
7PR
(0241) 53109
East
Jams from local strawberries and
raspberries, marmalade.
Contact: L Nicholson

Moniack Castle Meat and Game Preserves
Moniack Castle, Kirkhill, Inverness IV5
7PQ
(0463) 83283
Highlands
Jellies and sauces to complement
meat, game and fish (jellies made
from local wild berries: rowanberry,
hawthornberry, elderberry, sloeberry,
gooseberry), and mint jellies, juniper
chutney, dill sauce.
Contact: Philippa Fraser

Nicoll's of Strathmore Ltd
Douglastown, Forfar, Angus DD8 1TL
90307 63732
East
Heather, blossom, and blended Drambuie
honey.
Contact: James Nicoll

Pettigrew, J M
2 Oven Wynd, Kelso, Roxburghshire TD5
7HS
(0573) 24234
Borders
Chutneys, marmalades and mustards.
Contact: J Pettigrew

Scott, R & W
Clydesdale Preserve Works, Carluke
(0555) 70711
Glasgow
Traditional jams, jellies and marmalades.
Contact: George Benzie

Struan Apiaries
Burnside Lane, Conon Bridge, Ross-shire
1V7 8EX
(0349) 61427
Highlands
Pure Scottish blossom and heather honey.
Presentation packs with malt whisky, range
of stoneware pots, cut comb, bees wax in

small blocks, and furniture cream.
Contact: Hamish Robertson

11 Confectionery

Border Country Cousins
The Garden Factory, Lennel Road,
Coldstream, Berwickshire TD12 4EP
(0890) 2631
Borders
Fudge (butterscotch and whisky).
Contact: John C Balfour

Cameo of Edinburgh
15 West Telferton, Edinburgh EH7 6UL
(031) 669 6123
Confectionery made according to recipes of
A Ferguson, inventor of Edinburgh rock.
Handmade boiled sweets, Edinburgh rock,
cream sweets, Berwick cockles, soor
plooms, cinnamon balls.
Contact: D N Spratt

Crawford Candies
Pinefield Industrial Estate, Elgin
(0343) 547410/549071
Northeast
Scottish tablet.
Mail order.
Contact: Mark Whelan

Duncan's of Edinburgh
Beaverhall Road, Edinburgh
(031) 557 1958
Duncan's hazelnut bar, chocolates.
Contact: Bob Baxter

Ferguson, J & A
45 Grovepark Street, Glasgow G20
(041) 332 6084
Specialist chocolates, chocolate gingers and
caramel walnuts.
Contact: H Hirst

Gardiner's of Scotland
Turfholm Industrial Estate, Lesmahago,
Lanark ML11 0ED
(0555) 892992
Borders
Edinburgh Rock, Scottish toffee,
macaroons, snowballs, whisky fudge.
Contact: Tom Gardiner

Hills of Hawick Ltd
16 Commercial Road, Hawick TD9 7AQ
(0450) 73869
Borders
Hawick balls, soor plooms, Edinburgh
Rock.
Mail order.
Contact: William, Maureen or Richard
Smith

Jenny's Home Made Sweets (Edinburgh)
13 Baronscourt Road, Edinburgh EH8 7ET
(031) 661 4583

Plain tablet made with condensed milk, macaroons.
Contact: Walter E Innes
Millers
10 High Street, Jedburgh, TD8 6AG
(0835) 62252
Borders
'Jethart Snails' from original recipe, handmade boiled sweets.
Mail order.
Contact: W R Miller
Robertson (Orkney) Ltd
Cairston Road, Stromness, Orkney KW13 3bs
(0856) 850640
Fudge (whisky, rum and brandy), chocolate gingers.
Mail order.
Contact: James Robertson
Ross's of Edinburgh
Pentland Industrial Estate, Loanhead, Edinburgh EH20 9QR
(031) 440 1717
Specialists in traditional Scottish sweets. Edinburgh Castle Rock, rhubarb and peppermint rock, Berwick Cockles, barley sugar and butterscotch.
Mail order.
Contact: Graham Ross (fourth generation)

12 Trade organizations, food consortia, etc.

Aberdeen and District Milk Marketing Board
Twin Spires, PO Box 117, Buksburn, Aberdeen AB9 8AH
(0224) 696 371
Association of Scottish Shellfish Growers
Mo Dhachaidh, Appin, Argyll PA38 4BL
(0631) 73504
Contact: Gitte Salvarli
British Beekeepers' Association
National Agriculture Centre, Stoneleigh, Kenilworth, Warwickshire
(0203) 696 679
Contact: Michael Solley
British Deer Producers Society
Reediehill Deer Farm, Auchtermuchty, Cupar, Fife KY14 7HF
(0337) 28369
Contact: J Fletcher
British Food Information Service of Food from Britain
301–344 Market Towers, New Covent Garden Market, London, SW8 5NQ
(071) 720 7551/2144
Contact: Daphne MacCarthy
FFB UK Director of Marketing: Mary Curnock Cook
FFB Information Officer: Jay Fletcher

British Herb Traders Association
Sunnymead, West Pennard, Glastonbury, Somerset
(0458) 33573
Contact: J W Hancock
British Trout Association
PO Box 189, London SW6 7UT
(071) 381 1158
Contact: Amanda Courtney
Company of Scottish Cheese Makers
266 Clyde Street, Glasgow
(041) 221 4838
Represents all manufacturers of Scottish cheddar, and operates controls on quality with Quality Mark.
Contact: John Russell
East of Scotland College of Agriculture
Horticulture Dept, Crops, NLT Building, Bush Estate, Penicuik, Midlothian EH22 0PY
(031) 445 1786
Contact: Stuart Ainslie
Farm Shop and Pick your Own Organisation
Agriculture House, Knightsbridge, London SW1X 7NJ
(071) 235 5077
Contact: Jane Connor
Galloway Gourmet Foods
Dee Walk, Kirkcudbright, DG6 3DQ
(0557) 30905
Southwest
Food consortia.
Handmade Cheese of Scotland
Nairnside Farm, Cawdor, Nairn, 1V12 5XS
(06677) 621
Represents seven specialist cheesemakers from the Highlands and Islands to the Borders. Produces a variety of hand-made cheese (soft, hard and blue cheese from cows', goats' and ewes' milk).
Retail and catering, UK and export.
Contact: David Rose
Herring Buyers Association
46 Moray Place, Edinburgh EH3 6BQ
(031) 225 4548
Highlands and Islands Development Board
Bridge House, 20 Bridge Street, Inverness 1V1 1QR
(0463) 234171
National Farmers' Union of Scotland
17 Grosvenor Crescent, Edinburgh EH12 5EN
(031) 337 4333
Contact: Bill Romanis
Naturally Scottish
Suite S, Kirkton Business Centre, Livingston Village EH54 7AYT
(0506) 412833
Scottish Food Promotion Executive, sponsored by some sectors of the Scottish

agricultural and food industry, the Scottish Development Agency and the Highlands and Islands Development Board. Organizes exhibitions and retail promotions.
Contact: Colin Whimster or Tamara Luke

North of Scotland Milk Marketing Board
Claymore House, 29 Ardconnel Terrace, Inverness IV2 3AF
(0463) 232 611
Contact: David Watt

Scotch Quality Beef and Lamb Association
13th Avenue, Edinburgh Exhibition and Trade Centre, Ingleston
Edinburgh EH28 8NB
(031) 333 5335
Contact: Ian Brown

Scotch Whisky Association, The
20 Atholl Crescent, Edinburgh EH3 8HF
(031) 229 4383
Represents the principal firms of distillers and blenders (not retailers) engaged in the Scotch whisky industry, and has about 140 members, protects and promotes the interests of Scotch whisky and the industry.
Contact: Colonel H F O Bewsher

Scottish Agricultural Organisation Society Ltd
19 Clairmont Crescent, Edinburgh EH7 4JW
(031) 557 3060
Contact: Edward Rainy–Brown

Scottish Association of Master Bakers
4 Torphichen Street, Edinburgh EH3 8JQ
(031) 229 1401

Scottish Cooking Holidays
Waterside, Maryburgh, Dingwall, Ross-shire 1V7 8DW
(0349) 61320
Highlands
Miscellaneous holidays which include demonstrations of Scottish dishes and trips to local hotels specializing in Scottish food.
Contact: Rosalie Gow (cookery writer)

Scottish Federation of Meat Traders' Association
Hay's Auction Market, Needless Road, Perth PH2 0JW
(0738) 37472

Scottish Gourmet
The Thistle Mill, Station Road, Biggar
Monthly selection by Mail Order Club. Scotch beef and lamb, Ramsay's Bacon, Caledonian cheeseboard, Scott's Kitchen cakes, Scottish game in season, sometimes North Ronaldsay Lamb, free-range pork, etc.
Contact: Arthur Bell

Scottish Milk Marketing Board
Underwood Road, Paisley, Ayrshire PA3 1TJ
(041) 887 1234

Scottish Salmon Board
Drummond House, Scott Street, Perth PH1 5EJ
(0738) 35973
Contact: Andrew Gray

Scottish Salmon Growers' Association
Drummond House, Scott Street, Perth PH1 5EJ
(0738) 35420
Contact: William Crowe

Scottish Salmon Smokers' Association
33 Melville Street, Edinburgh EH3 7JF
(031) 220 2256
Contact: Archie Coulson

Sea Fish Industry Authority, The
10 Young Street, Edinburgh EH2 4JQ
(031) 225 2515

Shetland Salmon Farmers' Association
80 Commercial Street, Lerwick, Shetland ZE1 0DL
(0595) 5579

Tayside Regional Industrial Office
Tayside Regional Council, Tayside House, Dundee DD1
(0382) 23281

Women's Farming Union
Central Office, Crundalls, Matfield near Tonbridge, Kent TN12 7EA
(0892) 722 803
Contact: Elizabeth Browning, Joan Cremer
Scottish Co-ordinator: Mrs Clover Mack, Flaff Cottage, Woodhaven, Wormit, Fife DD6 8PT
(0382) 541774

Index

GENERAL

RECIPES